D0919678

WITHDRAWN

Mixing Memory and Desire

Mixing Memory and Desire

The Waste Land
and
British Novels

Fred D. Crawford

The Pennsylvania State University Press
University Park and London

For Matt and Doris Nitecki

Library of Congress Cataloging in Publication Data

Crawford, Fred D.
Mixing memory and desire.

Includes bibliographical references and index.
1. English fiction—20th century—History and criticism.
2. Eliot, T.S. (Thomas Stearns), 1888–1965. Waste land.
3. Eliot, T. S. (Thomas Stearns), 1888–1965—Influence. I. Title.
PR885.C7   823'.91'09   82-447
ISBN 0-271-00308-1   AACR2

CONTENTS

ACKNOWLEDGMENTS

I have received help from many people in the course of my research. I am grateful to The Institute for the Arts and Humanistic Studies of Penn State University for the faculty research grant which enabled me to visit the manuscript collections of twenty-five American libraries. I wish to acknowledge the staffs of these libraries (listed in the order I visited them) for their cooperation in allowing access to their holdings: Archives and Special Collections (The Marion E. Wade Collection), Wheaton College; The Special Collections Department, Northwestern University Library; Memorial Library Archives, Marquette University; Special Collections Department, The University of Iowa Libraries; The Bancroft Library, The University of California at Berkeley; Department of Special Collections, Manuscripts Division, Stanford University Libraries; Department of Special Collections, The University of California at Santa Barbara; The Huntington Library; Department of Special Collections, The University Research Library, The University of California, Los Angeles; The Humanities Research Center, The University of Texas at Austin; Special Collections, The University Libraries, The University of Arkansas; Rare Books & Special Collections, Washington University Libraries, Washington University (St. Louis); Department of Rare Books, Cornell University Library; Archives, Manuscripts, Rare Books, The George Arents Research Library at Syracuse University; Special Collections, Colby College Library; The Houghton Library, Harvard University; The Beinecke Rare Book and Manuscript Library, Yale University Library; Rare Books and Manuscripts, The Butler Library, Columbia University; The Henry W. and Albert A. Berg Collection of American and English Literature, The New York Public Library, Astor, Lenox and Tilden Foundations; Rare Books & Special Collections, Princeton University Library; The Treasure Room Manuscript

Collection, Haverford College Library; The Manuscripts Division, The Library of Congress; Manuscripts Department, Alderman Library, The University of Virginia Library at Charlottesville; Manuscripts Department, The University of North Carolina at Chapel Hill; The Rare Book Room, Pattee Library, The Pennsylvania State University. For permission to review restricted material, I wish to thank James O. Brown, Richard Elman, Mrs. Stanley H. Hillyer, and Mrs. Diane Pike.

For their permission to quote from previously unpublished material, I wish to acknowledge the holders of copyright: Alister Kershaw, Literary Executor for Richard Aldington; Conrad W. Oberdorfer and G. d'Andelot Belin, Trustees under the will of Amy Lowell; Francis Powys and the Estate of John Cowper Powys; The Rev. Walter Hooper and the Trustees of the Estate of C. S. Lewis; and Muriel Spark. I am also grateful to Anthony Burgess, Valerie Eliot, Rumer Godden, William Golding, Graham Greene, Christopher Isherwood, Alister Kershaw, Iris Murdoch, Anthony Powell, Lord C. P. Snow, and The Hon. Mrs. Henry Yorke (Mrs. Henry Green) for their responses to my inquiries.

Professor Dean Baldwin proofread portions of the manuscript, and Richard Winslow also reviewed parts of the study and ferreted out obscure articles on Eliot. Professor Audrey T. Rodgers provided helpful criticism, and Professor James E. Miller, Jr., offered sound advice for manuscript revision. John M. Pickering and Peter Ross Sieger of Penn State Press provided several helpful critiques. Professor Chet Wolford offered several observations, eased the tedious process of revision, helped to edit the manuscript, and demonstrated the incredible labors he will cheerfully perform in the name of friendship.

I owe my greatest debt to Stanley Weintraub, Research Professor of English at Penn State. He provided the original idea of this study, reviewed my manuscript at several stages, supplemented my research with helpful information, and supported my efforts in several other ways.

PREFACE

A Comment on Method

Although Eliot's criticism and his other works have contributed to his impact on modern literature, the focus of this book is the influence of *The Waste Land* on British novels. This raises several problems inherent in all studies of influence but particularly severe in this one. *The Waste Land* is probably the most allusive poem in the English language. As a result, numerous Thames Maidens, drowned sailors, typists, fortune tellers, neurasthenic women, empty chapels, Fisher Kings, spiritual blights, unreal cities, and Waste Lands which appear in British novels also appear in Eliot's sources, which were accessible to modern novelists. Although several images and themes may have become more widely known through the novelists' access to *The Waste Land,* other possible sources include Spengler, Nietzsche, Burckhardt, Shakespeare, Joyce, Gibbon, Wordsworth, Dante, Milton, Marlowe, Browne, Vergil, Bunyan, Dickens, Thackeray, Fielding, Keats, Huysmans, Proust, Wilde, Shaw, Ortega y Gasset, the Bible, Madame Blavatsky, Jessie Weston, Medieval Romance, Restoration Drama, Conrad, the tradition of dystopian novels, and several others. Many themes, images, and figures in Eliot's poem existed before Eliot appropriated them, and the novelists were capable of knowledge of Eliot's sources independent of Eliot. A full enumeration of parallels between *The Waste Land* and modern British novels would result in a study ten times the length of this one, without addressing the possibility of coincidental use of common sources.

Another difficulty of the study derived from my beginning by immersing myself in *The Waste Land*. It made sense at the time and still seems as logical as not, but as a result I read literally hundreds of

novels with Eliot's lines ringing in my head. Single words such as
"dust," "April," "fragments," and the like, on the novelist's page, trig-
gered a sensation of recognition that did not reflect the novelist's use of
The Waste Land as much as it did my own. To complicate this problem,
The Waste Land has a related effect described by James E. Miller, Jr.:

> As the poem became overly familiar through over-use, it was reduced to
> a kind of shorthand way of making references to modern life. And
> modern life seemed to oblige in remarkable ways, by confirming the
> simple observation that it was indeed a waste land—air pollution, gar-
> bage heaps, chemical poisons, plastics that would not disintegrate, phys-
> ical and moral corruption that stunned the senses and the mind.[1]

That *The Waste Land* is compatible with aspects of modern life which
developed after 1922 does not prevent the novelist from experiencing
life and drawing his own conclusions from it. Isherwood's Berlin, for
example, results from his observations there, not from Eliot's portrait
or from earlier portraits of modern despair or unreal cities or spiritual
blight. The poem appears to me to epitomize the spirit of its age, but
its peculiar aptness at seeming to describe events and conditions which
occurred after its publication (due to the presence of Tiresias, no doubt)
does not displace a novelist's direct or indirect knowledge of the conditions of his time or place.

Even when a novelist alludes directly and deliberately to another
work, his refashioning of what he borrows may so obscure his source
or modify it that the influence appears non-existent. Eliot addressed
this problem of influence when he commented on the presence of
Dante in *Little Gidding*:

> The intention . . . was . . . to present to the mind of the reader a par-
> allel, by means of contrast, between the Inferno and the Purgatorio,
> which Dante visited, and a hallucinated scene after an air-raid. But the
> method is different: here I was debarred from quoting or adapting at
> length—I borrowed and adapted freely only a few phrases—because I
> was *imitating*.[2]

The same principle of freedom in adapting is evident in *The Waste Land*.
Similarly, when novelists have "borrowed and adapted freely only a
few phrases" from *The Waste Land*, it becomes difficult to distinguish
between coincidence and influence. This problem becomes aggravated
because Eliot distilled motifs and archetypes which were in the air after
World War I and which novelists could have sensed or discovered had
Eliot never written. One could assert that *The Waste Land* brought the

motifs and archetypes to the awareness of every literary person, arguing that Eliot popularized the moderns' conception of their age. However, one could not prove it.

Another difficulty of discussing *The Waste Land* is the lack of agreement on what the poem means. Although Eliot himself insisted that
the poem was not an expression of modern disillusionment or a criticism of contemporary life, readers have frequently interpreted the
poem as a powerful statement of both. Edmund Wilson has emphasized the poem's scathing indictment of the dreariness and barrenness
of modern existence, finding in *The Waste Land* a protest against the
absence of belief; I. A. Richards, however, has taken the opposite tack
by asserting that the poem itself is completely devoid of systematic
statement or belief; F. R. Leavis has argued that the poem, delineating
a state of consciousness, ends exactly where it begins; Cleanth Brooks
has found spiritual affirmation in the poem's "renewing and vitalizing
of symbols"; and James E. Miller, Jr., following John Peter, has discovered evidence of Eliot's personal struggles embedded throughout the
poem. While these readings have all increased appreciation of *The Waste
Land*, no single interpretation has resolved every problem of coming to
terms with this elusive work, nor is one likely to. To complicate matters, there is scant evidence to connect a given novelist with a specific
interpretation of the poem.

In my attempt to resolve these problems, I have tried to impose the
following conditions on this study in the hope that, by not taxing
credulity too often, I might present a reasonable case.

1. Verbal echoes must refer directly to material unique to Eliot's *The
Waste Land*. For example, a reference to the Drowned Phoenician Sailor
or to the Blank Card (neither part of the traditional Tarot) or to the Man
With Three Staves (Eliot's name for the Three of Wands) derives from
The Waste Land; references to fortune-telling as such do not.

2. Novelists should not be subjected to an influence study unless
some evidence exists to verify some direct relationship between Eliot
and the novelists' work. When I selected novelists for this study, I
included only those who referred to Eliot in their correspondence and
published articles, included verbal echoes in the novels, or otherwise
provided some measure of support. I also relied on scholarly articles
and full-length studies which addressed issues of *The Waste Land*'s
influence on specific works. This secondary support also proved helpful in those instances where a novel evoked recognizable similarities to
the mood of *The Waste Land* with a minimum of allusions or direct
references to the poem.

3. Although interpretations of *The Waste Land* vary from "nihilistic"

to "Christian affirmation," only a given novelist's interpretation can be relevant in the discussion of that novelist's work. I have tried to avoid addressing the validity of different interpretations among the novelists and have limited identification between a novelist's interpretation and the continuing evolution of critical responses to *The Waste Land* except where the connection seemed striking.

4. To the extent such an attempt is feasible, the study of *The Waste Land*'s influence on modern British novelists should exclude other concerns. As a result, I have limited discussion to Eliot's presence rather than weighed his influence against that of others. If I do not mention Somerset Maugham, James Joyce, or D. H. Lawrence in my discussion of George Orwell, this does not mean that I feel Eliot's influence is the more persuasive or significant, but only the more relevant to this study.

5. The novelists' techniques, plots, characters, themes, settings, and other aspects of their art, for the purpose of this study, become pertinent only when they bear some relationship to *The Waste Land*. In many cases this draws attention from more significant and rewarding areas of a novelist's work, but considerations of space prevent a full-scale analysis of each novelist regardless of authorial merit or my desire to recognize it.

These conditions do not resolve all the problems of an influence study, but I hope they will mitigate some objections I anticipate from readers whose primary interest is the development of the novel rather than the impact of Eliot or of his most widely read poem.

All quotations from T. S. Eliot's *The Waste Land,* including the notes, follow *The Complete Poems and Plays: 1909–1950* (New York: Harcourt, Brace & World, Inc., 1952), and line numbers conform to this edition. I have maintained variances of spelling between American and English editions of the novels, idiosyncratic spelling in novelists' correspondence, and erratic punctuation except for obvious typographical errors.

INTRODUCTION

The Forms and the Extent
of The Waste Land's *Influence*

Paul Theroux's *The Great Railway Bazaar*, punning on an ethnic slur for Yugoslavs, includes a reference to the viability of *The Waste Land*:

> "You can imagine how these Jug policemen behave in third class," said Molesworth, in a rare display of social conscience.
> "'And still she cried and still the world pursues,'" I said, "'"Jug Jug" to dirty ears.' Who says *The Wasteland*'s irrelevant?"[1]

Sixty years after Eliot first published the poem, many believe that the Drowned Phoenician Sailor is part of the traditional Tarot pack without quite knowing where they obtained this misinformation. *The Waste Land*, in both England and America, has long been a firmly established part of "what the best dressed mind is wearing."

Many poets admit Eliot's poetical or critical influence, and in one sense Eliot may be regarded as the founder of modern poetry. He was not part of the early modernist movement, but *The Waste Land*'s appearance in October, 1922, revolutionized modern poetic technique as well as "defining" modernity. Of Eliot's influence, William Empson notes,

> I feel, like most other verse writers of my generation, that I do not know for certain how much of my own mind he invented, let alone how much of it is a reaction against him or indeed a consequence of misreading him. He has a very penetrating influence, not unlike an east wind.[2]

This influence has included negative as well as positive reaction. Victor Purcell, writing as "Myra Buttle," published a brilliant satire of *The Waste Land*. *The Sweeniad* (1957) parodied Eliot's lines as well as his pseudo-scholarly notes. Following the meter of the well-known opening lines, Purcell wrote,

> Sunday is the dullest day, treating
> Laughter as a profane sound, mixing
> Worship and despair, killing
> New thought with dead forms.
> Weekdays give us hope. . . .[3]

This familiar metrical pattern reappears in the satire:

> (Cloax is the vilest drink, gouging
> Pockets out of your giblets, mixing
> Frenzy and remorse, blending
> Rot-gut and white-ants.
> Jalap has a use. . . .[4]

To parody Eliot's ending and notes, Purcell includes the cryptic "··· --- ···" and defines it in a note: "The famous Morse signal of distress sent out by the Titanic on 14 April 1912. Here it is sent out by the inhabitants of the 'Unreal City.' No one answers it."[5] Purcell's parody embodies the techniques of *The Waste Land* which irritated contemporary readers most often—"scholarly" notes, irrelevant quotation, elitist appeal, departure from poetic tradition, and pointless obscurity.

Asked by *Esquire* to comment on the most overrated American writer, Harold Bloom immediately named T. S. Eliot:

> *all* of him, verse and prose; the academy, or clerisy, needed him as their defense against their own anxieties of uselessness. His neo-Christianity became their secular religion; his evasive idea of tradition became their mask, hiding their sense of being forlorn and misplaced. His verse is (mostly) weak; his prose is wholly tendentious.[6]

Karl Shapiro's "The Death of Literary Judgment" makes a similar point regarding Eliot's influence on modern poetry:

> Eliot invented a Modern World which exists only in his version of it; this world is populated by Eliot's followers and is not a reality. The Eliot population consists of a handful of critics and professors and a few writers of Eliot's generation, though one would think, reading modern

criticism and teaching from modern library textbooks, that there really is a kingdom of Modern Poetry in which T. S. Eliot is the absolute monarch and Archbishop of Canterbury in one.[7]

Shapiro not only underestimates Eliot's impact on poetry and criticism, but he also ignores Eliot's considerable impact on the novel. As E. K. Brown commented in 1938, "Anyone whose mind is well-stored with Mr. Eliot's images, if he reads widely in recent fiction, will be startled by the frequency with which these recur."[8]

Although Eliot's impact on modern fiction has been apparent since at least 1938, few have given the matter consideration beyond brief mention in criticism on British novelists. I think this has happened for two reasons. First, most have regarded Eliot's influence on American fiction more significant than his influence on British fiction. Several articles, one book, and at least one American doctoral dissertation have treated Eliot's influence on the novels of F. Scott Fitzgerald, Ernest Hemingway, William Faulkner, J. D. Salinger, Bernard Malamud, John Steinbeck, Kurt Vonnegut, Jr., and other American authors. However, the MLA bibliography lists only one article published on T. S. Eliot and any British novelist, a discussion of Anthony Burgess's *The Wanting Seed*.[9] This may reflect an assumption that the "American" Eliot would have his largest influence on American writers. Second, the interest in Eliot and *The Waste Land* has waned and revived, as Audrey Rodgers found: Following the "eclipse" that "Eliot's reputation . . . experienced in the fifties" there appeared "a proliferation of 'memoirs,' essays (over 100 in the '72 PMLA listing alone!), and over 40 full-length studies in a five-year period. . . ."[10]

A consideration of *The Waste Land*'s influence on modern British novels and novelists must note the difference between Eliot's private view of the poem and the almost universally accepted reading. Eliot himself addressed this problem directly:

> When I wrote a poem called *The Waste Land* some of the more approving critics said that I had expressed "the disillusion of a generation," which is nonsense. I may have expressed for them their own illusion of being disillusioned, but that did not form part of my intention.[11]

According to James E. Miller, Jr., in *T. S. Eliot's Personal Waste Land: Exorcism of the Demons*, Eliot's private interpretation would include himself as the Fisher King, Vivienne Eliot as the neurasthenic woman of "A Game of Chess," and Jean Verdenal as both Phlebas the Phoenician and the "you" to whom the poem's narrator speaks. However, this interpretation is not part of the use novelists have made of *The Waste*

Land's traditionally recognized meanings because it was not available to them until recently (John Peter's revealing 1952 article, on which Miller's study partly depends, was suppressed by Eliot and did not appear until 1969).

The extent and nature of *The Waste Land*'s influence vary among the seventeen writers of this study, from agreement to disagreement, from numerous references to isolated allusions, and even from successful to unsuccessful applications. Some writers who might belong in a study of Eliot's influence are not among the seventeen for a variety of reasons. Similarities between *The Waste Land* and the novels of Elizabeth Bowen, Ivy Compton-Burnett, Rosamond Lehmann, Mervyn Peake, and J. R. R. Tolkien appear to me coincidental. William Golding's resemblances to Eliot in most instances derive from Eliot's plays, not from *The Waste Land*. C. P. Snow's characters Sheila and Lewis Eliot, who appear to resemble Vivienne and T. S. Eliot superficially, resulted from pure coincidence—not only does Lewis Eliot derive largely from C. P. Snow, but Lord Snow took the name from Port Eliot in Cornwall. He has since regretted using the name precisely because of parallels to T. S. Eliot's life.[12] And Rumer Godden, some of whose novels owe their organization, content, imagery, and verbal echoes to Eliot's work, used not *The Waste Land* but the *Four Quartets*.[13] *The Waste Land* has influenced several novelists to a lesser degree, but not significantly enough to suggest that they be present in this study.

The novels of Virginia Woolf present an instance of *The Waste Land*'s influence easy to assert but difficult to prove. Because she valued Eliot's critical ability and poetic talents, particularly after meeting him in 1918 shortly after the Armistice,[14] Woolf perhaps naturally drew images and themes from *The Waste Land* in some of her novels, notably *To the Lighthouse* (1927) and *The Waves* (1931). Hogarth published the first English edition of *The Waste Land*, "and Virginia herself set *The Waste Land*, in this way absorbing the poem letter by letter, word by word, so that some of its imagery crept into her novels at a later time."[15] Eliot praised both Virginia and Leonard Woolf for the layout and pagination, which he found superior to those of the American edition. By 1924 Eliot felt secure enough in his friendship to speculate in a letter to Virginia Woolf whether the coming generation would profit from the writing of either.[16] For her part, Woolf mined *The Waste Land* in *To the Lighthouse*—conceived in 1925, written in 1926, and published in 1927—for several descriptions and images, and perhaps as well for a sense of despair, boredom, and aimlessness of the moderns. *The Waves* appeared four years later, and "F. O. Overcarsh called it 'in certain re-

spects a prose version of *The Waste Land.*'"[17] Woolf's early familiarity
with Eliot's poem and her appreciation of both poem and poet resulted
in the presence of *The Waste Land* in her novels, particularly when her
familiarity with *The Waste Land* led to refinement of her imagery. However, since she rarely went beyond such thematic parallels as Mrs.
Ramsay's desire to give, sympathize, and control, and did not include
specific verbal echoes from *The Waste Land*, Woolf's novels do not provide solid evidence of influence.

Apart from evolving critical reactions and attempts to explicate the
poem, the immediate impact of *The Waste Land* was extraordinary. Ap-
pearing shortly after the Armistice, the poem expressed the shock,
horror, disillusionment, and sense of emptiness which the war brought
to its generation. Samuel Hynes explicitly connects *The Waste Land* with
the war:

> the war book above all others in the 'twenties was *The Waste Land*, and
> no account of the forces that formed the 'thirties generation would be
> accurate that neglected that powerfully influential poem. Eliot had an
> acute sense of what he called "the immense panorama of futility and
> anarchy that is contemporary history," and he put that sense of history
> into his poem. And in 1922 contemporary history meant vestiges of the
> war: hence the two veterans who meet in the first part, and Lil's hus-
> band, who has just been demobbed, in the second, and the shouting
> and crying in part five, which Eliot's note identifies with the Russian
> Revolution. But beyond that, the world of the poem, with its heaps of
> broken images and its shocked and passive and neurasthenic persons, is
> a paradigm of war's effects, and of a world emptied of order and mean-
> ing, like a battlefield after the battle. And the *manner* of the poem—its
> ironic tone, its imagery, its lack of heroes and heroism, its anti-rhetorical
> style—is also a consequence of the war, an application of war-poet prin-
> ciples to the post-war scene.[18]

Edmund Wilson's 1922 reading of *The Waste Land* depended upon the
poem's political and sociological content, not on its poetic techniques.
When I. A. Richards developed a theory of criticism which treated *The
Waste Land* as a significant poem,

> he took for granted that the modern writer *must* accept a world without
> belief, because that was the philosophical point to which human history
> had come: that is to say, he dealt with the modern literary situation in
> long-range philosophical terms. . . . Second, he proposed that the way
> out of this situation, for the writer, was a *formal* one—Eliot had found a
> form for unbelief, so others could, too.[19]

While *The Waste Land* spoke eloquently to the generation of the war and to the literary generation immediately following it, the influence of the poem has changed over the years, and later critics, notably F. O. Matthiessen and Cleanth Brooks, have added to the possibilities of interpretation. The seventeen novelists of this study, divided into "contemporaries" of Eliot, writers between the wars, and writers after World War II, both reflect and anticipate the developing critical readings of the poem.

The Waste Land's influence on the modern British novel suggests a definite pattern. The initial response was to the power of Eliot's expression of a new-felt emptiness and meaninglessness in modern life, and novelists of the 1920s derived atmosphere, characters, and parts of their plots from the poem. The 1930s generation demonstrated several possibilities of influence, reacting to the subject of Eliot's poem, the atmosphere he described, specific techniques which Eliot found to express "unbelief," and even the proper relationship between images of the poem and a moral or ethical context. The novelists of the 1950s and 1960s, however, reveal the limitations of *The Waste Land*'s ability to continue shaping novelists' art, for these writers repudiate the moral tone of the poem and treat it as a literary event rather than as an accurate and living expression of the modern age. After sixty years, *The Waste Land* most often appears in a novel merely as reference or allusion for its own sake, at best peripheral to contemporary novelists' concerns. As critics and reviewers have grappled with *The Waste Land*, trying to identify the poem's meanings and to come to terms with *The Waste Land* as a poem, they have helped to form this pattern by altering readers' perceptions. The novelists, in their turn, have helped to "define" *The Waste Land* by their varied uses of it.

PART 1

The Waste Land's Early Impact

Many readers may question my selection of Richard Aldington, E. M. Forster, Ford Madox Ford, D. H. Lawrence, and Aldous Huxley for demonstrations of *The Waste Land*'s early impact. Of these five, Forster, Ford, and Lawrence had already established literary reputations, and when *The Waste Land* appeared, it included a clear echo of Huxley's first novel, *Crome Yellow*. To complicate matters, Aldington, Forster, and Lawrence frequently expressed their dissatisfaction with *The Waste Land* as well as their disapproval of T. S. Eliot. These considerations raise important issues regarding the nature of literary influence.

First, *The Waste Land*'s contributions to these novelists consisted of imagery, character, and suggestions of plot which were compatible with what the novelists had already determined to create. The effect of the poem was to enhance, rather than to shape, these novelists' art. The process by which an established novelist could combine previously stated themes with *The Waste Land*'s influence has been described by Roger Poole in his discussion of Virginia Woolf's use of the Philomel myth before and after *The Waste Land*'s appearance. After Poole remarks, "I think the influence of 'Tom' Eliot on Virginia in the years after the war is greater than has been realised,"[1] he notes that Woolf used birds singing in Greek (comparable to Eliot's lines on Philomel) in *Beginning Again* (1913), as well as referring directly to Eliot in *Mrs. Dalloway* (1925) and *The Waves* (1931). Obviously the first reference could not derive from *The Waste Land*, but Poole shows how Woolf's use of the image became more clearly defined as she developed a more heightened awareness of the image's symbolic import, partly through the offices of *The Waste Land*.

> I think that the associations are cumulative. . . . By the time Eliot had
> added his notation they had become the perfect symbol for a state of
> mind which, though apparently "insane" and definitely incomprehen-
> sible to the outsider, . . . is itself meaningful, indeed charged with
> meaning to the highest possible degree.[2]

The sources for post-*Waste Land* passages written by Forster, Ford, and
Lawrence are questionable since similar themes appear in pre-*Waste
Land* novels to some degree. However, the sheer number of characters
and images compatible with Eliot's poem and the more intense effect of
these in the post-*Waste Land* novels suggest that Eliot did influence
these established novelists to some extent.

The presence of Aldington, Forster, and Lawrence raises a second
problem. Since these writers frequently voiced their disapproval of
Eliot and of *The Waste Land,* how could they be subject to Eliot's influence? The problem seems to rest on the word "influence," which con-
notes approval or agreement as well as impact. For me, the issue is
Eliot's presence rather than the novelist's attitude towards poem or
poet. Aldington, for example, satirizes Eliot and parodies the poem in
his novels, as he does with other writers (notably Ford and Lawrence)
in *Death of a Hero.* Although Aldington's art presents a reactive rather
than approving view of Eliot and of *The Waste Land,* the poem and poet
nevertheless have their place in Aldington's work and have occupied
the novelist sufficiently to affect his art. I would not argue that Aldington's reaction to *The Waste Land* was as significant as Henry Fielding's
artistic responses to Samuel Richardson's *Pamela,* but I do feel that
Aldington's negative views of Eliot and his poem, expressed in Aldington's art, are as indicative of Eliot's impact as would have been admir-
ing imitation. The impulse to refute, as Victor Purcell indicated by
choosing the pseudonym "Myra Buttle" (my rebuttal), is also a source
of inspiration and, as such, deserves consideration.

Eliot's influence on these five writers seems limited since several traits
of the novelists' style—particularly Forster's, Ford's, and Lawrence's—
antedated *The Waste Land.* Forster, Ford, and Lawrence, however, address the problems raised by Eliot's Fisher King and the enigmatic
thunder of "What the Thunder Said," while Huxley adapted several
Eliotian characters and images in his depiction of a modern Waste
Land.

1

RICHARD ALDINGTON

What Branches Grow Out of This *Stony Rubbish?*

Richard Aldington's relationship to T. S. Eliot and to *The Waste Land* was much closer than that of Forster, Ford, or Lawrence. Aldington's treatment of Eliot and the poem was *ad hominem*, and most critics who have discussed Aldington's novels and parodies have assumed that Aldington was bitter, jealous of Eliot, and even unable to restrain himself in his desire for revenge. Aldington was none of these. Eliot and Aldington established an early friendship, worked together on the *Criterion*, influenced each other's writing, showed every sign of remaining fast friends, and could have had one of the most fruitful and amiable relationships in literary history. Instead, they rarely saw each other after the mid-1920s, stopped corresponding shortly after Aldington's publication of *Stepping Heavenward* in 1931, and did not renew correspondence until shortly before Aldington's death in 1962. The rupture did not occur because one man was in the wrong, but because each man, not realizing the feelings and motives of the other, inadvertently offended the other. Had Aldington confronted Eliot on various points which offended him deeply instead of venting his frustration in letters to others, and had Eliot informed Aldington of the flaws in Aldington's interpretations of Eliot's attitudes and actions, both men might have avoided unnecessary pain. Eliot, however, remained genuinely puzzled by Aldington's "attacks" and Aldington did not understand why Eliot, for personal reasons, could not tolerate several of Aldington's statements.

The transition from Aldington's early friendship with Eliot to their subsequent break occurred gradually over the span of a decade. From Aldington's point of view, which included several mistaken assumptions regarding Eliot, Aldington was the victim of Eliot's opportunism, arrogance, and snobbery. Aldington resented the supposed ingratitude of a protégé, and he found evidence of Eliot's "inferiority" in *The Waste Land*'s pessimism, Eliot's limited knowledge and reading, and the literary strategies to which Aldington attributed Eliot's receiving the Order of Merit. Working with Eliot on the *Criterion*, Aldington felt himself regarded as the lackey of prima donnas' whims and the performer of others' drudgery. Certainly the decline of his own popularity and influence during the 1930s also rankled as Aldington watched Eliot's reputation continue to grow. Aldington's assumptions regarding Eliot and the subsequent impulse to satirize both the poet and *The Waste Land* developed slowly until his assumptions became hardened convictions. The development of Aldington's apparent enmity for Eliot is complex, but the process is necessary to any explanation of Aldington's satires of Eliot and *The Waste Land*.

Before the publication of *The Waste Land*, Aldington was Eliot's most ardent enthusiast, excepting Ezra Pound. In a series of letters to Amy Lowell (who remained unconvinced), Aldington urged her to regard Eliot as a serious poet. Aldington was sufficiently immersed in the literary life of London to inform Lowell, in 1917, of his associations with Ezra Pound (since 1912), Harold Monro, F. S. Flint, Ford Madox Hueffer (Ford), W. B. Yeats, D. H. Lawrence, and H.D.[1] In 1920, when the *Times Literary Supplement* published an anonymous review of a modern American poetry anthology,[2] praising Edgar Lee Masters and omitting other modern poets, Aldington complained to Lowell of the omission of Eliot: "It seems to me insane to talk of modern American poetry, without mentioning [Eliot, H.D., and Pound]. Both Eliot & Pound are at least damned clever."[3] A month later, Aldington's praise became more enthusiastic after encountering resistance from Lowell, although he conceded that Eliot's "influence as a critic is much greater than as a poet. . . ."[4] After noting that he had sent a copy of the review to *Poetry* editor Harriet Monroe, asking her to reply to it, Aldington went on to complain about the *TLS* review, "a very supercilious article, which put Fletcher above everyone else and never mentioned H. D., Ezra, Eliot, Wallace Stevens, and several more; patronized you and put Lindsay above Sandburg!" Aldington appears genuinely happy at Eliot's success (7 April 1921): "He has had a positive ovation here & almost at a step reaches the first rank of contemporary critics. He can write anywhere and almost anything he chooses."[5] In a letter dated 26 August 1921, Aldington's concern has shifted to Eliot's mental health and lack of money:

> I am rather delayed by having to rush off from time to time to save
> people from nervous breakdowns. I think Eliot is so ill that he will
> die—he is working in a London bank & trying to write as well. It is a
> disgrace to England that so talented a man is not given a pension. . . .[6]

A month later, he again praised Eliot's talent and urbanity,[7] but Eliot's
situation continued to trouble Aldington. He informed Lowell that
despite his efforts to convince Eliot to leave Lloyd's Bank, Eliot preferred the bank to the prospect of submitting to the whims of editors
for his living.

In 1922, Aldington's letters to Amy Lowell became more pragmatic.
On 5 May 1922 he tried to solicit ten pounds for an "Eliot fund,"
opening with "This is an official begging letter! T. S. Eliot is very ill,
will die if he doesn't get proper & complete rest for a long time."[8] This
was part of the ill-fated *Bel Esprit* scheme of Ezra Pound, an attempt to
provide Eliot a sufficient income to enable him to leave Lloyd's by so-
liciting private subscriptions. After Ezra Pound publicized the scheme,
Aldington wrote to Lowell that Pound had done so for his own public
acclaim,[9] and he continued as late as 18 July 1922 to urge Lowell to
contribute: "we have passed the £200 line. Surely you won't refuse £10
a year. If I can afford it, you can."[10] However, when it became apparent
that the scheme would not raise sufficient funds to guarantee Eliot an
income beyond one year, and when the publicity of the affair had
resulted in extreme embarrassment for Eliot, he indicated that he would
remain at the bank. Aldington's attempts to gain Lowell's support of
Eliot's poetry proved as futile as his attempts to solicit money. Amy
Lowell referred to Eliot on 4 April 1923, expressing her doubts concerning him as a poet:

> I read Eliot's "Waste Land" with great interest, but I am more skeptical
> than ever. The book is immensely interesting as a record of a state of
> mind. As such, I think it is quite moving and startling, but I cannot find
> it poetry and I cannot help thinking that the state of mind itself is a
> pathological one. I think I should call it war hysteria if I were asked to
> analyze it; it seems to me the state of mind which a good many of the
> men of that generation are in. They are getting out of it over here, little
> by little.[11]

Aldington's attempts to convince Lowell of Eliot's worth reveal the
sincerity of his admiration for Eliot's work and concern for Eliot's situation.

The shift from the tone and substance of these letters to the impression Aldington has left upon most critics rests on several factors. Aldington seems to regard Eliot as a protégé who has surpassed his

patron, and who has shown ingratitude and indifference to one who had tried to advance Eliot's reputation and improve Eliot's financial position. Writing to John Atkins in 1958, Aldington recalled that he "introduced two other writers to the *TLS* in the early 1920's. One was called T. S. Eliot and the other Herbert Read!"[12] Valerie Eliot notes that in 1919, Eliot received "a request from Bruce Richmond to write occasional leading articles for the *Times Literary Supplement*."[13] That request resulted from what Aldington later described as "the most complicated piece of diplomacy I have ever undertaken." Richmond, "after about six months of cautious work," agreed to lunch with Eliot, despite the influence of "opposition writers" who had prejudiced Richmond against Eliot. Despite an awkward beginning, not improved by Eliot's sporting "a derby hat and an Uncle Sam beard he had cultivated in Switzerland," the meeting ended well. "Afterwards Richmond made a discreet Oxonian jest about the beard, but when we next met Tom it had vanished; and all was forgotten and forgiven."[14] Aldington misdated this episode "about 1922," but it was certainly the initial meeting with Richmond which led to Eliot's writing lead articles for the *TLS*.

Aldington's major grievance concerning Eliot was the magnitude of Eliot's later reputation, which Aldington felt was primarily the result of sycophancy, luck, and literary strategy. Writing to John Atkins in 1957, Aldington claimed that

> Eliot managed to cash in on the work done by Ford, [Wyndham] Lewis, Pound and myself, because F., L., and I did 3 years in the army, and Pound cleared out in 1919. Eliot sucked up to the bishops and the dons and the editors and the reviewers—and got his reward.[15]

Although Aldington, a combat veteran, resented the advantages which accrue to wartime civilians, his resentment rested on assumption rather than fact. Before Aldington and Eliot met, Eliot, "preoccupied with trying to find some way in which he could be useful to the country," confronted a solid wall of bureaucratic inertia:

> Having been rejected for active service owing to a congenital hernia and tachycardia, he applied to the Intelligence branch of the United States Navy, only to discover that he would have to enlist as a seaman and take an examination in a number of subjects. This was too slow and uncertain, so he turned his attention to the Army, where the Quartermaster Corps had been suggested. No sooner had he collected about sixteen "excellent" recommendations from various English officials, than he ran into a lieutenant engaged in starting a Political Intelligence section, who was quite sure that Eliot was the man he wanted. . . . A week

or so later, Eliot heard that Washington had cancelled the project. He was referred next to a major in charge of the ordinary Army Intelligence, who thought he would obtain a commission. . . .[16]

A later promise from the Navy Intelligence led Eliot to abandon the Army, problems of American versus British citizenship complicated matters further, and as a result Eliot remained a civilian despite his efforts to serve. Had Aldington been aware of these difficulties (which Eliot explained in a letter to John Quinn in November 1918), perhaps his feeling that Eliot had profited from the military service of others, such as himself, would not have developed into resentment.

Another irritation, which Aldington mentioned to John Atkins in a letter dated 22 June 1957, was Eliot's reputation as a founder of the modernist movement. As Aldington stated, Ford Madox Ford "sponsored the 1912 modernist verse (then modernist) which for some odd reason got attributed to Eliot though he turned up several years after us—he imitated us, not we him!"[17] Ironically, Eliot stressed the same point in a letter to Henry Treece, correcting factual errors in Treece's talk on modern poetry. Eliot informed Treece, who had included Eliot in a 1913 gathering of modern poets, that he had not come to England until the following year.[18] However, Aldington regarded exaggerations of Eliot's reputation as Eliot's doing, and the preferential treatment accorded to Eliot, compared with that accorded to his predecessors, further annoyed Aldington. Writing to Rachel Annand Taylor in 1950, Aldington criticized a *Festschrift* being prepared for Pound's birthday:

> Need I say that the publication seems to be chiefly about T. S. Eliot O.M.? Incidentally, not one of Ezra's pre-Eliot surviving friends (e.g. Carlos Williams, H.D., Flint,) is included, and it seems I was included because someone happened to recollect my associations with him "long ago, when we used to take Ezra seriously" as Lorenzo [D. H. Lawrence] used to say derisively.[19]

Whenever Aldington reflected on Eliot's reputation, his comments were on the order of "The race is not to the swift, nor the battle to the strong." He wrote to Alan Bird that "The highly paid writers of the last 40 years have not been the best, and those honoured are not the best. Gold medals and O.Ms. for the Audens and Eliots—calumny and even persecution for [D. H.] Lawrences and Aldous Huxleys."[20] He described T. E. Lawrence's writing and production of *Seven Pillars of Wisdom* as "a masterly campaign of literary strategy beyond even the powers of T. S. Eliot"[21] and called Eliot, after T. E. Lawrence, "the biggest fraud and cleverest literary strategist and self-advertiser of this century. It is interesting to note how the English intellectuals have allowed themselves to be cowed by a series of American dictators, from Russell Lowell to Berenson and Eliot."[22]

Although he did not refer to the problem in his autobiography, *Life for Life's Sake*, Aldington's association with Eliot on the *Criterion* led to even greater resentment. Aldington felt that he had not received due credit for his efforts on behalf of the magazine and that Eliot and others had not shown proper respect for his literary capabilities. Earlier Eliot had confided in Aldington and had accepted Aldington's criticism of his poetry. However, when Eliot criticized one of Aldington's articles, Aldington took offense at Eliot's "pompous" tone. On 17 July 1922, Eliot wrote to Aldington to say that he was surprised at Aldington's reaction, that he had not criticized Aldington so severely as Aldington had criticized him, and that if Aldington was able to dish it out, he ought also to be able to take it.[23] Except for this exchange, however, Aldington and Eliot remained on good terms. On 18 November 1922, Eliot confided to Aldington that he intended to see a solicitor about a possible libel suit against the Liverpool *Post* (concerning what the *Post* had published regarding the *Bel Esprit* affair),[24] and the tone of subsequent letters between the two was cordial. By 1924, however, Aldington felt that he was being exploited and complained, not to Eliot but to Harold Monro:

> I don't see why you should blackguard me about the Criterion. I did a hell of a lot of work for it, gave suggestions, procured authors, acted as secretary, tried to get subscriptions, got people interested in it, and all for a pound a week! I had continuously to put aside other work to answer Eliot's letters for him; I found him difficult to work with and I also found I was absolutely paralysed mentally by the snobbish attitude of the "Criterion."[25]

Aldington, however mistakenly, felt the others regarded him as a hack "allowed" to help members of a literary elite. The year before Aldington wrote his complaint to Monro, Eliot had been suffering from surprisingly similar pressures. Aldington knew that Eliot and Vivienne were having difficulties, but he might have been surprised at the anxiety and even hysteria implicit in Eliot's letter to John Quinn dated 12 March 1923:

> I am now in the midst of a terrific crisis. I wish to heaven that I had never taken up the *Criterion*. It seemed a good thing, and it is a good thing, but although it is a pity to drop such a promising beginning I may very soon have to drop it and I am quite sincere when I wish that I had

never undertaken it. It has been an evergrowing responsibility. . . . I think the work and worry have taken 10 years off my life. I have sunk the whole of my strength for the past 18 months into this confounded paper, when I ought to have been minding my business and doing my own writing. . . . In order to carry on the *Criterion* I have had to neglect not only the writing I ought to be doing but my private affairs of every description which for some time past I have not had a moment to deal with. I have not even time to go to a dentist or to have my hair cut, and at the same time I see the *Criterion* full of most glaring defects which I could only avoid by having still more time for it to devour, and at the same time I am simply unfit to take risks which in any case I should not be justified in taking . . . I am worn out, I cannot go on.[26]

Had Aldington and Eliot discussed the matter with each other instead of with Monro and Quinn, perhaps the ultimate crisis of their friendship would not have occurred.

One matter which Eliot would not discuss, and of which Aldington surely was ignorant, was the role of Eliot's private life in *The Waste Land*. John Peter, in an article quickly suppressed by Eliot in 1952, argued that one can read *The Waste Land* as dramatic monologue:

At some previous time the speaker has fallen completely—perhaps the right word is "irretrievably"—in love. The object of this love was a young man who soon afterwards met his death, it would seem by drowning. Enough time has now elapsed since his death for the speaker to have realized that the focus for affection that he once provided is irreplaceable. The monologue which, in effect, the poem presents is a meditation upon this deprivation, upon the speaker's stunned and horrified reactions to it, and on the picture which, as seen through its all but insupportable bleakness, the world presents.[27]

As James E. Miller, Jr., has subsequently revealed, this reading is compatible with Eliot's pre-*Waste Land* experiences and with earlier drafts of *The Waste Land* unavailable to Peter. In France, Eliot developed a close friendship with Jean Verdenal, who died during the war. Grieving for his lost friend, Eliot precipitously entered his disastrous marriage to Vivienne. If, as Miller has argued, Eliot is the Fisher King, Vivienne the neurasthenic woman of "A Game of Chess," and Jean Verdenal the person to whom the Fisher King speaks,[28] then Eliot would have been extremely sensitive to any remark about the poem which came too close to this view. Perhaps dreading that Aldington was aware of Eliot's grief for Verdenal and its effect on his relationship with Vivienne, Eliot met Aldington's comments on the poem with cold rage. Eliot, who often demonstrated laudable restraint when he was baited, had absolutely no tolerance on this subject. Aldington, unaware of the importance of Eliot's "personal" interpretation and occasionally carried away by his own sense of parody and satire, often struck a nerve. If Aldington was baffled by Eliot's sensitivity, Eliot may have felt threatened by Aldington's persistently satiric references to the poem.

As early as 15 November 1922, Eliot wrote to Aldington that he regarded *The Waste Land* as "a thing of the past as far as I am concerned and I am now feeling toward a new form and style."[29] If he had hoped to discourage comments on his poem, Eliot was disappointed. Conrad Aiken, describing how he once jokingly referred to the poem as *An Anatomy of Melancholy*, noted Eliot's "icy fury" and statement "There is nothing melancholy about it!"[30] When Aiken explained that the reference was not to the poem's content but to the number of quotations in the work, Eliot accepted Aiken's jest. When Aldington regarded *The Waste Land* critically, he usually emphasized the unacknowledged quotations and depressing quality of the poem, but when he joked about the poem Eliot took the jest in a context different from that which Aldington had intended, and was offended. A typical instance of Aldington's attitude and humor appeared in his letter to F. S. Flint (8? April 1923):

> I fear I have offended T. S. Eliot with one of my untimely (yet timeless) jests. He went to the country for a short holiday, so I wrote and asked him if he was cultivating his waste land. Ominous silence! I haven't dared to work off a more complex and perfidious jest, which is: That T.S.E. is rumored to have been offered a title, that he is to call himself Viscount Criterion, with the motto "Re-Joyce, for the Kingdom of Heaven is waste land." (Arms "Three high brows rampant, gules").[31]

Perhaps the second jest would have revealed the harmless nature of Aldington's first remark in a way that Eliot could accept, but "cultivating his waste land," implying an identification between Eliot and the Fisher King, was too close to home for Eliot. In 1925 Aldington resigned from the *Criterion*, but by then both his attitude towards *The Waste Land* and Eliot's sensitivity to that attitude were firmly established. As Aldington wrote to Harold Monro shortly before he resigned, "Why can't we admit without humbug all the horrifying truth and yet say: 'All the same, my dear philosophers and Waste Landers, I don't mean to be put off by you and shall enjoy my few years of existence as much as any gilded fly.' "[32]

At least four years before the publication of *Death of a Hero*, Aldington's attitude towards Eliot and *The Waste Land* included several opinions which appear in Aldington's novels: the poem is depressing, fragmented, overrated, intellectually pretentious, obscure, and even plagiaristic; the poet is arrogant, ridiculous in his desire for recognition as an Englishman, and pompous. Personalities aside, however, Aldington never publicly questioned Eliot's poetic genius beyond its alleged misuse.

> RA, in 1930, said, "It is insane to question Eliot's genius as a poet or his extreme skill as a critic. What can be attacked, and should be, is his expressed and implied attitude to life; and the over-intellectual over-specialized type of poetry he has created as a refuge from life."[33]

His objections resemble early critics' reactions to *The Waste Land*. Despite his lack of appreciation for poem and poet, however, Aldington borrowed from *The Waste Land* even in the process of lampooning Eliot. In *Death of a Hero* (1929), Aldington combines satire of Eliot with direct borrowing. The lampoon is heavy-handed, including a parody of Eliot's statement in his preface to *For Lancelot Andrewes* (1928), in which Eliot identified himself as "classicist in literature, royalist in politics, and Anglo-Catholic in religion":

> As for Mr. Waldo Tubbe, who hailed (why "hailed"?) from the Middle Western districts of the United States, he was an exceedingly ardent and patriotic British Tory, standing for Royalism in Art, Authority in Politics, and Classicism in Religion.[34]

This description, mocking Eliot's Missouri origins, English ancestry, editorial policy, and "Americanized Toryism," readily identifies Tubbe as Eliot.

Throughout the novel, Aldington creates a bleak atmosphere for a modern London which has become an urban Waste Land. George Winterbourne, the protagonist, perceives the modern blight in all its horror and commits suicide shortly before the Armistice by standing upright in the trenches. His parents, wife, and lover are completely indifferent to his death. In the tradition of Eliot's *Waste Land* women, George's mother's attitude towards her husband was "exasperation with him for existing at all and for interrupting her love affairs" (*DH*, 5). Her reaction to George's death is not the sorrow of the bereaved mother, but relief from modern boredom.

> The telegram from the War Office . . . went to the home address in the country, and was opened by Mrs. Winterbourne. Such an excitement for her, almost a pleasant change, for it was pretty dull in the country just before the Armistice. She was sitting by the fire, yawning over her

twenty-second lover—the affair had lasted nearly a year—when the servant brought the telegram. It was addressed to Mr. Winterbourne, but,
of course, she opened it; she had an idea that "one of *those* women" was
"after" her husband; who, however, was regrettably chaste, from cow-
ardice. (*DH*, 5–6)

Mrs. Winterbourne consoles herself by immediately dragging her lover
to bed. George's wife, Elizabeth, and his mistress, Fanny, seem relieved to learn of his death. They combine the indifference of Eliot's
typist and the "sophistication" of the Thames Maidens, as well as
resembling modern women described by D. H. Lawrence in *Women in
Love* (1920).

> Elizabeth and Fanny were not grotesques. . . . They both had that rather
> hard efficiency of the war and post-war female, veiling the ancient pred-
> atory and possessive instincts under a skilful smoke-barrage of Freud-
> ian and Havelock Ellis theories. To hear them talk theoretically was most
> impressive. They were terribly at ease upon the Zion of sex, abounding
> in inhibitions, dream symbolism, complexes, sadism, repressions, maso-
> chism, Lesbianism, sodomy, et cetera. Such women, you thought; no
> sentimental nonsense about *them.* No silly emotional slip-slop messes
> would ever come *their* way. (*DH*, 17)

Comparing pre-war with wartime London, Aldington described the
change in terms of increasing drinking and carnality, both of which
play prominent roles in *The Waste Land.* "Pre-war London was comparatively sober. Numbers of women did not even drink at all, and cock-
tails and communal copulation had not then been developed to their
present state of intensity" (*DH*, 122).

Aldington's capsule description of man is substantially his impression of "The Burial of the Dead": "For man is an ambulatory digestive
tube which wants to keep alive, and Death waits for him" (*DH*, 136). In
two pointed authorial comments, Aldington states that the blight on
the land results from man's spiritual blight. At the end of the prefatory
chapter, Aldington addresses the reader directly on this issue:

> That is why I am writing the life of George Winterbourne, a unit, one
> human body murdered, but to me a symbol. It is an atonement, a
> desperate effort to wipe off the blood-guiltiness. Perhaps it is the wrong
> way. Perhaps the poison will still be in me. If so, I shall search for some
> other way. But I shall search. I know what is poisoning me. I do not
> know what is poisoning you, but you are poisoned. Perhaps you too
> must atone. (*DH*, 29)

Early in his first chapter, Aldington reinforces this Waste Land crisis: "Rummy old England. Pox on you, you old bitch, you've made worms' meat of us. (We've made worms' meat of ourselves)" (*DH*, 34).

In addition to resemblances which may be largely coincidental, Aldington included verbal echoes from *The Waste Land*. Echoing Ophelia's mad speech (*Hamlet*, IV, v, 72–73), Eliot closed the pub scene of "A Game of Chess" with the barkeeper's "Good night, ladies, good night, sweet ladies, good night, good night" (l. 172). Aldington used a similar passage to address one of his characters: "Good-night, Elizabeth, good-night, sweet, sweet Elizabeth, good-night, good-night" (*DH*, 155). (Although Aldington's source, like Eliot's, could be Shakespeare, one should note that Aldington, after Eliot, addressed the echo to a female of "low" character.) Immediately after his caricature of Eliot as Waldo Tubbe, Aldington parodied Eliot's note defining "Shantih" as "The Peace which passeth understanding." The passage also suggests the imagery of debris in the Thames which opens "The Fire Sermon": "Sunday in London. In the City, nuts, bolts, infinite curious pieces of old metal, embedded in the black shiny roads, frozen rivers of ink, may be examined without danger. The peace of commerce which passes all desolation" (*DH*, 111). George Winterbourne realized he was in a Waste Land and refused to remain there, preferring suicide to modern life. In the novel, Aldington creates a modern setting as bleak, barren, and depressing as *The Waste Land*'s, even borrowing Eliot's images and words. Despite his claim that *The Waste Land* is depressing and therefore an inappropriate picture of life, Aldington has written a novel which requires, for its final effect, a similar awareness of Waste Land squalor in modern life and pity for George, who, like Eliot's Fisher King, perceives this squalor in all its horror.

Georgie, in *The Colonel's Daughter* (1931), also lives in a Waste Land. Her matrimonial prospects are bleak:

> Georgie wasn't pretty, Georgie wasn't rich, and thousands and thousands of the young men lay dead in rows, or they lived on a couple of hundred a year with no prospects, or they were rich and she never saw them, or they were flabby and wanted to be kept, or they were scattered from Honduras to Hong-Kong, from Labrador to the Straits, administering the Greatest-Empire-in-the-World, or they laboured in unhealthy climates (with one year's leave in three or five) making a thousand a year, and dying, or at best growing yellow and liverish, so that wholesale petrol, copra and coffee, rubber and tea, metals and minerals, might be lavishly at the disposal of Horace the Patriot and his pals.[35]

Georgie has other problems, including the sterility of life in general
and the drabness of her person. Aldington links the plight of Georgie
directly with the War. Purfleet declaims,

> "I know what you are going to say—they fought not for money, but from
> patriotism, sense of duty, love of country. Two minutes' silence! *You* and
> the other millions did 'your duty.' Result: the extinction of a generation
> of men, the misery of their women, and utterly senseless 'peace,' and
> the enrichment of noble-hearted men like our old pal Stimms." (CD, 50)

The vision of human relationships as either the dispassionate carnality of Eliot's young man carbuncular or the neurotic lust of the woman
in "A Game of Chess" dominates the novel, with a difference. Aldington's satire of sexual promiscuity is in sharp contrast to Eliot's disapproving, even prudish, depictions. This contrast receives emphasis
when Eliot himself enters the novel. Aldington lampoons Eliot more
directly in this novel, using two separate characters. The first, mentioned only once, is clearly T. S. Eliot, critic: "But Mr. Judd felt for
Colonel Smithers that 'considerable respect' which our eminent natu-
ralised critic, Mr. T. S. Pym, feels for a very few select native authors"
(CD, 65). The other caricature depicts Eliot's attitude towards sexuality
as Aldington interpreted it. When Lizzie Judd's pregnancy results in a
belated proposal of marriage from Tom, the community feels disappointment at being cheated out of melodramatic suicide or infanticide.
The village splits into two factions, one accepting and the other op-
posing Lizzie. The latter group includes "the Rev. Thomas Stearn (the
Methodist divine)" (CD, 109). The Reverend Mr. Stearn's attitudes towards sexual license reflect the prudish tone of *The Waste Land*, in
contrast to Aldington's satiric view. After "Mrs. Wrigley went into the
mercenary siren trade in a small but energetic way" (CD, 177), Thomas
Stearn appears extremely stupid when Mr. Wrigley represents himself
as a wronged husband, whose actual grievance is his wife's refusal to
share the proceeds:

> In his interview with the Reverend Thomas Stearn, that dissenting di-
> vine of high principles, Mr. Wrigley to some extent dissembled. The
> question of interests was not mentioned, but Mr. Wrigley laid great
> emphasis on the distress and misery of a motherless and wifeless home.
> . . . The Reverend Mr. Stearn melted with charity, and promised his aid;
> but his interview with Mrs. Wrigley was tempestuous and unsatisfac-
> tory. Among many other unsavoury epithets she called him "a stinking
> bible-puncher," "a measly drab-begotten ditch-delivered creeping jesus,"
> "a dram-drinking old hypocrite," and divers other unapostolic and less

quotable things. Mr. Stearn re-read John Knox's Monstrous Regiment of Women and denounced her and her loathly paramour (naming no names, however) in good set terms from the pulpit. Mr. Wrigley, who had never before been guilty of such excess, attended Chapel twice every Sunday, and gave such evident tokens of his regeneration that he might almost have qualified to recite his sins for the edification of out-of-door sects. (*CD*, 204–05)

Aldington's depiction of Eliot was not so direct as his caricature in *Death of a Hero*, but the ridicule may have been painful to Eliot, particularly in its implications of prudery, hypocrisy, and pomposity.

Neither *Death of a Hero* nor *The Colonel's Daughter* presented lampoons or parodies with which Eliot could not live, but *Stepping Heavenward* (1931) contained too personal and too effective an attack for Eliot to ignore. Answering a question about libel actions, Aldington wrote to Alan Bird,

> I don't think Pound could do anything about libel, but I'm not so sure of Eliot. When Chatto's did Stepping Heavenward as a Dolphin, Faber rang up Cha les Prentice (publishers behind the author's back!) and tried to persuade him to withdraw it. When Prentice (being a good friend of mine) refused F. hinted at action for libel, to which Prentice had the perfect reply that 1000 copies had been issued by Orioli a year before and Eliot had not complained.[36]

Writing to Richard Church in 1963, Eliot informed him that although he was willing to write something about Aldington and although he pitied Aldington, he could not write very much. Referring to *Stepping Heavenward*, Eliot stated that its publication had ended their relationship.[37] The book was far more serious to Eliot than satiric portrayal of his published attitudes or linking his name with buffoonery. In *Stepping Heavenward* Aldington presumed to write about Eliot's domestic difficulties with his first wife, presenting Ezra Pound as Lucas Cholmp, Vivienne Eliot as Adèle Paléologue, and T. S. Eliot as Jeremy Cibber (the allusion to Pope's nemesis Colly Cibber reflecting Aldington's opinion of Eliot's public acclaim).[38] Certainly Aldington crossed the bounds of taste. Perhaps at the time he was unaware of how close his satire came to the problems of Eliot's first marriage, but it is impossible to countenance some of Aldington's statements.

Stepping Heavenward contains a thinly disguised *ad hominem* attack on Eliot, mocking Eliot's American background, education, criticism, marriage to Vivienne, naturalization, and conversion to the Anglican church. Cibber is an emotionless, arrogant, and hypocritical strategist

whose works lack merit and whose success lacks validity. Cibber, edu-
cated at Harvard, spends a year at the Sorbonne, finds in England "his
spiritual home . . . in the ancient matrix of his race,"[39] determines to
become "either Historiographer or Laureate" (*SH*, 39), studies under
"Tibbitts" (Irving Babbitt), and writes papers "with the closest attention
to exactness of thought and precision of statement" (*SH*, 45). Aldington
explains Cibber's appearance of self-possession in a paraphrase of Eliot's criticism:

> This, as we now know from Cibber and his followers, is the mark of true
> greatness—to restrain not only the outward expression of emotion but
> emotion itself until nothing remains but the pure intellect and the pure
> spirit of contemplation. (*SH*, 46–47)

This statement derives from Eliot's "Tradition and the Individual
Talent":

> Poetry is not a turning loose of emotion, but an escape from emotion; it
> is not the expression of personality, but an escape from personality. But,
> of course, only those who have personality and emotions know what it
> means to want to escape from these things.[40]

Aldington distorted Eliot's largely misunderstood statement, already
susceptible to satire, by making absence of emotion an attribute of the
man, rather than of the man's dispassionate expression in his art.
Alluding to Eliot's "Imperfect Critics," Aldington writes of "the famous
'oblique' method which Cibber made so formidable, i.e., always to
create by destruction, to seek truth for oneself by exposing the errors of
others" (*SH*, 47). The attack focuses on the limitations of Cibber's (and
therefore Eliot's) "oblique method":

> Cibber's positive contributions are little short of meagre. Where he ex-
> celled was in pointing out the errors of others. Thus, while a man may
> spend eight or ten years in the composition of a book, Cibber could
> pick out all its faults in as many days, while the writing of one of the
> brilliant "exposure" essays would not occupy him more than six months.
> Thus, he acquired the reputation of always knowing more than the most
> learned, of possessing more abilities than the most talented. (*SH*, 63–64)

Eliot's reputation for learning was a sore point with Aldington, who
remarked frequently that Eliot was not so well-read as he seemed.
Writing to Alan Bird (18 July 1955), Aldington commented,

Of course the depreciation of Swinburne is rot, but then the trouble
of these war-fret years is the power of groups of sham intellectuals,
who haven't read (where would they find time?) and simply parrot
somebody like Tom Eliot (who I know reads damn little) or Leavis or
Richards.[41]

Aldington mentions Cibber's "*A Plea for Royalism in Western Europe*
(unfinished)," alluding to Eliot's "Four Elizabethan Dramatists: A Preface to an Unwritten Book," and emphasizes the extent to which Cibber's success rested on the efforts of Lucas Cholmp (Ezra Pound). The
pointedness of Aldington's comments on Eliot's poetry, criticism, early
background, and personality, complete with verbal echoes, would not
have been enough for Eliot to wish to suppress the book, but Aldington moved into more personal matters in a way literally unforgivable.
Some of his statements resemble those of John Peter in his 1952 article
(Eliot was more successful in his efforts to suppress the article than he
had been in his earlier attempt to stop publication of *Stepping Heavenward*).

Adèle, like Vivienne Eliot, becomes progressively more neurotic and
Aldington expressly blames Cibber for Adèle's condition. (Miller asks,
"In the meantime, what have Eliot's biographers made of Vivienne?"[42]
Aldington comes very close to Miller's analysis of Vivienne as the
neurasthenic woman of *The Waste Land* in *Stepping Heavenward*.) Cib-
ber receives sympathy for working in a haberdashery after he has
acquired a literary reputation, and the *literati* blame Adèle. In the novel,
Adèle's neurasthenia was aggravated by the blame she received for
Cibber's financial difficulties, and Aldington attempts to vindicate her
at Cibber's expense:

> Adèle became more and more unhappy. It is always *rather* unpleasant to
> live with a genius, but quite awful when he is a Cibber. . . . So long as
> Mrs. Cibber had the honour to be inscribed in the correct register, got
> her oats and fig-leaves, and received social consideration by reflection,
> what the devil else could she want? So many a time poor Adèle gazed
> into the mirror, clutching her hair distractedly, and whispering: "I'm
> going mad, I'm going mad, I'm going mad." (*SH*, 115)

The description recalls the neurasthenic woman of "A Game of Chess,"
also derived from Vivienne. Ultimately, Adèle "ran away with a young
man, and plunged into a life of hectic dissipation in Berlin. As the sole
reward for years of devoted misery she begged Cibber to divorce her"
(*SH*, 120). Apart from the distortion of the situation, Aldington's ver-

sion is cruel to both Eliot and Vivienne, but the crowning touch is
Cibber's reason for his conversion to the Catholic church:

> It almost looks as if Cibber had been waiting for an event of this kind to
> make his decision, though here again it is always possible that the real
> difficulty was to resolve into harmony the innumerable subtleties of that
> great and wonderful mind. At any rate, a fortnight after Adèle's deser-
> tion, Cibber was "received"—thereby making the divorce impossible.
> (*SH*, 120–21)

Cibber's entrance into the church becomes a deliberate and petty act of
vengeance. At this point Aldington stops his saint's life and proceeds
to the "universally known" sequel of his hagiography—Cibber inspires
a rash of conversions and England returns to Catholicism. Cibber dies
and becomes the first full American saint.

In the course of this pseudo-biography, *The Waste Land*'s pessimism
receives allusive criticism. Cibber writes "Notes on the Provincial Itinerary of the Emperor Antoninus," and Aldington's description indicates that he is parodying *The Waste Land*:

> At first sight it seems impossible that so abstruse a work should have
> such epoch-making consequences; but then, as we all know, it is the
> method and not the substance of a work which makes its value. And
> Cibber had method. The Itinerary itself was relegated to foot-notes,
> while the notes, cast in the form of a commentary, became the text.
> In the opening pages Cibber politely but decisively annihilated every
> living historian of eminence except Cholmp. Then, in passages of un-
> paralleled eloquence, now known to every schoolboy outside the great
> public schools, he lamented the decay and disappearance of so many
> once great and prosperous cities. (*SH*, 110)

This suggests the presence of notes at the end of *The Waste Land*, the
dedication to Ezra Pound, the falling towers of the Unreal Cities, the
familiarity of such lines as "April is the cruellest month," and the
comparison of past and present throughout the poem.

> Then deepening his organ-notes in a diapason of despair, he almost
> groaned that it was Too Late, that all Authority was doomed, and that
> nothing was left for the Noble Spirit but contemplation of the grave and
> the scurry of rats over the withered hopes of Mankind. (*SH*, 105)

Writing of the Itinerary's immediate reception, Aldington notes that
"two of Cholmp's stand-bys praised it extravagantly" (perhaps in ref-

erence to Conrad Aiken's favorable review of *The Waste Land*), that the book "had the sort of bad press which is very good for a reputation," that the book sold approximately five hundred copies, and that within a fortnight everyone raved about Cibber, "so original and *depressing*" (*SH*, 105–06). "In spite of his intellectual and social triumphs, life for him was almost equally compounded of dust and broken bottles. Broken bottles and dust he gave his followers" (*SH*, 114). In Cibber's home, "On the mantelpiece were a skull and a stuffed rat—emblems of Life and Death" (*SH*, 117).

This work, as a satire, has its merits, but as a portrait of Eliot it is a distortion. However, in a letter to Alan Bird dated 19 October 1952, Aldington maintained that he was "glad that 20 years ago I published my portraits of Cibber and Charlemagne Cox in Soft Answers"[43] (*Soft Answers* included both *Stepping Heavenward* and *Nobody's Baby*), apparently still unaware of the cruelty implicit in the work. At least *Stepping Heavenward* had a purgative effect, for Aldington seemed no longer compelled to lampoon Eliot in his novels.

All Men Are Enemies (1933) does not attack Eliot at all, but it does present the love story of Tony Clarendon and Katha in a Waste Land world. The novel begins with a statement from Isis which predetermines Tony's life.

> "Yet I am a goddess, and this is my gift. Since I am doomed to wander seeking always the lost fragments of Osiris, my lord, so do I doom this man always to wander seeking the lost fragments of a beauty which is lost, a peace which cannot be, an ecstasy which is a dream, a perfection which cannot exist."[44]

In *The Waste Land*, man has lost and continues to repress his hope. Tony early encounters hope's denial. When he asks his father, "what is *your* definition of God?" his father replies, "God is the exact equivalent of Shakespeare's ducdàme—a word to call fools together," and "Tony went empty away" (*AM*, 28). Tony equates the loss of meaning in the modern Waste Land with the absence of any positive values: "Everything that made life beautiful and interesting seemed to have been destroyed or smirched or violated in some way. . . . Even solitude was poisoned" (*AM*, 153). In answer to Helen's question of why Tony married Margaret, Tony replied in terms of a Waste Land: "Why do any of us marry? we set out hopefully after the mirage and finally grow accustomed to the desert" (*AM*, 304). This novel, without mentioning Eliot at all, expresses a sense of futility and disillusionment which is also present in *The Waste Land*.

Rejected Guest (1939) mentions Eliot specifically but does not attack him. Describing a literary coterie of which he disapproves, Aldington writes that "There was the school of sacristans, who talked about Maritain as if they had read him, and rowed about Gerard Manley Hopkins and T. S. Eliot. . . . Except for Wyndham Lewis and Eliot, they were nobodies."[45] Eliot appears only in this reference, but evidence of the Waste Land world is abundant. David, the illegitimate son of a noble scion (who has died before acknowledging the child to his family) grows up in a social, intellectual, and physical Waste Land. In a comment worthy of Bernard Shaw, Aldington defines David's major problem: "People are not interested in the problem of bastardy. It is simply biology without culture" (*RG*, 3). Despite the "better" intentions of the parents of the neighborhood urchins, David's illegitimacy makes him an outcast from his peers: "True, the parents had respected the innocence of their dear little children and had spelled the word, b-a-s-t-a-r-d, forgetting that the fifty millions or so spent on education had borne some fruit and the darlings could already spell all the dirty words in the language" (*RG*, 39). David's mother, who regards herself as an actress although her room and board derive from a profession of more ancient repute, limits culture to name-dropping gossip. David's uncle is worse:

> Politically he was a Bung, professing with violent incoherence a brand of Tory democracy which would have staggered Disraeli. He had a rabid dislike for what he called "theory," which might be defined as all knowledge he did not possess himself, a vast field. (*RG*, 31)

The physical world in which David develops is a blighted prison, which Aldington identifies as a "waste land":

> When David escaped from the box of Gordon Terrace, it was only to a larger prison. Like two fostering arms of the mother goddess, Industry, railway embankments stretched north and south and sharply cut the horizon. Smoke and coal-dust swept across the streets of small houses and left them gritty or greasy with thin black mud. Under the northern embankment was a noisy main street with shops and trams, but the nearer streets were almost empty and too wide with the melancholy of defeated pretentiousness. There were meagre unsuccessful trees in iron corsets, some of them dead, just dumped there and left untended because for some reason decaying saplings in the pavement are respectable. The fronts of the houses were all red brick with yellow sandstone window frames and the backs were yellow brick; and the concrete yards all ended in a bit of waste land. . . . Holding someone's hand David

walked through these streets, in a drift of sooty dust or under a fine grey rain, and looked wide-eyed upon civilization. (*RG*, 27–28)

Martindale provides David with a vision of the future that is worse than the past, a "brutalitarian epoch" dominated by lust for world power. Aldington does not resist an opportunity to mock the familiar opening line of *The Waste Land*: "April, we know, is the cruellest month; but at Saint-Australe it was beautiful. . . . As it was the most attractive part of the whole year, everybody went away except David, Mr. Martindale, and Prince Alleoti" (*RG*, 289).

Although Aldington's *Life for Life's Sake: A Book of Reminiscences* (1941) frequently mentions Eliot, most of Aldington's comments are either extremely favorable to Eliot or focus on a minor absurdity, such as Eliot's tipping his hat to the guard at Buckingham Palace. After the publication of *Stepping Heavenward* and Eliot's violent reaction to it, Aldington learned (as he should have known earlier) that he had wounded Eliot deeply, and in the future he exercised more restraint in his public utterances about Eliot. He included such details in his autobiography as Eliot's being the only one in London to offer Aldington a place to stay when he visited (*Life*, 238), commented that Eliot was surprisingly sensitive to the beauties of nature (*Life*, 260), and even praised Eliot's editorship of the *Criterion* (*Life*, 265). Aldington confined his negative comments to private letters. His published lecture on the poetry of Pound and Eliot criticized aspects of Eliot's poetry without denying Eliot's poetic genius, and Aldington no doubt felt to the end of his days that Eliot's reaction was much more violent than his satire itself justified. Part of the difficulty in the relationship of these two men, aside from their unwillingness to communicate mutual grievances to each other, involves Aldington's sense of satire. Commenting on his first two novels, Aldington noted that "I gave a certain amount of freedom to a satirical verve, which amused me and those who shared my views and annoyed the people it was meant to annoy. Can a satirist ask for more?" (*Life*, 373–74). As he discovered, a satirist must ask for more.

Aldington has been underrated as a novelist, partly due to the public and critical reactions to his debunking biographies of Norman Douglas and T. E. Lawrence. By 1961, partly owing to the influence of those who were offended in one way or another by Aldington, his books were out of print in his own country, although they enjoyed widespread popularity in the USSR, Czechoslovakia, Italy, Poland, and elsewhere in Eastern Europe. Aldington was considerably disappointed. "In September 1929, when I sat in the Paris café reading the letters and telegrams about Death of a Hero, it seemed reasonable to think that I had achieved such ambitions as I possessed. By September 1939 nothing was left" (*Life*, 403). Comparing his own scholarship, criticism, poetry, and novels with the "meagre" work of Eliot, and having difficulties keeping his work in print while Eliot was winning such honors as the Nobel Prize and the Order of Merit, Aldington associated Eliot's success with his own lack of success. Had he desired, he could have made his frustration public rather than confining his more bitter comments to private letters. Instead, he continued to write, and in the process he reversed the nature of his public comments on Eliot while coming closer to the spirit of *The Waste Land* in his later novels. Aldington's pessimistic novels approached the impression of disillusionment that *The Waste Land* made on most early readers, but Aldington and Eliot felt that their work and philosophy were incompatible. Nevertheless, Eliot's presence became an important aspect of Aldington's satire.

2

FORSTER, FORD,
and LAWRENCE

Faint Reverberations of Thunder

When *The Waste Land* appeared in 1922, E. M. Forster, Ford Madox Ford, and D. H. Lawrence had already established solid reputations as literary figures with distinctive, innovative styles. Nevertheless, Eliot's presence can be discerned to some extent in the post-1922 novels of all three. The novelists do not attempt to recreate a Waste Land for its own sake, but they draw from Eliot's poem to further their own purposes, revealing in the process that while they may have arrived at a Waste Land view not necessarily dependent on Eliot's, *The Waste Land* has some measure of responsibility for embellishing it.

E. M. FORSTER's *A Passage to India*

E. M. Forster disliked *The Waste Land* for what he called its obscure "scrap-heap" of quotations. However, George H. Thomson notes that Forster, in *A Passage to India*,

> now seriously accepts the inverse proposition that man must sustain and give life to the earth. The physical universe becomes part of man's spiritual burden. And like the universe of T. S. Eliot's poem, its characteristic aspect is that of a wasteland.
> The wasteland also invades man's sense of the beautiful, robbing him of the grace and dignity and formality of art.[1]

Forster's known preoccupation with the poem, his post-*Waste Land* completion of the Marabar Caves episode, and the relationship between Eliot's thunder and Forster's echo suggest that Forster found what he required to complete his novel in *The Waste Land*.

Forster did not appreciate *The Waste Land* as much as he did Eliot's earlier work. In *Abinger Harvest* (1934), Forster wrote that during World War I,

> The people I really clung to in the worst days were those who had nothing tangible to offer: Blake, William Morris, the early T. S. Eliot, J. K. Huysmans, Yeats. They took me into a country where the will was not everything. . . .[2]

However, in a 1929 article in the New York *Herald Tribune* Book Section, Forster raised several objections to Eliot's poem by asking specific questions:

> Who is the drowned sailor in it? What does the scrap-heap of quotations at the end signify? Is it helpful, here and elsewhere, to know where the quotations come from? or to read Miss Weston's "From Ritual to Romance" or the other authorities recommended in the notes?[3]

Objecting as much to the defenders of the poem as to the obscurity of the lines, Forster ironically concludes that "When there are difficulties, the fault is always ours,"[4] and then proceeds to explain what

> "The Waste Land" is about. It is about the fertilizing waters that arrived too late. It is a poem of horror. The earth is barren, the sea salt, the fertilizing thunderstorm broke too late. And the horror is so intense that the poet is disinclined to state it openly. . . .
>
> He is difficult because he has seen something terrible, and (underestimating, I think, the general decency of his audience), has declined to say so plainly.[5]

Forster believed that Eliot had mitigated life's horror and that Eliot's obscurity results from his reluctance to express the emptiness of modern life in direct terms. Forster did not shrink from explicit statements of the modern horror in *A Passage to India*.

When Forster returned to his manuscript of *A Passage to India* after allowing it to gather dust for a decade, he had resolved the problem of composition which had caused him to abandon the novel before the war. He had begun writing it in 1913 and within a year had substantially completed the first seven chapters, a portion of chapter 12, and some supplementary material for chapters 8, 12, and 14,[6] but the crucial visit to the Marabar Caves was not yet worked out at the time when he gave up on the manuscript and put it aside. Oliver Stallybrass notes that "it is clear that this central episode caused the author an unusual amount of trouble; it seems probable, indeed, that this is one reason why the book was not completed around 1913."[7] Forster resolved this "central episode," the excursion to the Marabar Caves, between 1922 and 1924. The Marabar echo suggests direct refutation of Eliotian thunder and may well have resulted from Forster's reading of Eliot's poem.

The echo of the Marabar Caves presents the horror of an empty universe which Mrs. Moore and Adela Quested cannot evade. At the same time the echo destroys both Mrs. Moore's faith and Adela Quested's hopes for love or marriage. In *The Waste Land* the thunder speaks three times: "DA/*Datta*" (give), "DA/*Dayadhvam*" (sympathize), and "DA/*Damyata*" (control). Although the voice of Eliot's thunder can imply a positive meaning in nature, the horror of Forster's echo is the absence of any meaning or hope. When Mrs. Moore emerges from the cave, she

> did not wish to repeat that experience. The more she thought over it, the more disagreeable and frightening it became. . . . the echo began in some indescribable way to undermine her hold on life. Coming at a moment when she chanced to be fatigued, it had managed to murmur, "Pathos, piety, courage—they exist, but are identical, and so is filth. Everything exists, nothing has value." If one had spoken vileness in that place, or quoted lofty poetry, the comment would have been the same— "ou-boum." If one had spoken with the tongues of angels and pleaded for all the unhappiness and misunderstanding in the world, past, present, and to come, for all the misery men must undergo whatever their opinion and position, and however much they dodge or bluff—it would amount to the same. . . . it robbed infinity and eternity of their vastness, the only quality that accommodates them to mankind.[8]

Mrs. Moore tries to fight the despair which takes hold of her, consoling herself that whatever happens to her—sunstroke, madness—the world will go on, but she realizes that "she didn't want to write to her children, didn't want to communicate with anyone, not even with God. She sat motionless with horror. . ." (*PI*, 150). In Eliot's poem the narrator heard the thunder offer a way to live in the modern Waste Land. The words are in another language, however, and *The Waste Land*'s inhabitants are unable to learn from the thunder's cryptic message. Forster's echo, incomprehensible because it has no hope to offer, destroys at least two people by making them perceive the lack of meaning beyond the physical realm.

Eliot's "What the Thunder Said" was philosophically incompatible with Forster's vision of the universe, and Forster's criticism was that Eliot left the ultimate horror unspoken. The Marabar Caves episode seems designed to repudiate Eliot's positive fragments of the wisdom of the East, while it meets the objections Forster raised to *The Waste Land*.

Ford Madox Ford's *Parade's End*

Several critics have noted the impact of *The Waste Land* on Ford Madox Ford's tetralogy, *Parade's End*. Ford and Eliot corresponded, referring to the poem as early as 25 February 1923. In August of that year, Eliot wrote to Ford that "There are *I* think about 30 good lines in The Waste Land. Can you find them? The rest is ephemeral."[9] After praising the poem for its coherence and unity, Ford confessed that he had not found the specific lines Eliot mentioned, so Eliot identified them for Ford in October: "They are the 29 lines of the water-dripping song in the last part."[10] Ford, appreciating the poem when English critics, according to Eliot, were "too timid even to admit they dislike it,"[11] adapted some of its lines and meaning in the tetralogy. Paul Wiley notes that Ford's myth, "in its recognition of the merchant and of the place of Christianity within the tradition . . . has something in common with Eliot's in *The Waste Land*, both writers employing an inclusive symbol recalling sources of order prior to the Christian synthesis,"[12] and Robert J. Andreach finds similarity in Ford and Eliot's views of the modern world in the tetralogy and in *The Waste Land*:

> The literature of our time may be sounding the death knell for our sick civilization, but Ford's immense novel gives an affirmative answer to the question posed in *The Waste Land*: "Shall I at least set my lands in order?"[13]

In *The Good Soldier* (1915), published before the appearance of *The Waste Land*, Ford addressed many of the problems which pervade his tetralogy, but a brief examination of his approach in the earlier novel reveals how the influence of *The Waste Land* may have affected Ford's later work. Ford, through the eyes and deficient sensibilities of a flawed narrator, described a relationship between John Dowell (the narrator), his wife Florence, Edward Ashburnham, and Edward's wife Leonora. Florence and Leonora are both cruel and vindictive, in their fashions. Florence engages in an adulterous affair with Edward, and Leonora ultimately drives Edward to suicide. Edward represents the declining British aristocracy, and the narrator eventually buys part of Edward's estate, anticipating the effect of the influx of American dollars which Ford will develop in *Last Post.*

However, sufficient differences exist between *The Good Soldier* and the tetralogy to suggest a change in Ford's perspective after the publication of *The Waste Land.* Despite Florence's nine years' infidelity with Edward, her deceit regarding her "heart," and her disregard for her husband, she becomes a sympathetic character. Her misfortune of marriage to the most insensitive of men and her understandable attraction to Edward mitigate disapproval of her behavior, as does her suicide, inspired by her dread that an earlier affair with the disreputable Jimmy (about which Edward already knows) will be revealed to her husband. The nine years' infidelity to her husband is also nine years' faithfulness to Edward—unlike *Waste Land* women, Florence is not gratuitously promiscuous. Leonora's cruelty to Edward results from his immoral conduct, and she becomes embittered towards him only after she has done everything in her power to win his love and to protect him, including her achievement of retrieving the income that Edward had lost at the gaming tables. Edward, whose troubles result from his inability to control his impulses, remains oblivious to his role in such consequences as the death of Maisie Maidan and the unhappiness of his wife. The narrator, emotionally deficient, also remains unaware of his complicity in "the saddest story" that he relates.

What separates *The Good Soldier* from the tetralogy—and from *The Waste Land*—is our sympathy for the women. If Leonora seems cruel or vindictive, her sheltered upbringing and Edward's actions partly justify her. In *The Waste Land* and in the tetralogy, the actions of Thames Maidens and Sylvia Tietjens seem to proceed from feelings of boredom or indifference, not from the pained outrage or crushed hopes of Leonora. In *The Waste Land* the moderns' religion is the superstition of Madame Sosostris. In the tetralogy, Sylvia's grasp of religion also is essentially superstitious. Leonora, however, genuinely suffers from a compromise of her religious values which she believes is damning and over which she had no control (her father, arranging her marriage with Edward, neglected to stipulate that children of this union receive instruction in the Catholic faith). Women in *The Waste Land* and Sylvia in the tetralogy attempt to find some outlet for frustration or boredom in adulterous liaisons. When Leonora considers an adulterous relationship, however, she cannot bring herself to commit it (after Edward's suicide she marries the man with whom she had attempted an affair). Although Leonora and Edward constantly perform actions which are unethical or immoral, what distinguishes them from *The Waste Land's* people and the characters of the tetralogy is their clearly defined moral perspective and their suffering and remorse when they fail to live up to it. Only Tietjens in the tetralogy has this trait. After the publication of *The Waste Land*, Ford's characters have changed in this regard.

While the first three novels of the tetralogy include several motifs and images of *The Waste Land* which may result merely from a shared perception of the post-War crisis, I find two arguments for *Waste Land* influence especially convincing: the number of allusions is unusually high for coincidence, and the resolution of Tietjen's dilemma could be a gloss for "What the Thunder Said." *Some Do Not . . .* (1924) describes the problems of Christopher Tietjens before and during the early years of the War and emphasizes the barrenness and ugliness of the modern world. Tietjens, the last Tory, looks about him and sees nothing but decline and decay in morals, British institutions, and the value of life. Unlike Ashburnham, Tietjens is not part of the decline. Tietjens sees his own life in terms of blight, and, like the Fisher King in the Grail myth, he blames the blight of the land on the blight of humanity: "He considered the base of the fountain that was half full of leaves. This civilization had contrived a state of things in which leaves rotted by August. Well, it was doomed!"[14] Several of the images and characters introduced in *Some Do Not . . .*—the Waste Land of modern civilization, boredom, indifference, the absence of Christianity—recur throughout the tetralogy, receiving more emphasis as the series progresses.

No More Parades (1925) emphasizes the decline of the British aristocracy and institutions. In *The Waste Land*, the young man carbuncular, who becomes the archetypal modern "lover" in his emotionless assault on the typist, is only an undistinguished and unpalatable "small house agent's clerk" (l. 232), despite his assurance. Perowne, briefly Sylvia's lover until she becomes bored with his mediocrity, also represents modern man diminished:

> Major Wilfrid Fosbrooke Eddicker Perowne of Perowne, the son of his mother, was one of those individuals who have no history, no strong proclivities, and no, or almost no, characteristics. He had done nothing, his knowledge seemed to be bounded by the contents of his newspaper for the immediate day; at any rate, his conversation never went any farther. He was not bold, he was not shy: he was neither markedly courageous nor markedly cowardly. (*NMP*, 392)

While the novel's use of *The Waste Land* has shifted from the barrenness of the land to the mediocrity of its inhabitants, the general state of decline remains dominant.

Ford originally intended *A Man Could Stand Up—* (1926) to conclude

Parade's End. The novel continues descriptions of a physical and spiritual Waste Land, but the change in Christopher Tietjens seems to reflect the critical comment of I. A. Richards, whose appendix to *Principles of Literary Criticism* (1926) asserted that some readers of *The Waste Land* discover "not only a clearer, fuller realisation of their plight, the plight of a whole generation, than they find elsewhere, but also through the very energies set free in that realisation a return of the saving passion."[15] This "realisation" did not occur in *The Good Soldier*, but it appears in the tetralogy. Tietjens, realizing that the older order has ended, prepares to make a place for himself in the new order. This requires that he "lower" himself.

> The war had made a man of him! It had coarsened him and hardened him. There was no other way to look at it. It had made him reach a point at which he would no longer stand unbearable things. . . . What he had been before, God alone knew. A Younger Son? A Perpetual Second-in-Command? Who knew. But to-day the world changed. Feudalism was finished; its last vestiges were gone. It held no place for him. He was going—he was damn well going—to make a place in it.[16]

This note of optimism, of the "saving passion," occurs within the Waste Land atmosphere which has appeared earlier in the tetralogy. Other parallels, which could be coincidental, resemble the images of *The Waste Land*. After his predictions of the War in *Some Do Not . . .* , Tietjens again functions as a Tiresias figure. This time he sees the future in terms of men's individual destinies:

> He wished these intimations would not come to him. He found himself at times looking at the faces of several men and thinking that this or that man would shortly be killed. He wished he could get rid of the habit. It seemed indecent. As a rule he was right. (*Man,* 125)

Like Eliot's Tiresias, Tietjens departs from the Tiresias myth by concerning himself with the fates of common men.

Last Post (1928), while continuing earlier themes, develops elements of *The Waste Land* which have received slight emphasis in the earlier novels. Mark Tietjens, refusing to speak or act in the modern world, "wanted to be out of a disgustingly inefficient and venial world, just as he, Mark, also wanted to be out of a world that he found almost more fusionless and dishonest than Christopher found it" (*LP,* 240). *Last Post* also contains unmistakable imagery from the poem. The most overt use of *The Waste Land* is Ford's adaptation of the Fisher King, who

> was fishing in the dull canal
> On a winter evening round behind the gashouse
> Musing on the king my brother's wreck
> And on the king my father's death before him. (ll. 189–92)

Christopher Tietjens is exactly in this position. He has reason to muse on his brother's wreck, for when Mark learned that the English would not invade Berlin to lay waste to Germany, he determined never to speak or move again. Functioning as an invalid, Mark is emotionally and physically a "wreck." Since Mark is Tietjens of Groby and Christopher is technically his "heir," Christopher's situation corresponds to the Fisher King's succession after his father and elder brother. Mark Tietjens "did not speak. Not to them, not to anybody. He was finished with the world. He perceived the trend of its actions, listened to its aspirations, and even to its prayers, but he would never again stir lip or finger. It was like being dead—or being God" (*LP*, 229). Christopher also has reason to muse on "the king my father's death before him." Mark, acting on misinformation, had informed his father that Christopher had impregnated Valentine Wannop, daughter of the elder Tietjens's closest friend. Stunned and saddened by the "news," the elder Tietjens committed suicide, making it appear a hunting accident. Christopher is not fooled by his father's ploy although Mark, initially aware of the truth, convinces himself that his father's death was indeed accidental. Christopher yields to no such self-serving illusion and constantly considers his father's death, the effect it will have on his own son, and the position in which he and his brother find themselves. When Eliot placed the Fisher King myth in *The Waste Land*, he distorted it by omitting the myth's suggestion that the Fisher King will be succeeded by a virile young man. Ford has made the same omission in *Last Post*.

D. H. Lawrence's *Lady Chatterley's Lover*

Although he often disagreed with Eliot, D. H. Lawrence also included aspects of Eliot's *The Waste Land* in his novels. F. R. Leavis, James C. Cowan, Samuel A. Eisenstein, and William York Tindall have found *Waste Land* influences in such works as *St. Mawr* and *Kangaroo*.[17] *Lady Chatterley's Lover* includes several parallels to *The Waste Land*, and C. E. Baron has found a direct connection between the novel and Eliot:

> Along with the Garnetts, Michael Arlen, T. E. Lawrence and other contemporaries who were unceremoniously bundled into *Lady Chatterley's*

Lover, Eliot, too, appears to receive his would-be placing. At any rate Sir Clifford Chatterley approaches very closely to the thoughts and language of "Tradition and the Individual Talent": "'After all,' he said in a declamatory voice, 'one gets all one wants out of Racine. Emotions that are ordered and given shape are more important than disorderly emotions. . . . The modern world has only vulgarized emotion by letting it loose. What we need is classic control. . . .'" This was written at the very time at which Middleton Murry was debating "romanticism" and "classicism" with Eliot in the pages of *The Criterion*.[18]

In addition to this version of Eliot's critical pronouncement, the novel abounds in references to a modern Waste Land. Most of Lawrence's social and psychological observations of the modern world appeared before *The Waste Land* in earlier novels. Nevertheless, elements of *The Waste Land* appear in *Lady Chatterley's Lover*.

Describing the third version of the novel, Mark Schorer notes that "the dramatic presentation of a true marriage is permitted to speak for itself, and the fact that this true marriage must exist in a wasteland leaves the end of the third version in some uncertainty, which is supremely right."[19] Lawrence's Waste Land, however, resembles Edmund Wilson's sociological description of Eliot's poem. According to Wilson,

> the terrible dreariness of the great modern cities is the atmosphere in which "The Waste Land" takes place—amidst this dreariness, brief, vivid images emerge, brief pure moments of feeling are distilled; but all about us we are aware of nameless millions performing barren office routines, wearing down their souls in interminable labors of which the products never bring them profit—people whose pleasures are so sordid and so feeble that they seem almost sadder than their pains.[20]

In early descriptions, Lawrence evokes this spirit. The workers, like the workday crowd streaming over London Bridge in "The Burial of the Dead," lack hope. Perhaps what was "terrible" and "mysterious" about these men in Lawrence's novel was the sense that they are in hell, like Eliot's clerks. The lack of hope which characterizes Eliot's Waste Land, and which indeed for Eliot has caused it, also appears throughout *Lady Chatterley's Lover*. Michaelis, whose seduction of Connie succeeds primarily because she is bored, "was hopeless at the very core of him, and he wanted to be hopeless. He rather hated hope" (*LCL*, 65–66). Writing to Connie, Mellors says, "There's a bad time coming. . . . If things go on as they are, there's nothing lies in the future but death and destruction, for these industrial masses. I feel my inside turn to water sometimes. . ." (*LCL*, 373).

The opening words of the novel, which suggest Eliot's "heap of broken images" and the "fragments" which the Fisher King has shored against his ruins, also summarize the prevailing mood of *The Waste Land*:

> Ours is essentially a tragic age, so we refuse to take it tragically. The cataclysm has happened, we are among the ruins, we start to build up new little habits, to have new little hopes. It is rather hard work: there is now no smooth road into the future. . . . (*LCL*, 37)

The ultimate solution to the problems of modern life, formulated by Mellors, specifically answers the Fisher King's question, "Shall I at least set my lands in order?" (l. 426). Mellors states his solution:

> "I'd wipe the machines off the face of the earth again, and end the industrial epoch absolutely, like a black mistake. But since I can't, an' nobody can, I'd better hold my peace, an' try an' live my own life: if I've got one to live, which I rather doubt" (*LCL*, 282).

Like Eliot's Fisher King, Mellors experiences a sense of futility in the midst of the horror that he perceives, and he cannot see beyond a personal solution.

That an emerging poet should have comparatively minor impact on established novelists would hardly be surprising. The wonder is that Eliot's *The Waste Land* did have a perceptible effect on the shaping of the novels of Forster, Ford, and Lawrence. Forster, in his struggle to reconcile the central episode of *A Passage to India*, seems to have found a solution in his reaction to "What the Thunder Said." Ford, completing his tetralogy, structured his plot so that *Last Post* functions as a gloss on some lines from *The Waste Land*. Even Lawrence found some of Eliot's lines useful, albeit in the process of rejecting Eliot's philosophy. Whereas Forster and Ford found *The Waste Land* helpful in their efforts to resolve problems of plot, Lawrence recognized the relevance of *The Waste Land*'s lines to his depiction of the conflict between man's natural desires and the industrial epoch.

3

ALDOUS HUXLEY

Withered Stumps of Time

When Aldous Huxley read *The Waste Land* he must have felt a shock of recognition, for his *Crome Yellow* (1921) featured a Mr. Scogan who dressed up as a fortune-teller and called himself Madame Sesostris. Like Eliot's Madame Sosostris, Scogan has limited knowledge and is fraudulent—he uses the "office" of seer to predict a meeting between a young woman and a romantic stranger, and the next week he hastens to fulfill this self-serving prophecy. Samuel Hynes writes that "Waugh was the first English novelist to see his own time as a period *entre deux guerres,* and that peculiar location gives his novel a good deal of its tone of human helplessness and aimlessness,"[1] but the claim may be more justly made for Huxley. In *Crome Yellow,* seven years before Waugh's first novel, the seer Sesostris

> prophesied financial losses, death by apoplexy, destruction by air-raids in the next war.
> "Is there going to be another war?" asked the old lady to whom he had predicted this end.
> "Very soon," said Mr. Scogan, with an air of quiet confidence.[2]

In *Point Counter Point,* also written before *Decline and Fall,* the subject of the next war crops up frequently. Rampion argues that "the next war and the next revolution will make it only too practical" to scrap the machine, and with sobering accuracy Philip Quarles (in 1928) records that Rampion gives "the present dispensation ten years."[3]

Responding to Grover Smith's query regarding the Sesostris/Sosostris connection, Huxley wrote on 3 March 1952,

I used to see a good deal of T. S. Eliot during and just after the first
World War. Whether he did me the honour of reading anything I wrote,
I don't know. And anyhow Sesostris-Sosostris is an intrinsically occult
name, made, as it is, of whispers and a snake's hiss. The good king
who, in Herodotus, conquered all Asia and reigned almost as long as
Queen Victoria is irrelevant. The real point is the sound of the name,
with the suggestion, perhaps, of a male in fortune teller's clothing—and
in *Crome Yellow*, of course, the incident was borrowed, with modifica-
tions, from the fortune telling scene in *Jane Eyre*.[4]

Despite Huxley's modest disclaimer, it seems likely that Eliot borrowed
the name from Huxley, and it is more likely that Huxley adopted much
of the perspective implied in *The Waste Land*, at least in his acceptance
of the problems of modern life. Hynes notes that

"By the end of the 'twenties," Aldous Huxley wrote in 1937, "a reaction
had begun to set in—away from the easy-going philosophy of general
meaninglessness towards the hard, ferocious theologies of nationalistic
and revolutionary idolatry. Meaning was reintroduced into the world,
but only in patches. . . ." Was he right? In a way he was, but like most
turns of mind this one was more complicated than it seemed. The philosophy of general meaninglessness—by which I suppose he means the
Waste Land vision—was never easy-going; there was from the beginning a note of nostalgic regret at the passing of nobility and belief, and
certainly the literary expression of it—*The Waste Land* itself, *Point Counter
Point*, *Vile Bodies*—acknowledged the need for a reintroduction of meaning. But as the 'twenties became the 'thirties, it was only a need; the
ferocious theologies were still to come.[5]

Huxley's novels, reflecting the trend from "general meaninglessness"
to "the need for a reintroduction of meaning," mark a turning point in
the story of *The Waste Land*'s influence. In his early novels, Huxley
accepts Eliot's description of modern life without attempting to place
Eliot's imagery into any philosophical context. *Point Counter Point*, however, experiments with the techniques of dislocation and juxtaposition
which Eliot had mastered as it seeks meaning in the lives of its characters. By the time Huxley wrote *Eyeless in Gaza*, he combined experimentation with form and relocation of meaning, creating a vision of modernity which owes much to *The Waste Land*. While Huxley's novels
borrow heavily from Eliot's poem, they reflect Huxley's unique view of
the problems of modern life. Since Huxley's novels, except for *Crome
Yellow*, appeared after *The Waste Land*, the compatibility of Huxley's
characters and images with Eliot's is less likely to be coincidence than
to be indebtedness on the part of the developing novelist.

In *Antic Hay* (1923), Huxley includes several modern problems which have received expression in *The Waste Land*. The artist Lypiatt finds himself alone in a meaningless world:

> "I look about me," and Lypiatt cast his eyes wildly round the crowded room, "and I find myself alone, spiritually alone. I strive on by myself, by myself." He struck his breast, a giant, a solitary giant. "I have set myself to restore painting and poetry to their rightful position among the great moral forces. They have been amusements, they have been mere games for too long. . . . People mock me, hate me, stone me, deride me. But I go on, I go on."[6]

Although closer to the senior Quarles than to Baudelaire, Lypiatt nevertheless describes a cultural desert with great feeling. *Antic Hay* includes several descriptions of general decay and decline in the modern world. The house in which Gumbril senior lives

> was a prematurely old and decaying house in a decaying quarter. The square in which it stood was steadily coming down in the world. The houses which a few years ago had all been occupied by respectable families, were now split up into squalid little maisonettes, and from the neighbouring slums, which along with most other unpleasant things the old bourgeois families had been able to ignore, invading bands of children came to sport on the once sacred pavements.
>   Mr. Gumbril was almost the last survivor of the old inhabitants. (*AH*, 23)

Modern boredom frequently plagues Huxley's characters. Rosie Shearwater, whom Gumbril, disguised as the Complete Man, has picked up, indicates the boredom of her life:

> She seemed, from her coolly dropped hints, to possess all the dangerous experience, all the assurance and easy ruthlessness of a great lady whose whole life is occupied in the interminable affairs of the heart, the senses and the head. But, by a strange contradiction she seemed to find her life narrow and uninteresting. She had complained in so many words that her husband misunderstood and neglected her, had complained, by implication, that she knew very few interesting people. (*AH*, 141)

Mrs. Viveash, also bored, pursues excitement with the same frenzy that the neurasthenic woman of "A Game of Chess" exhibits, with equally fruitless results: " 'Always the same people,' complained Mrs. Viveash, looking round the room. 'The old familiar faces. Never any one new. Where's the younger generation, Gumbril? We're old, Theodore. There are millions younger than we are. Where are they?'" (*AH*, 234). Gumbril also feels this sense of boredom: " 'Most of one's life is an *entr'acte,*' said Gumbril, whose present mood of hilarious depression seemed favourable to the enunciation of apophthegms" (*AH*, 238). Such an attitude results from insecurity and neurosis, at least in Gumbril's case. Even when he is with Emily, he cannot be happy: "Like a man on the night before his execution he looked forward through the endless present; he foresaw the end of his eternity. And after? Everything was uncertain and unsafe" (*AH*, 213). The Shakespeherian Rag, indicating the sterility of modern culture in "A Game of Chess," has its counterpart in *Antic Hay*. A popular tune in the novel is "What's He to Hecuba?":

> What's he to Hecuba?
> Nothing at all.
> That's why there'll be no wedding on Wednesday week
> Way down in old Bengal. (*AH*, 231)

The debasement of Hamlet's famous line into a popular ballad of unrequited love is literally a Shakespeherian Rag.

Eliot's "What the Thunder Said" contributes to *Antic Hay* by providing images of man's search for meaning in the universe, but Huxley maintains the fruitlessness of that search. Lypiatt, the self-styled preserver of culture, constantly feels his despair:

> "Death, death, death, death," he kept repeating to himself, moving his lips as though he were praying. If he said the word often enough, if he accustomed himself completely to the idea, death would come almost by itself; he would know it already, while he was still alive, he would pass almost without noticing out of life into death. Into death, he thought, into death. Death like a well. . . . He thought for a long time of the well of death. (*AH*, 291)

Contrasted to this despair, the hope of the Christian myth pales. Learning that Gumbril has overheard a conversation in a pub which alludes to unwanted pregnancy, Coleman

> exploded with delight. "Gravid," he kept repeating, "gravid, gravid. The laws of gravity, first formulated by Newton, now recodified by the immortal Einstein. God said, Let Newstein be and there was Light. And God said, Let there be Light; and there was darkness o'er the face of the earth." He roared with laughter. (*AH*, 90)

The characters in *Antic Hay*, like those in *The Waste Land*, feel that the burdens of modern life are too great for religious belief to mitigate. Even a scholar like Shearwater ultimately succumbs to superstition, clinging to the word "proportion" as superstitiously as *The Waste Land*'s moderns depend on Madame Sosostris's prophecies.

Point Counter Point (1928), like *Antic Hay*, draws frequently from *The Waste Land*. Huxley's techniques, which his character and spokesman Philip Quarles describes as "the musicalization of fiction" and the use of "parallel, contrapuntal plots" (*PCP*, 301), seem to owe as much to the motifs of *The Waste Land* as to the fugue, while the character Maurice Spandrell, for whom "Time and habit had taken the wrongness out of almost all the acts he had once thought sinful" (*PCP*, 159), derives from Eliot's description of Baudelaire. Huxley's experimentation with the "musicalization of fiction" and the "novel of ideas" recalls I. A. Richards's 1926 comment that *The Waste Land* presented "a music of ideas," and Huxley combines this technique with several images and motifs of the poem. The predominant impression of the novel, however, is the sterile quality of human existence, firmly within the tradition of *The Waste Land*. When Rampion, based on D. H. Lawrence, paints his "masterpiece," he depicts a progression which reveals an increasingly debased humanity:

> the van was composed of human monsters, huge-headed creatures, without limbs or bodies, creeping slug-like on vaguely slimy extensions of chin and neck. The faces were mostly those of eminent contemporaries. Among the crowd Burlap recognized J. J. Thompson and Lord Edward Tantamount, Bernard Shaw attended by eunuchs and spinsters and Sir Oliver Lodge attended by a sheeted and turnip-headed ghost and a walking cathode tube, Sir Alfred Mond and the head of John D. Rockefeller carried on a charger by a Baptist clergyman, Dr. Frank Crane and Mrs. Eddy wearing haloes, and many others. (*PCP*, 214)

Carling, whom Walter Bidlake has cuckolded, exclaims "What an age we live in! . . . Barbarous. Such abysmal ignorance of the most rudimentary religious truths" (*PCP*, 228). Spandrell, considering the relationship between God and the modern world, concludes that "Dust-bins had been his predestined lot. In giving him dust-bins yet again, the providential joker was merely being consistent" (*PCP*, 432). Rampion calls the moderns' hatred for life "the disease of modern man" (*PCP*, 120), and his masterpiece sketches the men of the twentieth century as "abortions" (*PCP*, 216).

In addition to these indications of modern blight, Huxley includes

allusions to specific passages from Eliot's "The Burial of the Dead."
One passage suggests the "violet hour" which Eliot used as a motif:
"They drove up to Gattenden, and the landscape of the Chilterns in
the ripe evening light was so serenely beautiful . . . reassuring as the
calm loveliness of beech trees and bracken, of green-golden foreground
and violet distances" (PCP, 386). After Spandrell and Illidge murder
Everard Webley and have difficulties placing his corpse in the back of
the car, Lord Edward deplores the waste of phosphorus in modern
burials of the dead, complaining that burying people in cemeteries
results in inefficient distribution. He would approve of planting the
corpse in the garden, as did Stetson in Eliot's poem.

Two aspects of "A Game of Chess" are present in *Point Counter Point*,
the neurotic boredom of the neurasthenic woman and the indifference
to human life represented by the talk of abortion in the pub. Lucy
Tantamount pursues pleasure frantically, mainly to avoid boredom.
She is a siren who cannot find satisfaction in love affairs but who
relentlessly tortures such pitiful weaklings as Walter Bidlake. She is
aware of her unhappiness and her nerves are shot. Marjorie Carling is
also hopelessly neurotic:

> "Sleep, sleep," she whispered to herself; she imagined herself relaxed,
> smoothed out, asleep. But, suddenly, a malicious hand seemed to pluck
> at her taut nerves. A violent tic contracted the muscles of her limbs; she
> started as though with terror. (PCP, 151)

The detached attitude towards human life, reflected in the scientific
description of cellular decomposition after Everard Webley's death, appears also in descriptions of the budding foetus which Marjorie Carling
carries.

> She looked ugly, tired, and ill. Six months from now her baby would be
> born. Something that had been a single cell, a cluster of cells, a little sac
> of tissue, a kind of worm, a potential fish with gills, stirred in her womb
> and would one day become a man—a grown man, suffering and enjoy-
> ing, loving and hating, thinking, remembering, imagining. . . . The
> astounding process of creation was going on within her; but Marjorie
> was conscious only of sickness and lassitude; the mystery for her meant
> nothing but fatigue and ugliness and a chronic anxiety about the future,
> pain of the mind as well as discomfort of the body. (PCP, 4)

For both Walter and Marjorie, the child has no existence except as an
impediment, both to Marjorie's mental and physical health and to Walter's freedom from obligation.

Like those in *Antic Hay*, the moderns trapped in the Waste Land of *Point Counter Point* find no solution to their problems. Rampion complains to Quarles that "The love of death's in the air" (*PCP*, 322), and Spandrell deliberately ends his own life by contriving a shoot-out with the police. Quarles notes that "The rush to books and universities is like the rush to the public house. People want to drown their realization of the difficulties of living properly in this grotesque contemporary world . . ." (*PCP*, 326). Rampion proposes a solution which answers in the affirmative the Fisher King's question of whether to set his lands in order: "Make the effort of being human. . . . In the meantime, at any rate, we must shovel the garbage and bear the smell stoically, and in the intervals try to lead the real human life" (*PCP*, 308). Yet the solace of religious belief is ludicrously inept in the novel. Charles Tantamount, an invalid with a passion for mathematics, pursues the Absolute with algebra because "It was the only sort of hunting possible to a cripple" (*PCP*, 140). Spandrell "hoped there was a hell for him to go to and regretted his inability to believe in its existence" (*PCP*, 222). Mr. Carling uses religion only to justify his outrage that Marjorie has run off with Walter Bidlake, and Rampion regards Christianity the source of "a sort of self-destruction" (*PCP*, 407). Marjorie Carling, however, after spending time with Mrs. Quarles, finds the consolation of faith in the same terms as those of Eliot's note defining "Shantih shantih shantih":

> "Happiness, happiness." Marjorie repeated the word to herself. Against the black vapours the hills were like emerald and green gold. Happiness and beauty and goodness. " 'The peace of God,' " she whispered, " 'the peace of God that passeth all understanding.' Peace, peace, peace . . ." (*PCP*, 363)

Like the Fisher King, in contrast to the others in *The Waste Land*, Marjorie seems to have found some positive meaning. However, despite her euphoria, the hope for resurrection does not soothe other characters in the novel, who continue to live miserably in a Waste Land.

Brave New World (1932) presents a futuristic Waste Land in which a sensitive or ethical person could not live. The world Huxley presents, which is in the tradition of dystopian novels, follows Edmund Wilson's political and sociological interpretation of *The Waste Land*'s "shattered institutions, strained nerves and bankrupt ideals."[7] The Savage ultimately retreats to a remote island in his futile quest for solitude, much as the Fisher King, turning his back on the "arid plain," deliberated setting his own lands in order. Huxley comments in his foreword that "This really revolutionary revolution is to be achieved, not in the external world, but in the souls and flesh of human beings."[8] Like Anthony Burgess's *The Wanting Seed*, *Brave New World* emphasizes sterility. When the Controller, Mustapha Mond, recalls Henry Ford's statement that "History is bunk," he echoes Eliot's "fear in a handful of dust" and the "Falling towers" of Unreal Cities:

> He waved his hand; and it was as though, with an invisible feather whisk, he had brushed away a little dust, and the dust was Harappa, was Ur of the Chaldees; some spider-webs, and they were Thebes and Babylon and Cnossos and Mycenae. Whisk. Whisk—and where was Odysseus, where was Job, where were Jupiter and Gotama and Jesus? Whisk—and those specks of antique dirt called Athens and Rome, Jerusalem and the Middle Kingdom—all were gone. Whisk—the place where Italy had been was empty. Whisk, the cathedrals; whisk, whisk, King Lear and the Thoughts of Pascal. Whisk, Passion; whisk, Requiem; whisk, Symphony; whisk. . . . (*BNW*, 22–23)

Unlike the progression of Eliot's poem, which proceeds from "civilization" to the "arid plain," the Savage moves from a Waste Land to a sterile civilization of the new world, and his reaction is that of Miranda: "'O wonder!' he was saying; and his eyes shone, his face was brightly flushed. 'How many goodly creatures are there here!'" (*BNW*, 94). Later he repeats his words with bitter irony as he discovers what the brave new world has done to the human spirit, and he tells Controller Mond that he finds the world "quite horrible." The civilization depends on drugs, conditioning, conspicuous consumption, a well-organized police force and intelligence system, and communal worship of a sort to maintain itself, yet the state does not satisfy the needs of its citizens beyond sensual requirements.

When neurosis reminiscent of the woman of "A Game of Chess" appears in the novel, it is a vestige of the "pre-modern" times of Henry Ford and Sigmund Freud. The Controller blames the family system for all neuroses which afflicted the "pre-moderns":

> "No wonder these poor pre-moderns were mad and wicked and miserable. Their world didn't allow them to take things easily, didn't allow them to be sane, virtuous, happy. What with mothers and lovers, what with the prohibitions they were not conditioned to obey, what with the temptations and the lonely remorses, what with all the diseases and the endless isolating pain, what with the uncertainties and the poverty—they were forced to feel strongly. And feeling strongly (and strongly, what was more, in solitude, in hopelessly individual isolation), how could they be stable?" (*BNW*, 27)

These futuristic descriptions of present life recall the neurasthenic woman in "A Game of Chess," whose nerves are bad and who tries to relieve her boredom. "The Fire Sermon" also has a counterpart in the novel. The Thames Maidens, free with their favors in an emotionless and remorseless context, are not far removed from the mores of the new world, in which everyone belongs to everyone else and fidelity is a mark of social inadequacy. As the Savage realizes of the "pneumatic" Lenina, whom he desires but who disgusts him by being indifferent to his sexual morality, "She thinks of herself that way. She doesn't mind being meat" (BNW, 62). (Huxley's use of "pneumatic" throughout the novel as a sexual compliment derives from the "pneumatic bliss" of Eliot's early poem "Whispers of Immortality.") Purgation, if not by fire, is important to the Savage. Even before he retreats to the lighthouse, the Savage purges himself of civilization by drinking hot water and mustard. Once he reaches his hermitage, his ritual of purgation becomes more intense.

> He pacified his conscience by promising himself a compensatingly harder self-discipline, purifications the more complete and thorough. His first night in the hermitage was, deliberately, a sleepless one. He spent the hours on his knees praying, now to that Heaven from which the guilty Claudius had begged forgiveness, now in Zuni to Awonawilona, now to Jesus and Pookong, now to his own guardian animal, the eagle. (BNW, 166)

Religion can provide no consolation, however, because instead of merely turning their backs on the hope of resurrection, the moderns have hopelessly divorced all Christian symbols from their meaning. Distorted quotations ("What man has joined, nature is powerless to put asunder," BNW, 14), and altered names (Charing-Cross to Char-ing-T, BNW, 41) prevent moderns from apprehending Christianity on a cognitive level. The crucifixion appears in the rituals of the Reservation, but Jesus is merely one god among many. When the Controller and the Savage converse, the Controller makes it clear that the state of modern civilization is the result of man's spiritual blight: "The gods are just. No doubt. But their code of law is dictated, in the last resort, by the people who organize society; Providence takes its cue from men" (BNW, 160). The Controller explains the suppression of knowledge of God as necessary and declares that "he manifests himself as an absence. . . . Call it the fault of civilization. God isn't compatible with machinery and scientific medicine and universal happiness. You must make your choice. Our civilization has chosen machinery and medicine and happiness" (*BNW*, 159). When the Savage argues that God is necessary to justify self-denial, the Controller responds, "But chastity means passion, chastity means neurasthenia. And passion and neurasthenia mean instability. And instability means the end of civilization. You can't have a lasting civilization without plenty of pleasant vices" (*BNW*, 161). Ultimately, Mond defines *soma* as "Christianity without tears" (*BNW*, 162). Although he fails to convince the Savage, he makes explicit the relationship between man's spiritual vacuity and his physical and emotional stability. The Savage, answering the question of the Fisher King, turns his back on this arid plain to set his own lands in order, and as he does so the thunder speaks:

> He was digging in his garden—digging, too, in his own mind, laboriously turning up the substance of his thought. Death—and he drove in his spade once, and again, and yet again. And all our yesterdays have lighted fools the way to dusty death. A convincing thunder rumbled through the words. (*BNW*, 173)

Because the moderns will not leave him in peace, setting his lands in order becomes committing suicide, which he feels the "convincing thunder" has urged. The only alternatives, as Huxley mentioned in his foreword, were lunacy and insanity.

Eyeless in Gaza (1936), which describes Anthony Beavis's search for meaning in life, abounds in the imagery of *The Waste Land*. Huxley's experiments with time, juxtaposing chapters set in different years, imitate Eliot's technique of dislocation. England is a Waste Land: "The train which carried Anthony Beavis into Surrey rolled through mile-long eczemas of vulgarity. Pills, soaps, cough drops and—more glaringly inflamed and scabby than all the rest—beef essence, the cupped ox."[9] When John Beavis, Anthony's father, mourns the death of his wife, "He knew that she was dead and that his bereavement was terrible. But he felt nothing of this bereavement—nothing except a kind of dusty emptiness of the spirit" (*EG*, 132). In several passages throughout the novel, Anthony reflects on the inadequacy of modern man, "people with some kind of hunch or deformity in their power of expression" (*EG*, 67), and he records in his notebook that "In a modern city it is possible to forget that such a thing as nature exists—particularly nature in its more inhuman and hostile aspects. Half the population of Europe lives in a universe that's entirely home made" (*EG*, 110). Part of Anthony's discontent with civilization is the absence of meaningful struggle:

"Civilization means food and literature all round. Beef-steaks and fiction magazines for all. First-class proteins for the body, fourth-class love-stories for the spirit. And this in a safe urban world, where there are no risks, no physical fatigues." (*EG*, 192)

Crossing foreign country with Mark, Anthony encounters a Waste Land more to his liking:

There was no shade, and the vast bald hills were the colour of dust and burnt grass. Nothing stirred, not even a lizard among the stones. There was no sight or sound of life. Hopelessly empty, the chaos of the tumbled mountains seemed to stretch away interminably. It was as though they had ridden across the frontier of the world out into nothingness, into an infinite expanse of hot and dusty negation. (*EG*, 358–59)

The physical ugliness, emotional emptiness, decline, and negation which Anthony sees around him are characteristic of Eliot's Waste Land world.

Boredom comparable to that of the women in *The Waste Land* plays an important role in the plot of *Eyeless in Gaza*. Mary, as a result of ennui, taunts Anthony about the possibility of his seducing Joan, the fiancée of Anthony's best friend Brian. Anthony hoped that Mary, in Gattick's presence, would have the decency to leave the matter be,

But he had reckoned without Mary and her boredom, her urgent need to make something amusing and exciting happen. Few things are more exciting than deliberate bad taste, more amusing than the spectacle of someone else's embarrassment. Before Gattick had had time to finish his preliminary boomings, she was back again on the old, painful subject. (*EG*, 276)

As a result, Anthony submits and kisses Joan, she decides that Anthony loves her, she writes a letter to Brian breaking their engagement, and Brian kills himself. Huxley's characters, like Eliot's, are often indifferent to others. Anthony notes in his diary that "That which besets me is indifference. I can't be bothered about people. Or rather, won't. For I avoid, carefully, all occasions for being bothered" (*EG*, 10). As Dr. Miller comments later, "They're probably quite right . . . It's indifference and hatred that are blind, not love" (*EG*, 395).

Because it is a search for meaning in a Waste Land, *Eyeless in Gaza* alludes often to the fifth section of Eliot's poem, "What the Thunder Said." Eliot implies a meaning for existence in "The awful daring of a moment's surrender" (l. 404), but Helen realizes that Anthony "had shut the door against her! He didn't want to be loved" (*EG*, 5). A "message" arrives from heaven when a dog falls from an open airplane and crashes next to Anthony and Helen, spattering them with blood. Anthony, who would prefer, in Eliot's words, to "keep the Dog far hence," treats the dog's landing as a joke, but Helen, upset, leaves Anthony, ending their affair. Recalling the dog, she thinks of it as a "sign from heaven, down comes the dog . . . Father Hopkins can't protect you from. . . . Bang!" (*EG*, 209). She sees Anthony and herself as lying in the Garden of Eden before the change wrought by the dog, and she complains that Anthony has written to her as if nothing significant had happened. She attaches an importance to the dog to which Anthony is insensible. Eliot's "heap of broken images" and the fragments which the Fisher King has shored against his ruins appear frequently in the novel. Most are fragments of memory, personality, and time. Anthony reflects that "Even the seemingly most solid fragments of present reality are riddled with pitfalls. What could be more uncompromisingly *there*, in the present, than a woman's body in the sunshine?" (*EG*, 15). He has suddenly recalled Brian's suicide, for which he is partly responsible, and realizes that the fragments of the present cannot protect him from the ruin of his past. Before killing himself, Brian wrote Anthony a letter in which he echoed Eliot: "I realize now that I'm all broken to pieces inside, and that I've been holding myself together by a continuous effort of will. It's as if a broken statue somehow contrived to hold itself together. . . . A statue at one moment, and the next a heap of dust and shapeless fragments" (*EG*, 372).

The denial of hope is a major part of Anthony's problem. Dr. Miller immediately recognizes this: " 'Yes, that sallow skin,' he repeated, and shook his head. 'And the irony, the scepticism, the what's-the-good-of-it-all attitude! Negative, really. Everything you think is negative.' Anthony laughed; but laughed to hide a certain disquiet" (*EG*, 376). Anthony has never had encouragement to find hope, however. His homosexual uncle James, after a sermon, snorts "Resurrection of the body, indeed! In A.D. 1902!" (*EG*, 27). When Mrs. Foxe reads scripture and the young Anthony can almost "hear the blows of the hammer on the nails" during the crucifixion, Mrs. Foxe (contrary to the Foxe who wrote *Book of Martyrs*) breaks the spell by talking about the

> "embroideries on the story. One must think of the age in which the writers of the gospels lived. They believed these things could happen; and, what's more, they thought they ought to happen on important occasions. They wanted to do honour to Jesus. . . . The wonderful thing

for us . . . is that Jesus was a man, no more able to do miracles and no more likely to have them done for him than the rest of us. Just a man. . . ." (*EG*, 71–72)

Anthony reads D. H. Lawrence's *The Man Who Died* but this does not satisfy him: "life, life as such, he protested inwardly—it was not enough" (*EG*, 245). Anthony continues to look at religion as a way of blaming one's shortcomings on someone else, or at least evading the consequences of one's actions. As he notes in his diary, "For English Catholics, sacraments are the psychological equivalents of tractors in Russia" (*EG*, 386). Yet despite these negative views of religion, Anthony ultimately becomes hopeful. Anthony, due to speak at a pacifist meeting and threatened with violence should he appear there, concludes that whatever "was in store for him, . . . he knew now that all would be well" (*EG*, 423). The source of this attitude, however, is the peace which Phlebas finds at the bottom of the ocean. Anthony thinks of peace in the imagery of "Death by Water":

> In peace, he repeated, in peace, in peace. In the depth of every mind, peace. The same peace for all, continuous between mind and mind. At the surface, the separate waves, the whirlpools, the spray; but below them the continuous and undifferentiated expanse of sea, becoming calmer as it deepens, till at last there is an absolute stillness. Dark peace in the depths. (*EG*, 421)

While Anthony has not found meaning in his life, he takes comfort in the peace which accompanies death.

Huxley's appreciation of Eliot was lifelong. In 1947, Huxley wrote of Eliot that "He is a man for whom I have always had a great affection (though I have never been very intimate with him, in spite of nearly thirty years of acquaintance) as well as a profound admiration."[10] While Huxley was certainly equipped to deal on equal terms with men of genius, he did not regard himself as a man of letters, and one consequence of this led Sybille Bedford to conclude that

> Aldous's most intimate friends, though men of high intelligence in their different ways and men of human quality (Lawrence, of course, stands entirely apart) were not the masters, the highbrows, the literary mandarins of his time, not, though he knew them all and was fond of many, Bloomsbury, not the Sitwells, not Morgan Forster or Tom Eliot.[11]

In 1963, in *Literature and Science*, Huxley revealed his feeling that Eliot's influence had a limit:

Eliot is a great poet because he purified the words of the tribe in novel, beautiful, and many-meaninged ways, not because he extended the field of subject-matter available to poetic treatment: he didn't. And this is true of most of his poetical successors. From their writings you would be hard put to it to infer the simple historical fact that they are contemporaries of Einstein and Heisenberg, of computers, electron microscopes and the discovery of the molecular basis of heredity, of Operationalism, Diamat and Emergent Evolution. . . .[12]

Huxley, praising Eliot's poetic technique and language rather than the "subject matter" of Eliot's poetry, reveals a limitation of The Waste Land's influence on the novel during the 1920s. Like Edmund Wilson and I. A. Richards, who between them established the general interpretation of The Waste Land that most subsequent critics and novelists would accept, the early Waste Land novelists reacted to Eliot's descriptions of the meaninglessness of modern life. Aldington, Forster, Ford, Lawrence, and Huxley seized on memorable lines and images of The Waste Land in their varied works on the futility and confusion of the post-War period, but solutions to the problem differed greatly, ranging from Forster's pessimistic view of a hostile universe to the personal solutions offered by Ford and Lawrence. The small measure of peace obtained by such characters as Aldington's Winterbourne, Ford's Tietjens, Lawrence's Mellors, and Huxley's Beavis resulted from withdrawal into a private sphere, resignation, or death.

Although Huxley felt that Eliot had not extended the "field of subject-matter available to poetic treatment," he indicated other aspects of Eliotian influence which were meaningful to him. Listing those books he would replace after his library burned, Huxley included "Eliot—because his is the most beautifully articulate voice of the generation to which I happen to belong."[13] Huxley's method of borrowing from The Waste Land reflects this attitude. In Antic Hay, the unmistakable presence of the Shakespeherian Rag lends credibility to Huxley's possible borrowing from The Waste Land's cultural desolation, modern boredom, and loss of meaning. In Point Counter Point, the presence of the "violet hour" and of Marjorie's comfort in "the peace of God that passeth all understanding" suggests that The Waste Land may be the source of more tenuous parallels. Eyeless in Gaza, which includes a literal Waste Land and the peace of Phlebas in the ocean's depths, also has other parallels to The Waste Land which receive emphasis from direct echoes of the poem. Huxley found The Waste Land helpful in his attempts to chronicle the spirit of the between-the-wars period.

PART II

The Waste Land's Influence
Between the Wars

The 1930s brought both new critical interpretations of *The Waste Land* and a greater variety of novelists' uses of the poem. In addition to Edmund Wilson's 1922 "sociological and political" reading of *The Waste Land* and I. A. Richards's 1926 discovery of a "form for unbelief" in the poem, Cleanth Brooks added a credible "theological" interpretation in 1939. For Brooks, "What the Thunder Said" reveals that "Eliot has been continually, in the poem, linking up the Christian doctrine with the beliefs of as many people as he can."[1] Eliot's "comments on the three statements of the thunder imply an acceptance of them, "[2] and even the quotations at the end relate to the general theme of Christianity. Noting that "Even a critic so acute as Edmund Wilson has seen the poem as essentially a statement of despair and disillusionment,"[3] Brooks blames such readings on "misconceptions of Eliot's technique," to which Brooks refers as "application of the principles of complexity."[4] For Brooks, "Eliot's theme is the rehabilitation of a system of beliefs, known but now discredited,"[5] which requires an indirect approach because

> the Christian terminology is for the poet a mass of clichés. However "true" he may feel the terms to be, he is still sensitive to the fact that they operate superficially as clichés, and his method of necessity must be a process of bringing them to life again. The method adopted in *The Waste Land* is thus violent and radical, but thoroughly necessary. . . . In this way the statement of beliefs emerges *through* confusion and cynicism—not in spite of them.[6]

For Brooks, Eliot's poem demonstrates that modern man is in the Waste
Land because he has turned his back on the Christian hope of resurrection.

Brooks sent a draft copy of his interpretation to Eliot in February
1937, inviting Eliot's criticism, and Eliot responded on 14 March 1937.
Eliot felt the interpretation was excellent and that Brooks's type of
study was worthwhile so long as it did not presume to reconstruct the
poet's method. Brooks's interpretation made Eliot feel that he had written more ingeniously than he had realized on a conscious level, but
Eliot limited his remarks to his appreciation of Brooks's article, feeling
that an author could not be very helpful with interpretive criticism.[7]

There seems to be little direct connection between Brooks's reading
and the new uses which novelists found for The Waste Land. Not only is
there scant evidence for causality between the critical interpretations
available and the novelists' borrowing from The Waste Land, but in
many cases the novelists, deriving a theological orientation elsewhere,
anticipated the critic. Also, the ten novelists of this section were as
varied in their interpretations as were Wilson, Richards, and Brooks.
However, the developing critical awareness of The Waste Land's possible meanings parallels the novelists' developing uses of the poem.

George Orwell, James Hanley, and Anthony Powell apply The Waste
Land in the sociological and political sense outlined by Wilson, all three
drawing from Eliot's poem to reinforce their separate conceptions of
modern crisis. John Cowper Powys, Henry Green, and Christopher
Isherwood seem closer to I. A. Richards's view of the poem. Those
whose views of modernity are compatible with Brooks's theological interpretation—Evelyn Waugh, Charles Williams, C. S. Lewis, and Graham Greene—developed their spiritual views before Brooks's article
appeared and were frequently opposed to Eliot in matters of religion.
Waugh also appeared to reject the notion of Eliotian influence on his
art after Waugh's novels developed an overtly Catholic perspective.
Greene's Catholicism also came to dominate his novels, but this occurred after Greene's discrimination between novels and "entertainments," a distinction partly dependent on Greene's use of The Waste
Land. The ten novelists demonstrate the range of The Waste Land's
influences on the modern novel. Greene reveals how his increased
appreciation of Eliot's work was essential to his development as a
novelist.

4

EVELYN WAUGH

A Handful of Dust

Evelyn Waugh so highly regarded T. S. Eliot at one time that he gently criticized his father, the critic Arthur Waugh, for regarding "Mr. T. S. Eliot and his côterie . . . as manifestly absurd."[1] Waugh cited his father's opinions in the ironical light of Eliot's later reputation:

> Of Mr. T. S. Eliot, little knowing (nor would he have cared a jot had he known) the great popularity the poet was to achieve before his own death, he wrote: "It was a classic custom in the family hall, when a feast was at its height, to display a drunken slave among the sons of the household, to the end that they, being ashamed at the ignominious folly of his gesticulations, might determine never to be tempted into such a pitiable condition themselves. The custom has its advantages; for the wisdom of the younger generation was found to be fostered more surely by a single example than by a world of homily and precept."
>
> This was the function he predicted for the future idol of the academies.
>
> I quote these judgements to show my father's limitations and his staunch loyalty to them.[2]

Waugh's willingness to borrow from *The Waste Land*, apparent in his early novels, decreased as he moved towards more "serious" themes in *Sword of Honour*, Waugh's World War II trilogy. Ironically, however, as Waugh's use of *The Waste Land* decreased, his novels moved closer to Cleanth Brooks's "theological" interpretation of Eliot's poem. In the process, Waugh also directed satire towards imitators of Eliot and critics whose "discovery" of Eliot's influence lacked substance.

Waugh's critics have tended to minimize the influence of Eliot's poem on Waugh's early work. Christopher Sykes, after dismissing El-

iot's influence on *A Handful of Dust* (1934), felt that Waugh had borrowed Eliot's phrase "inappropriately."³ According to James F. Carens,
Waugh's novels reveal Eliot's spirit but not his influence.

> While it cannot be demonstrated that T. S. Eliot influenced Waugh's
> satirical techniques, Waugh does seem to have shared the disillusion-
> ment and disgust to which *The Waste Land* gave quintessential expres-
> sion. In the political life of the nation, in the institution of the family, in
> the relation between the sexes, in the spiritual condition of his charac-
> ters, Waugh discerns only futility and sterility. All coherence is gone
> from the world he describes, as it is gone from the desolate world of
> Eliot's poem.⁴

(These conclusions are in the section of Carens's book entitled "In
the Waste Land." Later, Carens forms a triad of Waugh, Eliot, and
Greene on the basis of their religious convictions.⁵) While he is equating
Waugh's disillusionment and disgust with those apparent in *The Waste
Land*, stressing Waugh's satiric bent, and emphasizing the similarity of
attitude which led both Waugh and Eliot to change religious affiliation,
Carens provides evidence for another possibility. Several episodes in
The Waste Land (including the Madame Sosostris sequence, the liaison
of the typist and the young man carbuncular, and the pub scene) are
deliberately satiric, ridiculing the superstitions, "passions," and im-
morality of the modern age. Waugh, particularly in his early novels,
satirizes the same traits. Waugh's early use of *The Waste Land* resembles
that of the 1920s novelists, contrasting a meaningless modern world to
the glory of England's past, but his later works reflect more sophisticated use of his themes until, at the end of his career, he implies a
reading of *The Waste Land* only faintly anticipated by such earlier writers
as Ford and Huxley. Eliot, who lashed characters similar to those ap-
pearing in Waugh's novels, directly influenced Waugh's early satire.

Carens has noted that while Waugh's "early novels—all, excepting
Decline and Fall, written after his conversion—reveal no explicit Catholicism . . . , his conversion and the choice of a phrase from Eliot's poem
as the title of his third [*sic*] novel indicate that he was aware, early in
his career, of the condition of religion in the modern world."⁶ This
modern condition of religion is important to the spiritual atmosphere
of *Decline and Fall* (1928), particularly when Waugh reveals how shal-
lowly the characters consider religion and spirit. When Margot Beste-
Chetwynde introduces Mr. Sebastian Cholmondley ("Chokey") at the
school sports, the others react negatively to her affair with the black.
Oblivious or indifferent to the prevailing attitude, Margot says to the
company, "Let's go and talk to the Vicar about God. . . . Chokey thinks

religion is just divine.'"[7] The thoughtless attitude towards religion is also a trait of more agreeable characters. When Paul travels to Marseilles on Margot's behalf, unaware of the nature of her business, he becomes lost in the red-light district: "In a moment of panic . . . he turned and fled for the broad streets and the tram lines where, he knew at heart, was his spiritual home" (*D&F*, 359). As in *The Waste Land*, the modern city is the closest to spiritual home for modern man.

In addition to using motifs from *The Waste Land*, Waugh adopted one of Eliot's most characteristic methods. Eliot often added to his poem by quoting or slightly misquoting well-known lines out of context, such as the following distortion of Marvell and Day:

> But at my back from time to time I hear
> The sound of horns and motors, which shall bring
> Sweeney to Mrs. Porter in the spring. (ll. 196–98)

Using this technique in *Decline and Fall*, Waugh parodies Wordsworth's "Intimations of Immortality" through Grimes:

> "Our life is lived between two homes. We emerge for a little into the light, and then the front door closes. The chintz curtains shut out the sun, and the hearth glows with the fire of home, while upstairs, above our heads, are enacted again the awful accidents of adolescence. There's a home and family waiting for every one of us. We can't escape, try how we may. It's the seed of life we carry about with us like our skeletons, each one of us unconsciously pregnant with desirable villa residences. There's no escape. As individuals we simply do not exist. We are just potential homebuilders, beavers and ants. How do we come into being? What is birth?" (*D&F*, 313)

Similarly, Waugh's parody of Hamlet's "What a piece of work is man!" is bitterly ironical. Professor Silenus, the architect who resents the existence of human beings because their requirements for living alter his designs, exclaims,

> "What an immature, self-destructive, antiquated mischief is man! How obscure and gross his prancing and chattering on his little stage of evolution! How loathsome and beyond words boring all the thoughts and self-approval of this biological by-product! this half-formed, ill-conditioned body! this erratic, mal-adjusted mechanism of his soul: on one side the harmonious instincts and balanced responses of the animal, on the other the inflexible purpose of the engine, and between them man, equally alien from the *being* of Nature and the *doing* of the machine, the vile *becoming*!" (*D&F*, 330)

By exploiting associations that the reader already has with the original
passage, Waugh successfully emphasizes his satiric point regarding
Silenus's attitude and the nature of modern man.

In each of his next few novels, Waugh stresses one motif of Eliot's
poem as he begins his search for *The Waste Land*'s meaning. Unlike
Decline and Fall, *Vile Bodies* (1930) satirizes modern man's hedonistic
responses to boredom and spiritual emptiness. Samuel Hynes writes of
Vile Bodies,

> It is a novel set in actual London—the geography is correct, and the
> street names are real and in the right places. But it is a London novel
> only in the sense that *The Waste Land* is a London poem; the city itself
> is an Unreal City, a fantasy of modern life lived in the absence of
> values. . . .
>
> The comparison with Eliot is an apt one: the world of *Vile Bodies* is a
> Waste Land, only it is a Waste Land inhabited mainly by Bright Young
> People.[8]

Anticipating Anthony Powell's *Afternoon Men*, Waugh exposes the sterility and futility lurking behind the frenetic attempts of the young to
amuse themselves. In his prefatory note, Waugh comments that *Vile
Bodies* is by no means a sequel to *Decline and Fall*,[9] although Lady Metro-
land still thrives on the proceeds of her "Entertainment" company and
Lady Circumference reappears. It becomes clear that the world of *Vile
Bodies* is close to that of Paul Pennyfeather and to the decaying world
of Eliot's poem.

As in *Decline and Fall*, denial of hope is a major motif in *Vile Bodies*.
Waugh focuses on man's sexual frenzy in the absence of values instead
of offering belief as a solution, bringing Waugh's moderns into *The
Waste Land* tradition. Mrs. Melrose Ape, in the smoking room of the
ship, cannot refrain from delivering a sermon to the unfortunate pas-
sengers, and she stresses the absence of hope in the modern world:

> "We're going to sing a song together, you and me." ("Oh, God," said
> Adam.) "You may not know it, but you are. You'll feel better for it body
> *and* soul. It's a song of Hope. You don't hear much about Hope these
> days, do you? Plenty about Faith, plenty about Charity. They've forgot-
> ten all about Hope. There's only one great evil in the world today.
> Despair. I know all about England, and I tell you straight, boys, I've got
> the goods for you. Hope's what you want and Hope's what I got." (*VB*,
> 17)

On occasion there are grounds for hope ("a beneficent attention of
Providence" causes Miss Runcible's discarded cigarette to miss a bucket

containing gasoline), but for the most part there is no place for hope in this world. The denial of hope appears ironically: Nina's family home, pronounced by a Cockney cabdriver, is "Doubting 'All" (*VB*, 86).

Black Mischief (1932) more narrowly develops one major theme of *The Waste Land*, modern barrenness. Basil Seal's attempt to introduce "civilization" to the African state of Azania culminates in a "pageant of sterility." Basil explains the methods of birth control to the Emperor Seth (named for the Egyptian god of desert waste, enemy of the vegetation and fertility god Osiris), who asks,

> ". . . and another thing. I have been reading in my papers about something very modern called birth control. What is it?"
> Basil explained.
> "I must have a lot of that. You will see to it. Perhaps it is not a matter for an ordinance, what do you think? We must popularise it by propaganda—educate the people in sterility. We might have a little pageant in its honour."[10]

The satire of this modern trend continues when the pageant begins: "An orange and green appliquéd standard bore the challenging motto THROUGH STERILITY TO CULTURE" (*BM*, 249). After the banner has fallen, "Only one word was visible in the empty street. STERILITY pleaded in orange and green silk to an unseeing people" (*BM*, 253). While sterility is a modern ideal, the native Azanians reject that ideal in their consistent "misunderstanding" of western values. In the process of satirizing the pretensions of Europeans to civilize other peoples, Waugh points out the inherent savagery of the English and, incidentally, anticipates Huxley's *Brave New World* when Seth encounters a new idea:

> But the next day he was absorbed in ectogenesis. "I have read here," he said, tapping a volume of speculative biology, "that there is to be no more birth. The ovum is fertilised in the laboratory and then the foetus is matured in bottles. It is a splendid idea. Get me some of those bottles . . . and no boggling." (*BM*, 198)

Taking its title from the first section of *The Waste Land*, *A Handful of Dust* (1934) presents a Waste Land in which the philosophy of meaninglessness combines with a sustained plot. The title seemed inappropriate to Christopher Sykes: "The reference to T. S. Eliot's *Waste Land*, stressed by a four-line quotation from the poem, may have given the book a certain extra selling value, but the title was not apposite." Yet on the next page Sykes fairly contradicts his earlier statement:

In this book Evelyn manifestly took up graver attitudes and followed serious convictions. He had long been aware of the important and usually well-hidden fact that civilization is a frail structure, of the nature of durable but not thick ice under which lies chaos and its evil. These grave thoughts never interfere with the speed and skill of the narration. Evelyn's wise decision to confine their expressions to implication not only eliminated all moralizing (this we would expect) but eliminated any oppressive consciousness on the reader's side that this is, as it is unmistakably, a book with a message. Here, as it were, is the book's secret, and Evelyn's scrupulous care not to give the secret away makes it the more telling when the secret comes to light, as it must to any discerning reader. By his skilful disguise of his message as a comedy of manners, he achieved the very difficult feat of making the victim as hero a person to be taken seriously.[11]

Although Sykes seems to feel that Waugh's use of the epigraph and title from *The Waste Land* resulted from desire for sales, the evidence which Sykes provides for the superiority of *A Handful of Dust*—implicit moral, serious purpose, graver attitudes—is compatible with a reading of Eliot's poem. Stephen Jay Greenblatt focuses on the relationship between *The Waste Land* and *A Handful of Dust* in these terms:

Tony Last, literally imprisoned now in a literal wasteland, has nothing left of his dream but a heap of broken images. The fulfillment of Tony's humanism, his selfless devotion, his abnegation is an endless self-sacrifice enforced by a madman in the midst of a jungle. There is no City.[12]

Not only is *The Waste Land* "apposite" to Waugh's *A Handful of Dust*, but the novel marks Waugh's first (and, some argue, best) attempt to unify his satire into a mature, cohesive novel.

Evidence of the spirit of decline, as embodied in *The Waste Land* (and in Gibbon and Spengler before it), appears throughout the novel. Mrs. Beaver, who earns her living "decorating," is only a symptom of the modern age:

She was subdividing a small house in Belgravia into six flats at three pounds a week, of one room each and a bath; the bathrooms were going to be slap-up, with limitless hot water and every transatlantic refinement; the other room would have a large built-in wardrobe with electric light inside, and space for a bed. It would fill a long felt need, Mrs. Beaver said. (*HD*, 43)

Tony Last, the last remnant of a dying British nobility, is altruistic until his estate, Hetton, is threatened. Tony can sympathize with Brenda's affair with Beaver and is willing to help her financially within reasonable limits, but when Brenda demands so much alimony that Tony will not be able to maintain Hetton, Tony takes his stand and leaves Brenda penniless.

Waugh, as he has done in earlier novels, includes man's indifference to man as a major motif. While considering an affair with the decidedly mediocre John Beaver, Brenda reveals her lack of respect for him, describing him as

> "second rate and a snob and, I should think, as cold as a fish, but I happen to have a fancy for him, that's all . . . besides I'm not sure he's *altogether* awful . . . he's got that odious mother whom he adores . . . and he's always been very poor. I don't think he's had a fair deal." (*HD*, 53)

After Beaver and Brenda have become romantically entangled, Tony presumes to call Brenda when he is tight, and she exploits his embarrassment to teach him a lesson. After Brenda establishes her relationship with Beaver, she decides to provide Tony with a mistress. She selects Jenny Abdul Akbar, a lamentable choice. Polly Cockpurse, who originated the idea of pairing Tony with a mistress to keep Tony out of Brenda's way, consoles Brenda: "Anyway, this lets you out. You've done far more than most wives would to cheer the old boy up" (*HD*, 95). The most powerful expression of indifference comes after John Andrew dies in a hunting accident, which all concerned agree is "no one's fault": Brenda is relieved to learn that her son, not her lover, has died.

The denial of hope in the modern world is also important to the development of *A Handful of Dust*. The village vicar, supported by a living from Tony's father, is emblematic of the irrelevance of religion to contemporary life:

> His sermons had been composed in his more active days for delivery at the garrison chapel; he had done nothing to adapt them to the changed conditions of his ministry and they mostly concluded with some reference to homes and dear ones far away. The villagers did not find this in any way surprising. Few of the things said in church seemed to have any particular reference to themselves. They enjoyed their vicar's sermons very much and they knew that when he began to speak about their distant homes, it was time to be dusting their knees and feeling for their umbrellas. (*HD*, 33–34)

Even Tony is affected, for when Todd asks him "Do you believe in God?" Tony responds "I suppose so. I've never really thought about it much" (*HD*, 212). Religion provides no comfort at Hetton or in the jungle because Tony, like most moderns, ignores the hope implicit in the resurrection. Tony derives hope only from his own actions. When a prospector wanders into the village and Tony slips him a piece of paper with his name on it, Tony hopes. When help arrives, however, Todd manages to drug Tony and to convince the visitors that Tony has died. Another instance of hope, ironical, is that which the older generation commonly places in the younger. Young Teddy, whose love for Hetton rivals Tony's own, hopes "one day to restore Hetton to the glory that it had enjoyed in the days of his Cousin Tony" (*HD*, 224). There was no glory during the days of Cousin Tony, but Teddy clings to his hope. He sleeps in Galahad, the only uncomfortable room at Hetton, as befits one who, like Galahad, wishes to fulfill a Grail quest. Throughout the novel, religion provides no consolation, and those who place their hope elsewhere are quickly disappointed, too. Even Brenda, who believes that she loves John Beaver, soon learns that without money she cannot hold him.

Several incidents and figures in the novel appear to be based on *The Waste Land*. For example, early in the book when Tony is sitting on the bed, Brenda "leant forward to him (a nereid emerging from the fathomless depths of clear water)" (*HD*, 18). The Thames Maiden image suggested by this water-nymph metaphor is reinforced by Brenda's later infidelity with Beaver. When the naive Beaver attempts to kiss Brenda in the taxi and she rebuffs his attempt because it is clumsy, he first apologizes and then asks whether she really has minded. Brenda responds "Me? No, not particularly" (*HD*, 48), recalling the Thames Maiden who asks "What should I resent?" (1. 299).

The novel's title and epigraph are the only explicit references to *The Waste Land* in *A Handful of Dust*. In another sense, however, the novel, which focuses on the decline of Toryism, the decay of English values, the selfish adultery of moderns, and the hopelessness of a godless civilization, is *The Waste Land* written large, in which moderns who search for meaning find none. As Greenblatt has noted,

> Waugh refuses to create a merely sentimental picture of the achievements of the past at the moment of extinction; he insists, rather, upon recording in scrupulous detail the actual process of demolition. In Waugh's satiric vision, seemingly trivial events—the breaking up of a manor house, the redecoration of an old room with chromium plating, a drunken brawl in an Oxford courtyard—are symbols of the massive, irreversible, and terrifying victory of barbarism and the powers of darkness over civilization and light. Waugh's early novels . . . are chronicles of that awful triumph.[13]

After Waugh had realized this chronicle, he wrote several comic, far-
cical novels which evoke the mood of *The Waste Land* in isolated passages but bear little resemblance to it in subject matter or imagery.
Scoop (1937), a satire on journalism, *Put Out More Flags* (1942), a satire
of civilian opportunism in wartime, *The Loved One* (1948), a satire of
American funeral practices, and *The Ordeal of Gilbert Pinfold* (1957), a
fictional study of a mental disorder, share some of the poem's concerns
—indifference to others, the despair of modern man in a godless universe, and the squalor of modern life. During this period, Waugh may
have reacted to an exaggerated view of Eliot's influence on his art and
have deliberately avoided any overt connection between his work and
Eliot's poem.

  Brideshead Revisited (1945), "The Sacred and Profane Memories of
Captain Charles Ryder," is a serious treatment of the problems of living between the wars. Early in the novel the poem appears in a context
similar to the Earl of Birkenhead's memories of Oxford in the late
1920s, when Harold and William Acton "declaimed *The Waste Land*
through megaphones from balconies to bemused passersby. . . ."[14]
Waugh uses *The Waste Land* to satirize one character:

> After luncheon he [Anthony Blanche] stood on the balcony with a mega-
> phone which had appeared surprisingly among the bric-à-brac of Sebas-
> tian's room, and in languishing, sobbing tones recited passages from *The
> Waste Land* to the sweatered and muffled throng that was on its way to
> the river.
>   "'I, Tiresias, have foresuffered all,'" he sobbed to them from the
> Venetian arches—
>   "Enacted on this same d-divan or b-bed,
>   I who have sat by Thebes below the wall
>   And walked among the l-l-lowest of the dead. . . ."[15]

Here Waugh is lampooning Blanche, not *The Waste Land*; the poem
merely serves as a ready symbol of the cultural elite to which Blanche
aspires. Brideshead itself appears in a Waste Land context: "Foreigners
returning on post from their own waste lands wrote home that here
they seemed to catch a glimpse of the world they had believed lost for
ever among the mud and wire . . ." (*BR*, 179–80). The history of
Brideshead reveals that even it was built "in the waste hollows" (*BR*,
332), and that the blight has extended to the Marchmain family. Hopelessness confronting the Marchmains is a symptom of the modern age.

  Ryder, a middle-aged infantry captain, regards Hooper as a symbol
of modernity.

> In the weeks that we were together Hooper became a symbol to me of
> Young England, so that whenever I read some public utterance pro-
> claiming what Youth demanded in the Future and what the world owed
> to Youth, I would test these general statements by substituting "Hooper"
> and seeing if they still seemed as plausible. Thus in the dark hour before
> reveille I sometimes pondered: "Hooper Rallies," "Hooper Hostels," "In-
> ternational Hooper Co-operation" and "the Religion of Hooper." He was
> the acid test of all these alloys. (BR, 9)

The connection between Hooper's "Religion" and his lack of expectations becomes a major theme of *Brideshead Revisited*, for the plight of
moderns relates to their lack of religious faith. When the young Julia
finds that she must choose between Rex and her faith, her rupture
with the church is abrupt. When Rex agrees to convert to Catholicism,
his progress leaves much to be desired. Father Mowbray reports that
Rex

> "doesn't seem to have the least intellectual curiosity or natural piety.
>   "The first day I wanted to find out what sort of religious life he had
> had till now, so I asked him what he meant by prayer. He said: 'I don't
> mean anything. *You* tell me.' I tried to, in a few words, and he said:
> 'Right. So much for prayer. What's the next thing?' I gave him the
> catechism to take away. Yesterday I asked him whether Our Lord had
> more than one nature. He said: 'Just as many as you say, Father.'
>   "Then again I asked him: 'Supposing the Pope looked up and saw a
> cloud and said "It's going to rain," would that be bound to happen?'
> 'Oh, yes, Father.' 'But supposing it didn't?' He thought a moment and
> said, 'I suppose it would be sort of raining spiritually, only we were too
> sinful to see it.' " (BR, 192)

Rex's separation of religion from reality accords with the modern age.
Like *The Waste Land*, *Brideshead Revisited* connects the listlessness and
tedium which moderns face to their lack of faith in the resurrection.
Throughout *Brideshead Revisited*, Waugh alludes to the poem, adopts its
imagery, and draws from its major themes to write his first "serious"
novel.

Waugh's most ambitious work, the World War II trilogy entitled
Sword of Honour, includes *Men at Arms* (1952), *Officers and Gentlemen*
(1955), and *Unconditional Surrender* (1961). Unlike the earlier novels,
which owe much of their appeal to Waugh's sense of the absurd, or
Brideshead Revisited, which is a powerful treatment of serious human
problems, *Sword of Honour* combines the best of Waugh's wit with the
most serious of his themes. Throughout the trilogy, *The Waste Land* and

its imagery seem to appear in expressions of what is wrong with the world, but in *Unconditional Surrender* Waugh explicitly repudiates *The Waste Land* as a source of imaginative art.

Early in *Men at Arms*, "wasteland" describes Guy Crouchback's spiritual condition. He confesses in Italian because "Into that wasteland where his soul languished he need not, could not, enter. He had no words to describe it. There were no words in any language. There was nothing to describe, merely a void."[16] Several physical descriptions evoking *The Waste Land* also appear in the novel, most depicting the horrors of war. Corresponding to the physical blight of the Waste Land, the Modern Age also is blighted. Initially Guy feels that the war might be beneficial because "The enemy at last was plain in view, huge and hateful, all disguise cast off" (*MA*, 12). However, Lord Kilbannock, a journalist, announces the prevailing English spirit by describing what he wants from the war:

> "Once you're in, there's every opportunity. I've got my eye on India or Egypt. Somewhere where there's no black-out. Fellow in the flats where I live got coshed on the head the other night, right on the steps. All a bit too dangerous for me. I don't want a medal. I want to be known as one of the soft-faced men who did well out of the war." (*MA*, 27)

A major problem for the moderns at war is their reluctance to trust to faith of any sort. "Box-Bender looked self-conscious, as he still did, always, when religious practices were spoken of. He could not get used to it—this ease with the Awful" (*MA*, 33). The presence of *The Waste Land* in the blighted and sterile land of the Modern Age adds to the seriousness of the novel's theme. After his gift of whiskey has led to Apthorpe's demise, Guy feels the sense of despair characteristic of, if inexplicable to, the inhabitants of *The Waste Land*:

> Guy left the office unashamed. He felt shaken, as though he had seen a road accident in which he was not concerned. His fingers shook but it was nerves not conscience which troubled him; he was familiar with shame; this trembling, hopeless sense of disaster was something of quite another order; something that would pass and leave no mark. (*MA*, 247)

Unconditional Surrender continues themes reminiscent of *The Waste Land*, and when Ludovic submits a manuscript to Spruce, Waugh refers directly to the poem. After noting possibly libelous statements, Spruce continues,

"And besides these there seemed to me two poetic themes which occur again and again. There is the Drowned Sailor motif—an echo of the *Waste Land* perhaps? Had you Eliot consciously in mind?"

"Not Eliot," said Ludovic. "I don't think he was called Eliot."[17]

When writing, Ludovic was drawing entirely from his experience, so that this passage serves to deny influence of Eliot even when it appears obvious on a superficial level. Waugh may be reacting to the critical tendency to attribute Eliot's influence where it does not apply, with specific application to his own work. However, although Waugh can assert his lack of dependence on *The Waste Land* and demand due credit for his art, I doubt he could claim that Eliot's influence is entirely absent. His Waste Land differs markedly from Eliot's in many respects, but in others remnants of Waugh's earlier borrowings from the poem appear evident.

Against a Waste Land background, the absence of hope which Waugh has stressed in *Men at Arms* and *Officers and Gentlemen* continues. The man who feels most Job-like, most cut off from God and man, is Ludovic:

> Things had happened to Ludovic in the summer of 1941, things had been done by him, which, the ancients believed, provoked a doom. Not only the ancients; most of mankind, independently, cut off from all communication with one another, had discovered and proclaimed this grim alliance between the powers of darkness and justice. Who was Ludovic, Ludovic questioned, to set his narrow, modern scepticism against the accumulated experience of the species? (*EB*, 110)

As Guy explains to Kerstie in another context, "Perhaps when they *are* hurt, the tough suffer more than the tender" (*EB*, 195). Ludovic later publishes his *Pensées,* a greatly admired book which is part of the current literary genre of

> books which would turn from drab alleys of the thirties into the odorous gardens of a recent past transformed and illuminated by disordered memory and imagination. Ludovic in the solitude of his post was in the movement.
> Nor was it for all its glitter a cheerful book. Melancholy. . . . (*EB*, 245)

Hopeless, pained, melancholy, doomed—these describe the moods and feelings engendered by a physical Waste Land.

Coupled with the denial of hope is the sense of boredom felt by all the novel's characters except Gervase Crouchback. Despite their respective troubles, Guy and Virginia find that they are bored:

> "It was all quite true," Virginia shuddered. "The things that happen to one! Anyway that's all over. I've had a dreary war so far. I almost wish I'd stayed in America. It all seemed such fun at first, but it didn't last."
> "I found that," said Guy. "Not perhaps in quite the same way. The last two years have been as dull as peace." (*EB*, 167)

The hopelessness and boredom result from man's lack of faith in the Christian myth. While Virginia later believes religious faith easy to find and to keep, Guy, throughout the trilogy, has difficulty coming to terms with his religion and suggests that the Pope should take a more active role in world affairs. Gervase tells Guy, "you're really making the most terrible nonsense, you know. That isn't at all what the Church is like. It isn't what she's *for*" (*EB*, 6). Eventually Guy realizes that problems with his own faith have caused the feeling of emptiness in himself:

> "I don't ask anything from you"; that was the deadly core of his apathy; his father had tried to tell him, was now telling him. That emptiness had been with him for years now, even in his days of enthusiasm and activity in the Halberdiers. Enthusiasm and activity were not enough. God required more than that. He had commanded all men to *ask*. (*EB*, 81)

At the end of the novel, the question of sterility, barrenness, and despair in the modern world becomes a question of morality:

> "Is there any place that is free from evil? It is too simple to say that only the Nazis wanted war. These Communists wanted it too. It was the only way in which they could come to power. Many of my people wanted it, to be revenged on the Germans, to hasten the creation of the national state. It seems to me there was a will to war, a death wish, everywhere. Even good men thought their private honour would be satisfied by war. They could assert their manhood by killing and being killed. They would accept hardships in recompense for having been selfish and lazy. Danger justified privilege. I knew Italians—not very many perhaps—who felt this. Were there none in England?"
> "God forgive me," said Guy. "I was one of them." (*EB*, 305)

Waugh also emphasizes sterility in the novel. Ian remarks of Virginia, "Well, who else do you suggest for her? I daresay one of the Americans would be the best bet. The trouble is that, from the litter of contraceptives they leave everywhere, it looks as though they lacked strong philoprogenitive instincts" (*EB*, 113). Uncle Peregrine excites Virginia's mirth later by his lack of the same instincts:

> "Peregrine, have you never been to bed with a woman?"
> "Yes," said Uncle Peregrine smugly, "twice. It is not a thing I normally talk about."
> "Do tell."
> "Once when I was twenty and once when I was forty-five. I didn't particularly enjoy it."
> "Tell me about them."
> "It was the same woman." (*EB*, 175)

Earlier, like Liz in Eliot's pub scene, Virginia had decided to abort her unwanted child. Only after she has been unsuccessful in her attempt to locate "Dr. Akonanga, 14 Blight Street, W. 2" (*EB*, 102), does she change her mind. The combinations of sterility and blight in the novel resemble the relationship Eliot established in *The Waste Land*.

When Oates demonstrates his "Electronic Personnel Selector," it reminds Guy of a fortune-telling slot machine. Like Madame Sosostris, Oates can make nothing of a "blank card," and his next demonstration, which selects Guy for a specific mission, is not accurate. "Guy did not attempt to correct the machine on the point of his age, or of the extent of his Commando training" (*EB*, 29). Guy reflects that

> The card that had come popping out of the Electronic Personnel Selector bearing his name, like a "fortune" from a seaside slot-machine, like a fortune indeed in a more real sense—the luck of the draw in a lottery or sweepstake—brought an unfamiliar stir of exhilaration. . . . (*EB*, 52)

Like Madame Sosostris's clientele, the moderns who use this machine are essentially superstitious, a point made several times in the novel. In one instance, Dr. Akonanga, the abortionist whom Virginia could not find, is employed by the government to give key German personnel physical ailments and nightmares through voodoo. Later in the book, Guy encounters a conscientious objector who is "explaining his objections at length above the turmoil of jazz. They were neither political nor ethical but occult, being in some way based on the dimensions of the Great Pyramid" (*EB*, 147).

The Waste Land's influence on Waugh's novels forms an interesting pattern. In Waugh's early work, culminating with *A Handful of Dust*, one finds themes from *The Waste Land* as well as evidence of Waugh's willingness (at least in the novel's title and epigraph) to invite comparison of his vision and Eliot's. In his next several works, allusions to *The Waste Land* are not discernible. Then, in *Brideshead Revisited*, Waugh returns to *Waste Land* themes and, on occasion, draws attention to Eliot's poem. Finally, in *Sword of Honour*, despite its apparent compatibility with parts of Eliot's poem, Waugh wrote an explicit repudiation of *Waste Land* influence, perhaps because he had come to regret the associations drawn between his work and Eliot's poem and wished to be recognized in his own right.

5

ORWELL, HANLEY,
and POWELL

Rats' Alley

GEORGE ORWELL

In the novels of George Orwell, James Hanley, and Anthony Powell, the influence of *The Waste Land* seems grounded in a political and sociological interpretation consistent with Edmund Wilson's 1922 reading of the poem. Orwell, who felt that Eliot would have been a better poet had he developed a political stance in his later poetry, realized it was absurd to expect Eliot to become a champion of democracy, but he isolated one purpose which he felt Eliot could have pursued: "it is arguable that he would have done better to go much further in the direction implied in his famous 'Anglo-Catholic and Royalist' declaration. He could not have developed into a Socialist, but he might have developed into the last apologist of aristocracy."[1] Although Orwell felt that the solution to the modern problem was political, he described his Waste Land in Eliot's terms. Peter Stansky and William Abrahams, writing of Orwell's early reading, note that "he did not venture deep into the territory of the 'new,'" including works by T. S. Eliot.[2] They add that when the "'modern movement' was entering its decade of triumph," Orwell, in Burma, had no access to Eliot's works.[3] However, when describing the young Orwell beginning his teaching at Evelyn's School (a boys' preparatory school), Stansky and Abrahams write,

> Then came April, to a reader of *The Waste Land* inevitably "the cruellest month," and one ventures to think that the phrase would have occurred

to Blair, for more than one reason, arriving at a waste land of his own: a dreary prep school in a dreary suburban town. . . .[4]

Here lies the germinal relationship between Orwell and the poem. Confronting an essentially Waste Land world, Orwell associated his views with those of the poem and employed Eliot's imagery to describe this world. Eliot's view of the modern dilemma, reinforced by *Waste Land* imagery of what Orwell called the "ugliness and spiritual emptiness of the machine age,"[5] appears in Orwell's early novels. The "subject matter" of *The Waste Land* is the subject of *Keep the Aspidistra Flying, Coming Up for Air,* and even *1984.* In "Why I Write," Orwell claimed that "Every line of serious work that I have written since 1936 has been written, directly or indirectly, *against* totalitarianism and *for* democratic socialism, as I understand it."[6] (He addressed the issue "directly" after World War II in *Animal Farm* and *1984,* but "indirectly" in his pre-Spanish Civil War novel *Keep the Aspidistra Flying* and in his 1939 novel *Coming Up for Air.*)

Orwell's *Keep the Aspidistra Flying* (1936), the story of Gordon Comstock's abortive attempt to transcend the money-god by writing poetry in self-imposed poverty, is set in an urban Waste Land reminiscent of Eliot's. Orwell often refers directly to Eliot. Comstock, whose poetry collection *Mice* has immediately lapsed into well-deserved obscurity, bitterly surveys the arrangement of books on the poetry shelves of the bookshop, seeing, among other works, Eliot's.[7] On the town after an unexpected payment of $50 for one poem, Comstock "knocked down reputation after reputation. Shaw, Yeats, Eliot, Joyce, Huxley, Lewis, Hemingway—each with a careless phrase or two was shovelled into the dustbin" (*KAF,* 161). Although he expresses a contempt for Eliot—including a caustic reference to Eliot's having chosen the church over socialism and suicide (*KAF,* 88)—Comstock sees the world of London as a Waste Land much like Eliot's. The physical surroundings indicate the aesthetic emptiness of modern civilization. For Eliot's moderns in *The Waste Land,* culture consists of the "Shakespeherian Rag." In *Keep the Aspidistra Flying,* art is either a novel by Ethel M. Dell or a tasteless advertising poster. As Gordon reflects on the significance of what he sees, he combines the death wish, the sense of decay, and the loss of meaning which pervade *The Waste Land:*

> He gazed out at the graceless street. At this moment it seemed to him that in a street like this, in a town like this, every life that is lived must be meaningless and intolerable. The sense of disintegration, of decay, that is endemic in our time, was strong upon him. Somehow it was

mixed up with the ad-posters opposite. He looked now with more seeing
eyes at those grinning yard-wide faces. After all, there was more there
than mere silliness, greed and vulgarity. Corner Table grins at you,
seemingly optimistic, with a flash of false teeth. But what is behind the
grin? Desolation, emptiness, prophecies of doom. For can you not see, if
you know how to look, that behind that slick self-satisfaction, that titter-
ing fat-bellied triviality, there is nothing but a frightful emptiness, a
secret despair? (*KAF*, 16)

The poem which Comstock tries to write, *London Pleasures*, "two
thousand lines or so, in rhyme royal" (*KAF*, 30), shares some structural
features with *The Waste Land*. The poem is too ambitious for Comstock's talents, and Orwell's description of the poem's shortcomings
echoes both *The Waste Land* itself and the complaints of its severer
critics. Forster's chief objection to *The Waste Land* was the incoherence
of the lines quoted at the end, which the Fisher King introduces as
"These fragments I have shored against my ruins" (l. 431). Similarly,
Comstock's poem "had simply fallen apart into a series of fragments.
. . . —just fragments, incomplete in themselves and impossible to join
together" (*KAF*, 31). In Eliot's poem, a crowd in which "each man fixed
his eyes before his feet" (l. 65) moves across London Bridge. Orwell's
crowd is also anonymous, avoiding others' eyes:

> The crowd slid past him; he avoided and was avoided. There is some-
> thing horrible about London at night; the coldness, the anonymity, the
> aloofness. Seven million people, sliding to and fro, avoiding contact,
> barely aware of one another's existence, like fish in an aquarium tank.
> (*KAF*, 71)

Comstock explicitly equates London and hell: after making "a gesture
that comprehended the whole of Piccadilly Circus," he tells Ravelston,
"The lights down in hell will look just like that" (*KAF*, 168).

Unlike *The Waste Land*'s inhabitants (excepting the narrator), Comstock knows he is in a Waste Land, but his sin is the same as theirs—
he has repudiated hope. "April is the cruellest month" because nature
renews a promise that will lead to disappointment; the character who
addresses Stetson fears that "The corpse you planted last year in your
garden" might begin to "sprout" (ll. 71–72); and in the final section of
the poem,

> He who was living is now dead
> We who were living are now dying
> With a little patience (ll. 328–30)

Orwell includes all three attitudes in the novel. In a passage which protests the promise of April and mixes traditional imagery and modern jingles in an Eliotian manner, April is no harbinger of hope. The narrator cites traditional paeans to spring and then remarks,

> But how absurd that even now, in the era of central heating and tinned peaches, a thousand so-called poets are still writing in the same strain! For what difference does spring or winter or any other time of year make to the average civilised person nowadays? In a town like London the most striking seasonal change, apart from the mere change of temperature, is in the things you see lying about on the pavement. In late winter it is mainly cabbage leaves. In July you tread on cherry stones, in November on burnt-out fireworks. Towards Christmas the orange peel grows thicker. It was a different matter in the Middle Ages. There was some sense in writing poems about spring when spring meant fresh meat and green vegetables after months of frowsting in some windowless hut on a diet of salt fish and mouldy bread.
>
> If it was spring Gordon failed to notice it. (*KAF*, 222)

Describing the tombstone placed over Gordon's paternal grandfather (whose epitaph ends with the line, "He sleeps in the arms of Jesus"), Orwell notes the fervent hope of Samuel Ezekiel Comstock's descendants that the corpse not sprout:

> No need to repeat the blasphemous comments which everyone who had known Gran'pa Comstock made on that last sentence. But it is worth pointing out that the chunk of granite on which it was inscribed weighed close on five tons and was quite certainly put there with the intention, though not the conscious intention, of making sure that Gran'pa Comstock shouldn't get up from underneath it. If you want to know what a dead man's relatives really think of him, a good rough test is the weight of his tombstone. (*KAF*, 38)

Ravelston, expressing Eliot's position, comments "We've got to die before we can be reborn, if you take my meaning," but Gordon immediately rejects this notion: "We're dying right enough. I don't see much signs of our being reborn" (*KAF*, 85). Even the prevailing morality which Gordon attributes to modern life echoes the godless morality of modern man in Eliot's poem. Gordon notes that "Money is what God used to be. Good and evil have no meaning any longer except failure and success. Hence the profoundly significant phrase, to *make good*" (*KAF*, 43). Providing an economic motive rather than a spiritual source for guilt, Comstock claims that having no money is "the only thing in the world there *is* to be ashamed of" (*KAF*, 146). Gordon's solution to the blight of the modern world resembles the regenerative and purgative fire of "The Fire Sermon," for throughout the novel Gordon hopes for London's destruction in another war: "A few tons of T.N.T. to send our civilisation back to hell where it belongs" (*KAF*, 230).

Orwell's echoings of situations and specific lines from *The Waste Land* also contribute to the vision of modern life in *Coming Up for Air* (1939). George Bowling, traveling salesman for an insurance firm, comments on the barrenness of the modern world and defines himself in terms applicable to the characters in Eliot's *Waste Land*: "I'm vulgar, I'm insensitive, and I fit in with my environment."[8] Bowling finds a symbol for modern life in a milk-bar, where "nothing matters except slickness and shininess and streamlining" (*CUA*, 26). When Bowling bites into a sausage and discovers it is filled with fish, "It gave me the feeling that I'd bitten into the modern world and discovered what it was really made of" (*CUA*, 27).

Bowling ascribes modern civilization's problems in part to spiritual failure. Commenting on the number of sensational murders which the press features, Bowling finds the papers' reports inferior to "the old domestic poisoning dramas; . . . the truth being, I suppose, that you can't do a good murder unless you believe you're going to roast in hell for it" (*CUA*, 26–27). When Bowling recollects his mother's giving him a "second-hand copy of Foxe's *Book of Martyrs*," he remembers that he did not read it "though the illustrations weren't half bad" (*CUA*, 104). Bowling clearly makes himself a member of the Waste Land's majority when he decides, "I don't believe it made very much difference that what's called religious belief was still prevalent in those days" (*CUA*, 125).

As Eliot describes his crowd, so Bowling describes clerks rushing to work. Imagining the "best" time for Hitler to bomb London, Bowling thinks of "Some quiet morning, when the clerks are streaming across London Bridge" (*CUA*, 24). This crowd image recurs a few pages later:

> The usual crowd that you can hardly fight your way through was streaming up the pavement, all of them with that insane fixed expression on their faces that people have in London streets. . . . Enough noise to waken the dead, but not to waken this lot. I felt as if I was the only person awake in a city of sleep-walkers. (*CUA*, 29)

Orwell's novel also parallels Eliot's equating of the crowd flowing over London Bridge and the crowds in hell. During his visit to Professor Porteous (styled after Huxley's *Antic Hay* character of the same name), Bowling realizes that Porteous is not really alive and then relates this to his observation of crowds:

a curious thought struck me. *He's dead.* He's a ghost. All people like that are dead.

It struck me that perhaps a lot of the people you see walking about are dead. . . . There are a lot of people like that. Dead minds, stopped inside. Just keep moving backwards and forwards on the same little track, getting fainter all the time, like ghosts. (*CUA*, 188)

Bowling, recalling Eliot's Fisher King, was an avid fisherman. *The Waste Land*'s narrator describes a rat crawling

> softly through the vegetation
> Dragging its slimy belly on the bank
> While I was fishing in the dull canal
> On a winter evening round behind the gashouse
> Musing on the king my brother's wreck
> And on the king my father's death before him. (ll. 187–92)

Bowling's reminiscences include his brother's ruin and his father's death, and Bowling has no hope for a virile successor (which also distinguishes Eliot's Fisher King from the myth's). Bowling observes the problem of fishing in London: "A few dismal fishing-clubs plant themselves in rows along the banks of canals. . . . Now all the ponds are drained, and when the streams aren't poisoned with chemicals from factories they're full of rusty tins and motor-bike tyres" (*CUA*, 87). Bowling differs from the Fisher King in an important philosophical way, as he reveals in his reaction to his wife Hilda. For her the Fisher King's question is always answered with certainty—she will set her lands in order. To Bowling, however, this is not the proper outlook: "As for wars, earthquakes, plagues, famines and revolutions, she pays no attention to them. Butter is going up, and the gas-bill is enormous, and the kids' boots are wearing out and there's another instalment due on the radio—that's Hilda's litany" (*CUA*, 8). Hilda's attitude robs Bowling of comfort and pleasure because

> She does everything for negative reasons. When she makes a cake, she's not thinking about the cake, only about how to save butter and eggs. When I'm in bed with her all she thinks about is how not to have a baby. If she goes to the pictures she's all the time writhing with indignation about the price of the seats. (*CUA*, 161)

Thus in *Coming Up for Air*, Bowling's character and reactions to modern life are in accord with those of *The Waste Land*'s Fisher King, although Orwell indicates that he and Eliot will part company in their solutions to the dilemma of the modern world. Bowling has no intention to consider setting his lands in order. One objection which Bowling has to Porteous is the latter's insistence that modern civilization does not matter beside that of the ancients, and that there is no historical solution to modern problems. Bowling offers Porteous a vision of

> the bad time that's coming, but he wouldn't listen. Merely repeated that there's nothing new under the sun. Finally he hauls a book out of the shelves and reads me a passage about some Greek tyrant back in the B.C.s who certainly might have been Hitler's twin brother. (*CUA*, 185–86)

Bowling's motive for returning to Lower Binfield was to salvage something meaningful from the past to improve his future, but Porteous, like O'Brien in *1984*, either denies the relationship of past to present or uses the past to justify the events of the present. Bowling constantly worries about the effect of politics on the quality of his life. In *1984*, Winston Smith will learn that the ultimate source of his dissatisfaction with his existence has been the encroachment of politics on individual freedom.

Despite its political and futuristic orientation, *1984* (1949) also bears some resemblance to *The Waste Land* in its depiction of a decline in spiritual values. Winston's world view, like Gordon Comstock's and George Bowling's, includes recognition of an urban Waste Land:

> Were there always these vistas of rotting nineteenth-century houses, their sides shored up with balks of timber, their windows patched with cardboard and their roofs with corrugated iron, their crazy garden walls sagging in all directions? And the bombed sites where the plaster dust swirled in the air and the willow herb straggled over the heaps of rubble; and the places where the bombs had cleared a larger path and there had sprung up sordid colonies of wooden dwellings like chicken houses?[9]

The true horror of modern life, as recognized by Winston, is also the most haunting horror of *The Waste Land*: "It struck him that the truly characteristic thing about modern life was not its cruelty and insecurity, but simply its bareness, its dinginess, its listlessness" (*1984*, 63). Also in *1984* is a nearly exact quotation of Eliot's "I will show you fear in a handful of dust": O'Brien tells Winston, "We are the dead. Our only true life is in the future. We shall take part in it as handfuls of dust and splinters of bone" (*1984*, 145).

Although there is similarity between Winston's world and that of *The Waste Land*, the political orientation of *1984* precludes Eliot's influence except on a superficial level. Had Eliot's solution been more in agreement with Orwell's, connections between the poem and the novel might have been more useful to the novelist. However, Orwell's political solutions set his work apart from *The Waste Land*'s vision.

JAMES HANLEY

Like Orwell, James Hanley applied Eliot's images and motifs frequently to the Waste Land world of his novels. Hanley, who has not won regard as a prose stylist, often used Eliot's images and phrases in his writing. Little known in America in spite of twenty-six novels over the past fifty years, Hanley has focused on the social and economic problems of the lower classes. Unlike Jack London, however, Hanley refuses to romanticize the plight of the working class or to find any redeeming features in the hard life. London's writer in *The Sea Wolf* discovers and asserts his latent manhood, but Hanley's Arthur Fearon, who runs away to sea in *Boy* (1932), contracts syphilis and is mercifully smothered in his bunk by the ship's captain. Hanley's lack of formal education (he ran away to sea at thirteen) and his refusal to treat the ugliness of lower-class life in a romanticized manner have led to faint praise from such reviewers as Peter Hutchinson: "Hanley writes like a riveting machine, or a machine gun. He appears to know nothing, he clearly cares nothing, about shading and coloring. But it is evident that Hanley, with his profound insight into the lower depths, with his surging but well-leashed resentments, is a man to be closely watched."[10] Such varied individuals as T. E. Lawrence, Richard Aldington, and E. M. Forster have praised Hanley's novels, but the general agreement is that his experience and his ability to express it, while worthy, suffer from an unpolished, even graceless, style. Hanley wrote of the horrors of life in the slums, of life at sea, of work as a stoker, and of flight from authority. The world which Hanley viewed is a Waste Land world. Although Hanley wrote largely from his own experience of poverty, war, and the sea, he found images in *The Waste Land* which could enhance his hard-hitting style, adapting them to his own use as effectively as any of Eliot's drawing-room imitators could wish.

General references to *The Waste Land* abound in Hanley's novels. For example, in *The Furys* (1935), the Furys' home is clearly in a Waste Land, and when Anna Ragner, a usurer, appears in the novel, the reference becomes explicit: "At the back of the factory, standing detached on a small piece of waste land, stood Anna Ragner's house."[11] Hanley echoes lines from all five sections of *The Waste Land*. In a passage describing crowds of people "walking round in a ring," Hanley makes use of the Unreal City and Crowd motifs that were combined with a vision of London as hell in Eliot's poem. In *The Furys*, Professor Titmouse describes a mob scene in terms reminiscent of the Unreal City, and, like Eliot, invokes Dante's Inferno in his description:

> "Now! the people have begun to move. The police have charged them. Some hand has thrown a lighted paper into a shop. Listen to their shouting. The flames are rising. Arms ride the air, sticks, stones, and bottles fly, batons whizz past one's head. As the flames spread from shop to shop, flames which no mortal hand can now put out, those towering walls are thrown clear, one can see them perfectly. One can see them for what they are. Prisons, my boy. And who are these running people, these swearing crowds? Look! The light of the fires has caught them. Goblins from the Inferno. Ha ha!" (*Furys*, 343)

In *Levine* (1956), Pentony, speaking of a "community" of shanties that provide refuge for derelicts, describes it as

> "A place full of shadows, half-men coming round corners, men staring through windows, women just sitting, bits and ends of everything there, no centre, nothing with a meaning. And the climate. Entirely relaxed. It's neither hot nor cold. No change. Bits of people blowing about like paper."[12]

(The last sentence recalls *Burnt Norton* (III, 15): "Men and bits of paper, whirled by the cold wind.") Levine's reaction to the town is to note its "unreal" aspects: "I knew nobody and the town was strange. Narrow and dark, with its little huddle of shops, its ghost people fluttering about from one street to another. I never looked at them. I went right past them" (*L*, 137).

In *The Closed Harbour* (1952), the more hellish aspects of modern cities are seen from Labiche's perspective. "Thenceforth he climbed, laboriously, up and up, what Monsieur Follet had once described as climbing into hell."[13] Labiche, who works with the Saint Vincent de Paul Society in an attempt to perform good works, is familiar with the seamier side of the city. He is in the Waste Land but not of it. Unlike the others, he is aware of this condition and, despite the squalor and poverty which he encounters, is able to maintain that hope which denizens of Eliot's poem deny. Although Hanley only rarely allows one motif to dominate the imagery of a novel—the Lazarus motif in *The Secret Journey* (1936), the Hanged Man motif in *Hollow Sea* (1938)—he has used Eliot's imagery in all his works.

Hanley has also adapted lines from Eliot's "A Game of Chess" several times. Eliot's neurasthenic woman demands "Speak to me. Why do you never speak. Speak" (l. 112). Hanley's novels contain equivalent demands that, as in Eliot's poem, receive no suitable answer. Remembering life with her unresponsive parents, Grace Helling in *Levine* recalls, "I say nothing, there is nothing to say. Mother *knows*, father *knows*. There are no questions to be asked in this house, since there are none to answer" (*L*, 164). In Eliot's poem, repeated questions lead to a statement of absolutely no hope: .

> "What are you thinking of? What thinking? What?
> "I never know what you are thinking. Think."
>
> I think we are in rats' alley
> Where the dead men lost their bones. (ll. 113–16)

This exchange, as well as the line "Nothing again nothing" (l. 120) that closely follows it, is directly echoed in a conversation between Peter Fury and Sheila in Hanley's *An End and a Beginning* (1932):

> "What were you thinking about?" she asked. He did not answer. He hadn't actually heard, as though the words themselves had slipped out, velvet soft, crawled to the chair on which he sat.
> "What were you thinking about, Peter?"
> "Nothing," he said, "nothing," like the word had lain on the tip of his tongue all this silent hour, only waiting to drop. And as if to make sure that it had landed, he repeated, "Nothing."
> "What were you thinking about?"[14]

The recurring references to nervousness and boredom, the questions without answers, and the reliance on sex to relieve boredom, all of which appear in Hanley's novels frequently, derive from Eliot's *The Waste Land*.

One Tiresias figure appears. Professor Titmouse, who made unwelcome sexual overtures to Peter Fury when the two witnessed a riot in the city, disturbs Peter long after their encounter. Peter discovers that although Titmouse has become part of the past, his presence lingers:

> "What is the matter with me?" The feelings that ran riot in him were strange and terrifying.
> "*You are a young fool,*" said Professor Titmouse.
> Yes, that was who it was. That was the voice always raging in his ears. That was the person he had dreamed about.
> "*It is just that she cannot help it. Go up. She is waiting for you. Do not hesitate.*" And, as though the man in the deerstalker hat had lifted him

from the chair, Peter rose to his feet, opened the kitchen door and went
upstairs.

Professor Titmouse seemed to tramp behind him. (*Furys*, 502)

Professor Titmouse is as mystically present to the young Peter Fury's
imagination as Eliot's Tiresias is in the encounter between the typist
and the young man carbuncular. Professor Titmouse's prophetic lec-
tures and pervading presence seem reminiscent of Tiresias, while his
homosexuality may even suggest the hermaphroditic sexual ambiguity
of Eliot's Tiresias figure.

Eliot's "Death by Water" seems to appear frequently in Hanley's art.
Since many of the novels have the sea for their setting, the absence of
drowning would be surprising. In *The Closed Harbour*, however, Hanley's combination of drowning with a Lazarus figure parallels Eliot's
association between Lazarus and Phlebas: Marius "was drowned and
his ship was drowned, they were like Lazarus, trying to rise, their eyes
were clogged with death" (*CH*, 7). Parallels in Hanley's novels to Eliot's "What the Thunder Said" are more convincing. Unlike Eliot, however, Hanley does not emphasize a relationship between man's belief
and the blight of the modern world. Instead, he implies that man's
indifference to man is the source of the world's ills. Sheila's description
in *An End and a Beginning* of the thundering feet of the workmen
running to their jobs recalls "hooded hordes swarming." Eliot's "blood
shaking my heart / The awful daring of a moment's surrender" (ll.
403–04) may have suggested the song sung of Peter O'Garra in *The
German Prisoner* (1950):

> Not only the men, women, and children, but even the houses and roofs
> and chimney pots, the very paving stones, joined in song. They became
> humanized. And the song they sang was that Peter O'Garra's blood was
> heavy with surrender.
> "His blood is heavy with surrender," they sang.
> As soon as the blood is heavy with surrender *Act*. O'Garra had acted.[15]

The image of the key in "We think of the key, each in his prison /
Thinking of the key, each confirms a prison" (ll. 114–15) appears also.
In *The Last Voyage* (1931), Johnny Reilly comments "the heart is a terrible prison."[16] Almost immediately after his release from prison in *An
End and a Beginning*, Peter Fury checks into a sailor's hotel and demands
a key for his door, only to learn that no doors are locked there. Later,
thinking to himself about Sheila, Peter recollects,

> She moved, I heard her move, and I didn't want her, I wanted nothing,
> and I knew the words I couldn't find, they were buried deep down in

her, anchored there, steel words, they wouldn't budge, and she had only to turn a key, the simplest key in the world, and let them come in, and speak them to me. (*E&B*, 281)

When Felix Levine thinks about Grace Helling, he concludes, "She is my new prison, and there is one warder in this prison, and she is the warder also" (*L*, 144).

Hanley borrowed some motifs, such as that of the Hanged Man in *Hollow Sea*, as structuring devices, and introduced Tiresias figures in *The Furys* to provide commentary on a Waste Land world, but for the most part the echoes and allusions contribute to description of atmosphere. The poem has not changed Hanley's outlook on the modern world, but rather has reinforced his own perception of it. The recognition Eliot's lines evoke in the reader and the power they carry with them serve to emphasize those aspects of modern life which disturbed Hanley most—economic inequality, squalid poverty, physical and spiritual ugliness, man's indifference to man—and to provide more power to Hanley's style. By profiting from Eliot's poetic description of the modern world, Hanley has added force to his own description of the modern hell.

ANTHONY POWELL

Anthony Powell echoed Eliot to enhance the period atmosphere of his novels. Powell was reluctant to identify himself with Eliot's specific statements of position and, consequently, when he echoed Eliot in his novels, he rarely identified Eliot overtly or called attention to the reference, particularly in his early novels, *Afternoon Men* (1931) and *Venusberg* (1932). In 1953, reviewing a new edition of *Afternoon Men*, Jocelyn Brooke described the novel's early reception in Bloomsbury and found Eliot's influence, not from *The Waste Land* but from *Sweeney Agonistes*.[17] Powell, recalling Brooke's review, misremembered it as a comparison between *Afternoon Men* and *The Waste Land*, indicating that the *Waste Land* connection exists at least for him.[18] The novel contains counterparts for Eliot's neurasthenic woman, typist, and Thames Maidens, and focuses on the boredom of lust which dominates Eliot's "A Game of Chess." Fotheringham, editor of a spiritualist paper, indicates the absence of religion in the modern world but dismisses it as unimportant, and he refers to "the terrible waste lands of hopeless despair."[19] Susan Atwater contrasts to the other women in the novel as the Hyacinth Girl contrasts to the godless women of Eliot's poem. "Death by Water," "Unreal City," and "the violet hour" also have parallels in the novel. Yet the influence of these echoes on the plot, characterization, and even atmosphere of Powell's party novel is not great. *Venusberg* also contains references to the poem, particularly to Eliot's "Unreal City."[20] Neil Brennan has called "the Baltic capital [of *Venusberg*] a cross between the world of Beerbohm's *Zuleika Dobson* and that of Eliot's *The Waste Land*."[21]

In *A Dance to the Music of Time* (1951–1976), a twelve-volume work spanning a quarter of a century, Powell's references to Eliot are more direct but function to add authenticity to Powell's history of the age rather than to further characterization or action. For example, in *Casanova's Chinese Restaurant* (1960), Powell's characters mention both T. S. Eliot and *The Waste Land* by name, but in each case the mention is made only to enhance an evocation of the period in which the novel is set. After Moreland comments at length on the affront that signs of intelligence in others suggest to most men, and argues that he should "restrict" himself to "intelligent girls," Barnby asks sarcastically "What do you expect to do? . . . Give readings from *The Waste Land*?" Moreland replies that this is "Not a bad idea."[22] Later he tells Matilda "I was thinking the other day one might make an anthology of the banker poets . . . Guillaume Apollinaire . . . T. S. Eliot . . . Robert W. Service . . ." (CCR, 54). These two excerpts are exceptions, however; elsewhere Powell's references to *The Waste Land* and to Eliot are far less direct.

Echoes of Eliot's poem are heard most clearly in Powell's physical descriptions, such as the desolate and wasted scene which opens *Casanova's Chinese Restaurant*. Jenkins's comments on the period and its chaos also reflect the prevailing attitude in *The Waste Land*, so that anyone disposed to collect examples of "the absence of hope," "the presence of despair," and "the lack of meaning" will have no difficulty. However, Powell's novels include more convincing evidence of Eliot's influence in their direct evocations of Tiresias. In three characters, Tiresias's self-description—"throbbing between two lives"—applies directly. Jenkins, whom Robert Towers has described as a "voyeur,"[23] suggests that Tiresias who, in Eliot's distortion of the myth, has shifted from *voyant* to *voyeur*. Mrs. Erdleigh, telling Jenkins's fortune, says that "'You live between two worlds. . . . Perhaps even more than two worlds. You cannot always surmount your feelings.' I could think of no possible reply to this indictment."[24] Jenkins recognizes the same quality in Umfraville, who is living between two ages:

> Once I had thought of those people who had known the epoch of my own childhood as "older people." Then I had found there existed people like Umfraville who seemed somehow to span the gap. They partook of both eras, specially forming the tone of the post-war years; much more

so, indeed, than the younger people. Most of them, like Umfraville, were melancholy; perhaps from the strain of living simultaneously in two historical periods.[25]

In another character, Professor Sillery, the Tiresian association at first seems unlikely in the ironical description of Sillery's "powers" in *A Question of Upbringing*: to many encountering Sillery at the university,

> the Sillery legend was based on a kind of kaleidoscope of muddled information, collected in Sillery's almost crazed brain, that his boasted powers had no basis whatever in reality: others again said that Sillery certainly knew a great number of people and passed round a lot of gossip, which in itself gave him some claim to consideration as a comparatively influential person, though only a subordinate one. Sillery had his enemies, naturally, always anxious to denigrate his life's work, and assert that he was nothing more than a figure of fun; and there was probably something to be said at least for the contention that Sillery himself somewhat exaggerated the effectiveness of his own activities.[26]

Whatever the validity of Sillery's claims to powers of knowledge, however, a later reference specifically links him to Tiresias:

> Sillery, I thought, was like Tiresias: for, although predominantly male, for example, in outward appearance, he seemed to have the seer's power of assuming female character if required. With Truscott, for instance, he would behave like an affectionate aunt; while his perennial quarrel with Brightman—to take another instance of his activities—was often conducted with a mixture of bluntness and self-control that certainly could not be thought at all like a woman's row with a man: or even with another woman; though, at the same time, it was a dispute that admittedly transcended somehow a difference of opinion between two men.[27]

Later, Jenkins notices that when Miss Weedon sits near Sillery, she begins also to assume hermaphroditic powers, and when Miss Weedon and Sillery rejoin the others, they "at once abjured a great proportion of the hermaphroditic humours assumed by each of them for the purpose of more convenient association with the other."[28]

Powell has stated that allusions and references to *The Waste Land* in *A Dance to the Music of Time* are intended to contribute solely to the period atmosphere of the novels.[29] The direct references to Eliot, supplanted in the later novels by references to later works such as James Joyce's *Ulysses*, Virginia Woolf's *Orlando*, and D. H. Lawrence's *Lady Chatterley's Lover*, tend to support this approach. However, the Tiresian characteristics of Jenkins, Umfraville, and Sillery seem to owe their existence to Powell's response to *The Waste Land*, and in their case, Eliot's influence has been to shape major characters of the novel cycle. Throughout the twelve novels, written over a 25-year period, the continued presence of themes and images attributable to *The Waste Land*'s influence suggests more than an attempt to use *Waste Land* references merely to authenticate period atmosphere.

Orwell, Hanley, and Powell reveal, in their subordination of *The Waste Land* to political, sociological, and historical purposes, a limitation which interpretation can impose on *The Waste Land*'s influence. Like Edmund Wilson, these novelists found in Eliot's poem some justification for their views of the post-war crisis, and they found Eliot's images, motifs, and figures apt for their separate descriptions of the modern dilemma. Hanley and Powell, in addition, found the unifying devices of *The Waste Land* helpful. However, their perspectives on the significance of post-war changes differed from that of *The Waste Land*, which precluded their unqualified acceptance of the poem's implied attitude towards modern life. While the influence of *The Waste Land* is noticeable in the works of these three novelists, it remains subordinate to the novelists' separate views of the between-the-wars period.

6

POWYS, GREEN,
and ISHERWOOD

Out of the Dead Land

JOHN COWPER POWYS

The novels of John Cowper Powys, Henry Green, and Christopher Isherwood suggest that *The Waste Land* presented for these writers what I. A. Richards called "a clearer, fuller realisation of their plight, the plight of a whole generation," but without the "return of the saving passion" Richards found in *The Waste Land*. They also demonstrate that, by the late 1920s and mid-1930s, the presence of *The Waste Land*, and of Eliot, may have begun to pall. Powys, despite his early familiarity with and admiration for *The Waste Land*, only referred directly to the poem in one novel, *Weymouth Sands* (1934). In his public pronouncements, Powys often criticized Eliot's poem, referring to "that emotional-sardonic rattling of the tin cans of the world's rubbish-heap that you get in T. S. Eliot's *Wasteland*,"[1] and he disapproved of the poem's influence on modern poetry.[2] In his private correspondence, however, Powys indicated his appreciation for *The Waste Land* to Eric Barker: "It's so hard for me to get what these new poets are after! But I *do* like the 'Wasteland' by reason of having read it aloud so many times & because of its many quotations from the old great poets."[3] Powys also criticizes, in other letters, the pension eventually given to Eliot, but when he disparages Eliot, he unfailingly indicates that he still likes Eliot's most often quoted poem. He refers to "that . . . Aunt Sally T. S. Eliot whose Cocktail Party about crucifying a girl near an Ant Heal struck me as pure puritanical-catholic Inquisition sadism of the worst fanatical kind

—worse than the sadism of the Marquis of Sade. . . . but for myself I still like the Wasteland."[4] In *Weymouth Sands*, Powys acknowledged the influence of the poem by drawing unmistakable images and motifs from it.

When Powys used *The Waste Land* in *Weymouth Sands*, he relied more on parallels than on allusions, but near the end of the novel Powys referred specifically to a physical Waste Land. Magnus, wandering lost, "saw around him a domination of the artificial by the natural, it was the dominance of a 'natural' that in itself seemed a fragment of a derelict and deserted world. Across this Waste-Land drifted the stricken man. . . ."[5] Unlike Eliot's Waste Land, however, which is an artificial, urban environment, Powys's Waste Land is natural terrain. Ironically Magnus, like the inhabitants of Eliot's Unreal City, only recognizes a physical Waste Land when he is removed from a spiritual one.

The characters in *Weymouth Sands*, like the figures in *The Waste Land*, are bored, despairing, and even neurotic. Most of the female characters are as frenzied in their attempts to conquer boredom as the neurasthenic woman of "A Game of Chess." A sense of world-weariness makes Perdita Wane's memories ironical when she reflects that "There's a stone in Guernsey—Men and women used to sit on it, and it brought them luck. Uncle and I sat on it once and it brought *him* luck, for he died the next month" (*WS*, 357). Peg reveals that her problem with life is its unvarying routine:

> "Clever people laugh at such things," she thought, "and simple people cry at them. But they keep on repeating themselves. Everything repeats itself. Perhaps everything that's happening now, at this minute, in all these houses has happened, exactly the same, through all eternity. Undress; go to bed; sleep; wake up; kiss and get up; dress; kiss and pretend; do the same with the same; and go to bed again!" (*WS*, 84)

This also recalls Sweeney and Doris in their discussion in *Sweeney Agonistes* of a "cannibal isle," where there is

> SWEENEY: Nothing at all but three things.
> DORIS: What things?
> SWEENEY: Birth, and copulation, and death.
>   That's all, that's all, that's all, that's all,
>   Birth, and copulation, and death.
> DORIS: I'd be bored.
> SWEENEY: You'd be bored.

Perdita is no more capable of enduring monotony than is Doris or Peg.
Powys moves from general similarities to specific allusions when two

Waste Land figures, Phlebas the Phoenician and Tiresias, play minor roles in the novel. Jobber's comments on a ship's possible fate recall Phlebas:

> "Not much hope for the old Cormorant there . . . if she once got caught. She'd spin round like a top. There's a sea-hole under there, that goes down like a shaft. Think of those dark, slippery under-sea walls! Do 'ee suppose our two skeletons would go on whirling round and round down there, when the fishes had picked 'em shell white?" (*WS*, 352)

The image of the picked bones may recall "A current under sea / Picked his bones in whispers" (ll. 315–16). Sylvanus, after taking on some of Tiresias's prophetic characteristics, enters "Hell's Museum, like a wandering Teiresias" (*WS*, 515). (Powys, however, has used a different spelling of the seer's name from Eliot's.)

Powys's most direct use of *The Waste Land*, unmistakably deliberate, is the establishment of a Madame Sosostris motif. Gipsy May tells fortunes with both a regular deck and a Tarot pack. When she tells a fortune, she names a Tarot card with Eliot's unique phrase: "'Goodness!' she cried: 'The Man with Three Staves!'" (*WS*, 136). When Marret and Gipsy May argue after Marret recognizes the Hanged Man and upsets the cards to forestall Gipsy May's potentially unfavorable reading, the two women introduce the issue of Christian faith. Eliot's Madame Sosostris episode contrasts the superstition of the moderns with the faith in resurrection that moderns reject—Madame Sosostris does not "find / The Hanged Man" (ll. 54–55). Powys explicitly combines the two issues in Marret and Gipsy May's argument:

> "Tisn't fitting nor right," Marret countered, without a tremor in her voice, "to play with they Devil-Cards about he. They cards can tell of Hangings and Buryings for them as hasn't talked and walked with God, but when—" (*WS*, 141)

Later, after Gipsy May maliciously shaves off Sylvanus's moustache while Sylvanus sleeps, she blames The Man with Three Staves for her action (*WS*, 417). Another character, Cattistock, resembles the Hanged Man:

> What he really looked like—with his white face balanced above his new light-coloured over-coat, a garment that somehow suggested stables and the race-course—was the Hanged Man of Gipsy May's Tarot cards. His body had the rigidity of a corpse just then, owing to the intensity of his thought, and his features for the same reason had lost all intelligent and even intelligible expression. (*WS*, 445)

Near the end of the novel, the fortune-telling motif appears again, although the card has inexplicably changed: "'These lawyers are no good,' she [Gipsy May] announced confidentially and even gaily. 'Me cards were right! The Man with Two Staves was right!'" (WS, 574). As Madame Sosostris's warning "Fear death by water" was valid in the context of The Waste Land, so Gipsy May's predictions with the Tarot are essentially accurate. Powys's borrowing of the fortune-telling motif advances the novel's plot, while other allusions to The Waste Land enhance character delineation. Powys's allusions indicate that The Waste Land has had some influence on Powys's novel, and that Powys felt his fiction could derive some advantage from a judicious adaptation of Waste Land imagery.

HENRY GREEN

Unlike Powys, Henry Green usually reveals the influence of The Waste Land in his diction rather than in episodes or descriptions in his novels. Giorgio Melchiori has commented that "From the choice of words, colours and images it is obvious that the younger writer, during his formative years in the late 'twenties must have deeply felt the pervasive influence of the Eliot of The Waste Land; . . ."[6] Green injected imagery and diction from the early sections of The Waste Land into his prose, presenting the characteristic problems of modernity without posing a solution. John Russell, essentially agreeing with Melchiori, calls Green's attitude "nihilistic."[7] Green's novels depict moderns' disillusionment, superstition, and frantic efforts to relieve boredom through sexuality. The novels include counterparts for Eliot's Unreal City, Madame Sosostris, "violet hour," crowd, and burial of the dead, yet none of these parallels involves a direct verbal echo. However, Eliot's influence on Green is more direct in the parallels to "A Game of Chess" and "The Fire Sermon."

   Green has alluded to Eliot more subtly than most, preferring to leave thematic parallels to Eliot's poem unspecified. However, Melchiori has pointed out that the opening of "The Fire Sermon," describing the Thames, has provided a river scene in Living (1929):

> Here Eliot's river images fuse with the mechanical sound of the typist's gramophone, the music creeping upon the water, Elizabeth's pleasure barge and the narrow canoe on the Thames, which are all in this section of The Waste Land, to form Green's picture, a picture like Eliot's of lassitude and emptiness. And we should remember that the spectator of the scene, in Living, is one of Eliot's "loitering heirs of city directors."[8]

The futility of the moderns who try to resolve their problems through sexuality, represented by the indifferent response of the typist and the Thames Maidens to "passion" and by the boredom of the neurasthenic woman, frequently appears in Green's novels. Writing of *Loving* (1945), Russell notes that in "the contrasted splendor and decay of the scenes that celebrate Edie, in her hedonism and Raunce's unlovely desperation (that even makes him sick), there seem to be overtones of sterility that call to mind, say, Eliot's 'A Game of Chess.' . . ."[9] Although Green often celebrates loving relationships in his novels, he also satirizes modern sexual license in a manner recalling Eliot's disapproving moral tone.

Green borrowed more directly from two major sections of "A Game of Chess"—the "Cleopatra's barge" opening and the conversation between Lil and her friend in the pub. Melchiori, detailing the nature of Green's borrowing, pointed out parallels in diction between Eliot's opening lines and a passage from *Concluding* (1948):

> The Chair she sat in, like a burnished throne
> Glowed on the *marble,* where the glass
> *Held up* by standards wrought with fruited vines
> From which a *golden Cupidon* peeped out
> (Another hid his *eyes* behind his wing)
> Doubled the flames of sevenbranched candelabra
> *Reflecting light* upon the table as
> The glitter of her *jewels* rose to meet it,
> From satin cases *poured* in rich profusion;
> In vials of ivory and *coloured* glass
> Unstoppered, lurked her strange synthetic perfumes,
> Unguent, powdered, or liquid—troubled, confused
> And drowned the sense in odours; . . .
> . . . .
> Huge sea-wood fed with copper
> Burned *green* and orange, framed by the *coloured* stone,
> In which sad *light* a carvèd dolphin swam.
> Above the antique mantel was displayed
> As though a window gave upon the sylvan *scene*
> The change of Philomel, by the barbarous king
> So rudely forced; yet there the nightingale
> Filled all the desert with inviolable voice
> And still she cried, and still the world *pursues,*
> "Jug jug" to dirty ears.
> And other withered stumps of time
> Were told upon the *walls*; staring forms
> Leaned out, leaning, hushing the room *enclosed.*[10]

Melchiori quotes a parallel passage from *Concluding*, in which Green has assimilated Eliot's diction:

> Panelling around the *walls* was enamelled in white paint, as also the bedsteads with pink covers, the parquet floor was waxed and *gold*, *two* naked *Cupids* in cold white *marble*, and life size, *held up* a slab of *green* above a basket grate, while white and brown arms were stretched into the tide of a late afternoon *pouring by*; a redhead caught fire with sun like a flare and, out of the sun, *eyes*, opening to *reflected light*, like *jewels enclosed* by flesh *coloured* anemones beneath *green*, clear water when these yawn after shrimps, disclosed great innocence in a *scene* on which no innocence had ever shone, where life and *pursuit* were fierce, as these girls came back to consciousness from the truce of a summer after luncheon before the business of the dance.[11]

In addition to these parallels, Green's "redhead" who "caught fire with the sun like a flare" surely owes something to Eliot's lines almost immediately following those quoted by Melchiori:

> Under the firelight, under the brush, her hair
> Spread out in fiery points
> Glowed into words, then would be savagely still. (ll. 108–10)

Not only has Green appropriated several words and phrases from Eliot's poem, but he has adapted the context to minimize the difference between the woman preparing her toilette for an adulterous affair and the girls preparing for the school dance.

Similarly, Green has borrowed from Eliot's pub scene, which mentions the cause of Lil's physical deterioration: "(She's had five already, and nearly died of young George)" (l. 160). In *Caught* (1943), a similar character receives parallel description: "She 'ad a terrible time 'aving it, really, but as I said to 'er in the 'ospital, I says, . . . and she said to me, 'Not a word against Ted, mum,' . . ."[12] Green has drawn from the sections of *The Waste Land* which reflect the failure of human relationships to satisfy emotional needs without suggesting a solution. Green's borrowing has been of two types, directly from imagery and less directly from diction. The images directly identifiable as Eliot's are relatively few, and the use of the diction of *The Waste Land* is not only elusive at times, but may even be unconscious. Green's borrowing, however, has enriched his style.

CHRISTOPHER ISHERWOOD

Christopher Isherwood, like Powys and Green, also exploits selected lines and images of *The Waste Land* in his novels. Known primarily as W. H. Auden's collaborator in verse drama and as the author of *Goodbye to Berlin*, from which *Cabaret* was made, Isherwood wrote nine novels between 1928 and 1967. Including Isherwood in the "Auden Generation," Samuel Hynes attributes Isherwood's early appreciation of Eliot directly to I. A. Richards, who taught at Cambridge during Isherwood's undergraduate years. "Richards was the first English critic to develop a theory of modern poetry in terms of which *The Waste Land* was an important poem. His *Science and Poetry* (1926) takes what one might call a Waste Land view of the modern situation."[13] Describing his attitudes as of winter, 1926/27, Isherwood specifically referred to Eliot as "the master" and mentioned "Eliot's Dante-quotations and classical learning."[14] In his own novels, Isherwood drew often from *The Waste Land* to present his version of the modern world. In his foreword to *All the Conspirators* (1928), twenty-nine years after the novel first appeared, Isherwood addressed the roles of echoes in a novel, commenting that he can "excuse" his echoes of E. M. Forster and Virginia Woolf because "the author has actually learned a few lessons from these masters and put them into practice here. But the echoes of James Joyce annoy me, because they are merely echoes."[15] When he drew from Eliot's *The Waste Land*, however, Isherwood selected images which would advance the purpose of his novels rather than merely echo Eliot's poem.

Of *The Memorial* (1932), Alan Wilde has written that

> In the description of the crowd at one of Mary's concerts, for example, the abrupt transitions, the fragmented sentences, and the relative absence of ligatures provide the counterpart to the aimless fragments of unrelated chatter (obviously modeled on *The Waste Land*) and to the characters themselves, who are assembled for a discrete occasion and ready to disperse as soon as it is over.[16]

The novel has several specific passages reminiscent of *The Waste Land*, including an identification of an urban and artificial desert:

> At the top of the Ridge it was always cool; though Cheshire lay trembling in haze. Eric got off his bicycle for a few moments, liking to stand there, feeling on one hand the lonely country of cart-roads, broken

sign-posts, stone farms and walls, on the other the solemn wilderness
of tram-lines and brick and the tall mills scribbling the sky with their
smoke.[17]

More significantly, however, *The Waste Land*'s fifth section, "What the
Thunder Said," appears prominently in the novel. Edward seems based
on Eliot's Fisher King, as Wilde has pointed out:

> Indeed, his separateness gives him an almost mythic status in the novel:
> the Fisher King of Isherwood's 1930's Waste Land. Most self-conscious
> and self-aware of all the characters, constantly mobile and active, ulti-
> mately isolated from all the others, he epitomizes in his own life the
> sterility and aridity of all the lives in the book. In his search for some-
> thing that will excite him and make his life meaningful, in his efforts to
> allay his boredom and restlessness, there is a paradigmatic quality—the
> attempt of the self to break out of its limitations and find a resting place
> in an unsatisfactory world.[18]

A reader who attempts to find a solution for Edward's plight by turning to Isherwood's authorial voice will meet disappointment:

> As for Isherwood himself, although he implies a need for change, he
> offers little hope; the thunder speaks, as it does in Eliot's poem, but
> there are no healing rains—no way that the characters can find to give,
> sympathize, and control.[19]

Isherwood makes this explicit in Lily's thoughts when the Bishop prays
over Richard's tomb:

> She saw the tall monument, the work of a good Manchester firm, taste-
> fully executed and paid for by the large, easily afforded subscriptions of
> grateful business men. But Richard isn't here, she thought—she knew,
> with horror: Richard isn't anywhere. He's gone. He's dead. (*Memorial*,
> 103)

Eric expresses the "religion" of modern man in an outburst to Lily,
arguing against others' belief: "I don't just tolerate Religion; I loathe it.
All Religion is vile. And religious people are all either hypocrites or
idiots" (*Memorial*, 207). Eric, however, later converts to Catholicism and
then, according to his letter to Edward, finds "the most extraordinary
feeling of peace" (*Memorial*, 291). Yet Eric's feeling of peace is narrowly personal—almost every character suffers spiritual torments without finding any ease.

   The World in the Evening (1954) also suggests several images from *The*

Waste Land. The narrator is acutely aware of the sterility of the modern world.

> I came to a halt at the edge of the pool. It was brilliantly clean; not one leaf floating on its surface, not one speck of dirt on its tiled floor. God curse this antiseptic, heartless, hateful, neon mirage of a city! May its swimming pools be dried up. May all its lights go out for ever. I drew a deep dizzying breath in which the perfume of star jasmine was mixed with chlorine.[20]

The characters in the novel suffer the boredom which afflicts Eliot's figures. Monk regards himself as somewhat jaded, and he refers directly to Eliot when he describes this feeling: "The poets—except for T. S. Eliot—had lied; they pretended life was exciting. I now knew that it wasn't. The only valid emotion was boredom (or ennui, as I preferred to call it)" (*World,* 68–69).

In *Down There on a Visit* ((1962), Isherwood continues to suggest isolated images from *The Waste Land.* At one point Isherwood describes a desert waste: "The first plunge had got us over the ditch. Now we were rocking across a red, bumpy wasteland, baked into cracks by the sun. In the middle distance a column of dust moved hither and thither, like a stooping ghost."[21] A counterpart for Mr. Eugenides, who asked the narrator of *The Waste Land* "in demotic French / To luncheon at the Cannon Street Hotel / Followed by a weekend at the Metropole" (ll. 212–14), appears in the novel. The homosexual Machado "spoke to me from time to time in French, which I had great difficulty in understanding because of his fearful accent" (*Down,* 47). Alan Wilde finds the relationship between the narrator Christopher and Lancaster indicative of influence from *The Waste Land:*

> The major clue to Christopher's personality appears, however, not in the recurrent allusions to epic myth and epic drama but in the more discreetly symbolic reference (embodied in the name of the ship on which he makes his trip to visit Mr. Lancaster) to Coriolanus. That Isherwood had in mind those lines in *The Waste Land,* in which the second voice of the thunder offers its commandment to sympathize, is clear in terms both of the general significance of the story and of the more specific echo—in Christopher's comment about his cousin: "I just did not have the key to him it seemed"—of the central phrase in Eliot's passage. "Mr. Lancaster" is, in fact, predominantly concerned with Christopher's failure of sympathy, the result less of his ignorance and age than of his egoism, his entrapment, to borrow another of Eliot's images, within the prison of himself.[22]

The inability, and even refusal, of characters to find comfort in religious faith appears in *Down There on a Visit* when the narrator says of "E.M.,"

> He lives by love, not by will.
>   That last statement smells unpleasantly of the Christian religion. But E. M., of course, has no religion. If he did, he wouldn't be E. M. I must admit, he doesn't seem to loathe it as I do; in fact, when he talks about it, he's very moderate and open-minded. But, all the same, he's one more living proof that nobody who is really great can have any truck with that filth. (*Down*, 175–76)

Later, Christopher recalls a conversation in which "Dorothy had asked me if I saw any other meaning in life than the one you get through belief in communism. When I told her, No, she hadn't understood what I meant—that I saw no meaning in life at all" (*Down*, 232–33). Yet *Down There on a Visit* does have a "particular ethical system," according to Wilde, which

> finds its most cogent expression in Eliot's famous formulation: "So far as we are human, what we do must be either evil or good; so far as we do evil or good, we are human; and it is better, in a paradoxical way, to do evil than to do nothing: at least we exist."[23]

In the novel, although the characters reject religious faith, they do demonstrate their awareness of their power to do evil or good in relation to each other. Isherwood recognized what I. A. Richards called *The Waste Land*'s statement of the "plight of a whole generation," and he appropriated those images which were compatible with his interpretations of the problems of the age.

Powys, Green, and Isherwood demonstrate a significant change of emphasis and direction in novelists' indebtedness to Eliot's *The Waste Land*. After so many poets and novelists had felt the pervasive impact of Eliot's poem and had reflected that influence in their writing, identification with *The Waste Land* developed considerably less appeal for many writers. That influence, however, was none the less real. Powys, whose private correspondence showed a constant regard for *The Waste Land* over a considerable period, chose to restrict his applications of Eliot's imagery and themes to one novel, *Weymouth Sands*, yet borrowings from *The Waste Land*—Powys's fortune-telling motif and two Tiresian figures—advanced the plot and shaped some characters of the novel. Green, whose consciousness of Eliot's poem was sufficient to affect his diction and to contribute some specific scenes to a few novels, chose to retain these effects without calling attention to Eliot by direct reference. Isherwood, whose undergraduate years at Cambridge coincided with I. A. Richards's close attention to Eliot's poetry, focused on those lines of "What the Thunder Said" which supported his view of characters' need to sympathize with others, and their frequent failure to do so. These novelists' selection of specific *Waste Land* themes, to the exclusion of others, introduced a new sophistication which would reach its culmination in the novels of Anthony Burgess.

7

CHARLES WILLIAMS
and C. S. LEWIS

Unreal City

Even before Cleanth Brooks offered a positive, Christian interpretation of *The Waste land* in 1939, Charles Williams and C. S. Lewis borrowed from Eliot's poem to present the modern Waste Land in a theological perspective. While much of their reaction to the poem results from Eliot's conversion to the Anglican Church in 1927 and his public statements on faith in the modern world, Williams anticipated Brooks's interpretation of *The Waste Land* by almost a decade. In his 1948 preface to Williams's *All Hallows' Eve*, Eliot noted that "It was in the late 'twenties, I think, that I first met Charles Williams," and Eliot referred to their "acquaintanceship of some twenty years, which I am proud to think became a friendship."[1] Williams and Eliot corresponded about their work, and each influenced the other. Discussing Williams's use of "The Negative Way of approach to God" in his novels, Elizabeth Wright identifies three seekers of the Way who, "speaking from three different centuries of Christian history, lent the implication of their thought to Williams' understanding of the Negative Way": Juan de Yepes (St. John of the Cross), Søren Kierkegaard, and T. S. Eliot, citing the *Four Quartets* and *Ash Wednesday* as specific sources.[2] Charles Williams's novels abound in imagery from *The Waste Land*, apply myth in the manner of Eliot, and reveal Williams's willingness to borrow from Eliot's work. The most readily apparent connections between Eliot's poem and Williams's novels appear in the uses of the Grail myth in *War in Heaven* (1930), the Tarot in *The Greater Trumps* (1932), and the Unreal City in *All Hallows' Eve* (1945).

In *War in Heaven,* Williams structures his plot on the myth of the Grail, as Mary McDermott Shideler outlines it.[3] Summarizing the similarity of the Grail myths in the works of Lewis, Eliot, and Williams, Charles Moorman presents

> four major points concerning the relationship between the writers with whom I am to deal and the Arthurian myth: (1) that each of them looks at the Arthurian material as a whole structure rather than as a series of parts, as myth rather than as legend, (2) that each abstracts from that whole a single and generally agreed upon theme, (3) that this theme centers on the episode of the Grail quest, and (4) that these writers are committed by the literary tradition of the Grail (as well as by their own inclinations) to treat it as a purely Christian symbol. Each of the writers thus interprets the whole Arthurian myth as the exposition of a single religious theme—the failure of secularism in society.[4]

Whereas Eliot's use of the Grail in *The Waste Land* emphasizes the blight on the land and the quest for meaning, Williams's use emphasizes the power of the object which men desire for material ends. Describing the Grail in its literary context, Williams writes that

> The living light had shone for so long in his mind upon the idea of the Graal that it was by now a familiar thing—Tennyson and Hawker and Malory and older writers still had made it familiar, and its familiarity created for it a kind of potentiality. To deny it would be to deny his own past.[5]

Describing the literary tradition from which knowledge of the Grail has come to him, Kenneth lists the tradition of Eliot as well as that of Williams: "Malory—Tennyson—Chrétien de Troyes—Miss Jessie Weston" (*WIH*, 121). When Prester John describes himself, he merges his own identity with that of other mythical figures in a manner similar to Eliot's mixture of Phlebas, the one-eyed merchant, and Mr. Eugenides. If Tiresias is the eternal witness, and if "What Tiresias *sees*, in fact, is the substance of the poem," Prester John serves the same function in relation to the Grail myth:

> "I am a messenger only," the voice, if voice it were, uttered, "but I am the precursor of the things that are to be. I am John and I am Galahad and I am Mary; I am the Bearer of the Holy One, the Graal, and the keeper of the Graal. I have kept it always, whether I dwelt in the remote places of the world and kings rode after me or whether I removed to the farther parts of man's mind. All magic and all holiness is through me, and though men stole the Graal from me ages since I have been with it

for ever. Brother and friend, the night of His coming is at hand." (*WIH*, 204)

The resemblance between Prester John as a unifier of the Grail's history and Tiresias as the unifying force of the earlier *The Waste Land* suggests more than coincidence.

Another affinity which many have cited between Williams and Eliot, and which is more clearly a case of direct influence, is the use of the Tarot. David W. Evans invites attention to Eliot's use of the Tarot in *The Waste Land* "ten years, incidentally, before Williams wrote *The Greater Trumps*)"[6] and notes that Williams's use of the Tower resembles Eliot's: the tower is

> never quite being destroyed but continually resurrecting or reforming itself. Such is the way the falling towers of Jerusalem, Athens, Alexandria, Vienna, and London are presented in *The Waste Land*:
>> What is the city over the mountains
>> Cracks and reforms and bursts in the violet air
>> Falling towers . . .
>
> Portraits on the earliest Tarots occupied the whole card, but one later version makes use of the double-headed design familiar on modern cards. On the lower half of the sixteenth trump in this pack, the Tower appears in an inverted position like Eliot's towers "upside down in air . . . / Tolling reminiscent bells."[7]

In his use of the Tarot, Williams includes the cards Madame Sosostris has mentioned. Madame Sosostris describes "something" the one-eyed merchant "carries on his back, / Which I am forbidden to see" (ll. 53–54). Williams's Fool "had over one shoulder a staff, carved into serpentine curves, that carried a round bag, not unlike the balls with which the Juggler played. The bag rested against his shoulder, so that as he stood there he supported as well as bore it."[8] Eliot's Hanged Man is associated with Christ and with the Fisher King. Nancy at one point in the novel confuses them:

> The car slowed, wheeled as if sweeping round a curve in the road, and suddenly—despite herself—she screamed. For there, with light full on it, thrown up in all its terrible detail, gaunt, bare, and cold, was a man, or the image of a man, hanging by his hands, his body thrust out from the pole that held it, his head dropping to one side, and on it a dreadful tangled head-dress. It hung there right before her, and she only knew that it was the wrong way up—the head should have been below; it was always so in the cards, the Hanged Man upside down. But here the Hanged Man was, livid and outstretched before her, his head decked

but above. She screamed and woke. At least, everyone supposed she woke. Henry was solicitous and her father was irritable, and, after all, it was only a village war memorial with a rather badly done crucifix. (*GT*, 63)

The use of the "Unreal City" motif in *All Hallows' Eve* reveals more direct evidence of Eliot's influence than either the Grail or the Tarot. In an article entitled "The Image of the City in English Verse," Williams stated that he mentioned Eliot's *The Family Reunion* because "it carries within it the poetic hints of the civic union of the living and the dead."[9] Gunnar Urang identifies *All Hallows' Eve* as "the realm of the dead from the very beginning."[10] For Williams, as T. S. Eliot wrote in his preface to *All Hallows' Eve*, "There was no frontier between the material and the spiritual world."[11] Elizabeth Wright comments that "this purgatorial realm of the newly dead is itself London within the temporal London,"[12] so that Williams's *All Hallows' Eve*, like Eliot's *The Waste Land*, equates London with hell. To correspond to Eliot's "I had not thought death had undone so many," Williams often uses a crowd motif. In *Shadows of Ecstasy* (1931),

> terrible as the fear was, fear was not present alone; desire and loathing and the cruel darkness of abandoned souls walked in the midst of the crowds and took their pleasure as they could. Abominable things were done, which none saw or seeing stopped to prevent. Shrieks went up in hidden corners, and laughter and sudden silences answered them, silences hardly discernible in the general roar and themselves filled with the never-ceasing sounds of the guns.[13]

In *All Hallows' Eve*, however, the crowd scenes are more suggestive of the dead walking in the Unreal City. Lester Furnival, newly dead but not yet aware of it, surveys the city: "The bridge was as empty as the river; no vehicles or pedestrians here, no craft there. In all that City she might have been the only living thing" (*AHE*, 2). Lester, after she discovers her true state, wonders,

> what then could be done now? If neither Evelyn nor she herself had ever of old done anything, what could or should they do now—with nothing and no one about them? with only the shell of a City, and they themselves but shell and perhaps not even true shell? only a faint memory and a pang worse than memory? It was too much to bear. (*AHE*, 19)

As narrator, Williams comments that "The common likeness of the dead was greater than any difference between their living faces; they were both citizens of a remoter town than this London, and the other town was in this room" (*AHE*, 43). A description of London combines the litter which blights *The Waste Land*'s Thames, the bleakness of the modern world, and the anticipation of rain:

> The Thames was dirty and messy. Twigs, bits of paper and wood, cords, old boxes drifted on it. Yet to the new-eyed Lester it was not a depressing sight. The dirtiness of the water was, at that particular point, what it should be and therefore pleasant enough. The evacuations of the City had their place in the City; how else could the City be the City? Corruption (so to call it) was tolerable, even adequate and proper, even glorious. These things also were facts. They could not be forgotten or lost in fantasy; all that had been, was; all that was, was. A sodden mass of cardboard and paper drifted by, but the soddenness was itself a joy, for this was what happened, and all that happened, in this great material world, was good. The very heaviness of the heavy sky was a wonder, and the unutilitarian expectation of rain a delight. (*AHE*, 222)

Despite Lester's heightened awareness which allows her to accept the sordid aspects of reality without repudiating them, the physical description is of Eliot's London.

In one description of Lester's "Unreal City," Williams echoes Eliot's "Jerusalem Athens Alexandria / Vienna London / Unreal" (ll. 375–77). Lester reflects that

> There was no huge metropolis in which she would have been lost, and no single village which would itself have been lost in all that contemporaneous mass. In this City lay all—London and New York, Athens and Chicago, Paris and Rome and Jerusalem; it was that to which they led in the lives of their citizens. When her time came, she would know what lay behind the high empty facades of her early experience of death. (*AHE*, 189)

While Williams's use of the Grail and the Tarot do not in themselves demonstrate Eliot's direct influence, the verbal echoes which Williams includes in his novels are another matter. Combined with the elements of *The Waste Land* in *War in Heaven*, *The Greater Trumps*, and *All Hallows' Eve* is a Waste Land atmosphere which is present in all Williams's novels. While the major thrust of Williams's novels is not to suggest the emptiness of modern life, Williams uses that suggestion as a backdrop for the experiences with the occult and the mystical which form the struggles of his major characters.

Several descriptions in Williams's novels suggest the physical Waste

Land of Eliot's poem. In *War in Heaven,* in a description of Lord Mayor Street,

> There was a sufficient number of sufficiently dirty children playing in the road to destroy privacy without achieving publicity: squalor was leering from the windows and not yet contending frankly and vainly with grossness. It was one of those sudden terraces of slime which hang over the pit of hell, and for which beastliness is too dignified a term. . . . (*WIH*, 65–66)

The combination of present squalor and past glory is a hallmark of Eliot's poem, echoed in Williams's comparison of Roland with "the grocer's at the corner." In *The Place of the Lion* (1931), the description of the sere garden after Berringer's house has burned is of a Waste Land in miniature:

> The garden was changed. The flowers were withered, the grass was dry and brown; in places the earth showed, hard and cracked. The place looked as if a hot sun had blazed on it for weeks without intermission. Everything living was dead within its borders, and (they noticed) for a little way beyond its borders. The hedges were leafless and brittle; the very air seemed hotter than even the June day could justify.[14]

Also indicative of Williams's attention to *The Waste Land,* and more significant to Williams's purposes, is the spiritual vacuum in which modern man lives. Those of his moderns who think about spiritual values at all indicate that they cannot discover a meaning for their existence. *Shadows of Ecstasy* echoes Eliot's "We had the experience but missed the meaning":[15] "The Renascence knew the splendour but lost the meaning, and it was tempted by learning and scholarship, and ravaged by Calvin and Ignatius with their systems, and it withered into the eighteenth century" (*SE,* 73). In a possible reference to Eliot's "The Hippopotamus," *War in Heaven* indicates a modern attitude towards scripture:

> "Well, sir, I always understood that where Job scored over the three friends was in feeling a natural curiosity why all those unfortunate things happened to him. They simply put up with it, but he, so to speak, asked God what He thought He was doing. . . . As a mere argument there's something lacking perhaps, in saying to a man sitting on the dustbin, all over boils, 'Look at the hippopotamus.'" (*WIH*, 23–24)

Whenever modern man concerns himself with the Deity, he does so solely for secular ends. "At lunch Mornington had Mr. Batesby's scheme of Reunion explained at length by its originator. It was highly complicated and, so far as Kenneth could understand, involved everyone believing that God was opposed to Communism and in favour of election as the only sound method of government" (*WIH*, 99). Lionel claims "it is the ordinary religion disguised; it is the church-going clerk's religion. Satanism is the clerk at the brothel. Audacious little middle-class cock-sparrow!" (*WIH*, 168). The police inspector's views of the struggle between good and evil are also secular:

> The inspector's view of the devil was roughly that the devil was something in which children believed, but which was generally known not to exist, certainly not as taking any active part in the affairs of the world; these, generally speaking, were run by three parties—the police, criminals, and the ordinary public. (*WIH*, 221)

Damaris, having difficulties with her dissertation in *The Place of the Lion*, has no affinity for the beliefs of her subject, Abelard, and lacks a proper sense of proportion: "Perhaps the whole thing had better be in an appendix—*On the Knowledge of the World* . . . no, on *God's Idea of the World from Plato to Aquinas*. Something was wrong with that title, she thought vaguely, but she could alter it presently" (*PL*, 109).

Many Dimensions (1931) echoes Eliot's note that "Shantih" in the poem translates as "The Peace which passeth understanding,"[16] and in *The Place of the Lion* dry, sterile thunder appears at significant moments. Before the Archetypes appear comes "that crash of thunder, every now and then echoing all through the black sky. No lightning, no rain, only—at long intervals, just whenever she was going off to sleep at last —thunder, and again thunder" (*PL*, 16). Mr. Foster immediately connects this Eliotian thunder with its significance, but Anthony does not perceive it until later. When Anthony realizes the thunder's meaning, he recognizes that "the thunder—which was not thunder, he knew, but the utterance of the guardian of the angelical world—he certainly could not hear" (*PL*, 132). In the novel, Eliot and his thunder are both present. Anthony's cleaning woman

> had been broken of her original habit of putting everything straight, of thrusting papers away in drawers and pushing books back onto shelves —any book on any shelf, so that Spinoza and Mr. T. S. Eliot might jostle, which would have been quite suitable. . . . (*PL*, 206)

While Eliot has "upside down in air were towers / Tolling reminiscent bells, that kept the hours" (ll. 383–84), Williams has included among similar images "the Tower that fell continually" (*GT*, 178). Eliot's "bats with baby faces in the violet light" (l. 380) may have inspired Williams's "Why was he here among this crowd of bats with negro faces?" (*SE*, 187).

Throughout the novels Williams has developed imagery very close to Eliot's. In the context of Williams's entire achievement, Eliot's influence is readily apparent in Williams's descriptions of physical, cultural, and spiritual bleakness, in many attributes of his characters, and in some of the phrasing which Williams uses. In those novels where *The Waste Land*'s influence is marked (*War in Heaven, The Greater Trumps, All Hallows' Eve*), Williams develops a dominant motif of the poem to advance the novel's plot. (One novel not discussed in this chapter is Williams's *Descent into Hell* (1937), in whose protagonist, Peter Stanhope, some have detected a caricature of Eliot, no doubt based on that character's having written verse dramas. However, the character's physical description and critical pronouncements do not resemble Eliot's, nor do his actions. Except for one reference to his having imposed verse drama on the London theatre, Stanhope has virtually nothing in common with Eliot. Perhaps only enemies of Eliot can render recognizable, if distorted, representations of the poet.)

Unlike Williams, C. S. Lewis disagreed with Eliot on personal and philosophical grounds. Lewis and Eliot agreed that the modern age requires spiritual rebirth and that the problems of the modern world result from man's lack of faith, yet Lewis dismissed Eliot's brand of spirituality. He opposed Eliot's artistic and critical judgments, and he would be unlikely to concede the extent to which his novels resembled *The Waste Land*. Lewis often referred to Eliot, but hardly in a flattering context. Writing to Bede Griffiths in an undated letter (probably 1931 or 1932), Lewis commented that

> What I did think—and still do think—was that an influential school of thought both in your church and mine—were very antagonistic to idealism, and in fact were availing themselves of the general secular reaction against 19th century thought, to run something which they call Neo-Scholasticism as the cure for all our evils. The people I mean are led by Maritain on your side and by T. S. Eliot on ours. Perhaps I over-rate their importance. I hope I do, for I confess there is no section of religious opinion with which I feel less sympathy.[17]

Lewis objected to Eliot's "high-brow" approach to religious questions, and found Eliot's attitude dangerous. Of his *The Pilgrim's Regress* (1933), after admitting to Canon Claude Chavasse that

his book was over-bitter and uncharitable, Lewis said, "What I am at-
tacking in Neo-Angular is a set of people who seem to me . . . to be
trying to make of Christianity itself one more high-brow, Chelsea, bour-
geois-baiting fad" and "T. S. Eliot is the single man who sums up the
thing I am fighting against."[18]

Preferring a more direct approach to faith, Lewis rejected Eliot's over-
intellectualized approach to religious doubt.

In *The Pilgrim's Regress*, Lewis parodies Eliot:

In the *Regress* John meets three pale men from the North (which throughout the book represents the way of reason and system). They are Mr.
Humanist, Mr. Neo-Angular, and Mr. Neo-Classical (thin disguises for
aspects of Irving Babbitt, Eliot, and perhaps T. E. Hulme). They were
brought up by Sigismund (Freud), attended the university at Eschropolis
(the cynical twenties), and though they have serious differences, they
are united in their undying hatred of romantic nonsense.[19]

Lewis preferred the theology of Charles Williams to that of Eliot because Williams did not neglect the positive, natural, and romantic aspects of faith.

Lewis believed with Williams that man must endure the protests of
Nature against Grace. He must not, indeed he cannot, suppress Nature
(including the body and the pleasures of the senses) on the grounds that
these things are evil. Williams spoke of two Ways: the Affirmation of
Images (Romanticism) and the Rejection of Images (Asceticism). . . .
Lewis would chide Eliot and other Counter-Romantics for being unnec-
essarily ascetic.[20]

The issues of Neo-Scholasticism and Eliot's high-brow approach to religion appear throughout Lewis's letters. Writing to Sr. Magdelena on 7
June 1934, Lewis comments that "Of scholastic philosophy and theology you probably know much more than I do. If by any chance you
don't, stick to Gilson as a guide and beware of the people (Maritain in
your church, and T. S. Eliot in mine) who are at present running what
they call 'neo-scholasticism' as a fad."[21] When the subject of Eliot arises
in his correspondence, Lewis is consistent in his diction—the comparison with Maritain and the label "fad" appeared in Lewis's earlier letter
to Griffiths.

Lewis also took exception to Eliot as poet and critic. Writing to
Charles Williams on 20 July 1940, Lewis describes Revolution Thompson's *Preludes*, an autobiography in verse, and compares Thompson
favorably with such poets as Eliot.

In fact, as I shall say to him in acknowledging it, "poetry" with the Eliots and Audens has become such a loss that the real thing now mainly survives in verse not intended to be fully serious—e.g. there is more real poetry in *Punch* than in the high brow periodicals.[22]

Lewis advised Theodora Bosanquet not to submit Charles Williams's *All Hallows' Eve* to Eliot: "Not Eliot at any price. He couldn't understand one word of C. W.'s book."[23] Praising E. R. Eddison's novel *Oroboros* in a bantering Middle English style, Lewis wrote that

> yf (wh. heven forbidde) I were its ownlie reder, yet the ioye you hadde in the inventioun and indyting of the said book and I in the reading in it sholde of themselves aloone utterlie outweigh and ouergo all the clam jamfrey and whymperinges of the rakehellie auctours in these latter daies, as the Eliots, Poundes, Lawrences, Audens, and the like.[24]

In his allusions and references to Eliot, Lewis specifies that he disapproves of Eliot's "Neo-Scholastic," high-brow approach to theology; that he distrusts Eliot's perceptions as a critic of literature; and that he rejects what he considers "negative" and despairing tones in Eliot's poetry.

His disapproval of Eliot's attitudes suggests that resemblances between *The Waste Land* and Lewis's novels may result from common sources, such as Jessie Weston's *From Ritual to Romance*, rather than from direct borrowing on Lewis's part. In his space trilogy—*Out of the Silent Planet* (1938), *Perelandra* (1943), and *That Hideous Strength* (1945)— Lewis applied several images, motifs, and themes which appear in Eliot's *The Waste Land*, but these, particularly Lewis's Fisher King, differ significantly from Eliot's. Occasionally, Lewis's descriptive passages are close enough to Eliot's to suggest some influence.

The Waste Land early indicates modern man's rejection of the Son of Man, who "cannot say, or guess, for you know only / A heap of broken images" (ll. 21–22). When the King and Queen of Perelandra ascend after successfully resisting the temptation of their Eden, Ransom prostrates himself before them and echoes Eliot's poem:

> When at last he raised his eyes from the four blessed feet, he found himself involuntarily speaking though his voice was broken, and his eyes dimmed. "Do not move away, do not raise me up," he said. "I have never before seen a man or a woman. I have lived my life among shadows and broken images.[25]

Eliot's "The Fire Sermon" includes the lines

> The river bears no empty bottles, sandwich papers,
> Silk handkerchiefs, cardboard boxes, cigarette ends
> Or other testimony of summer nights. (ll. 177–79)

The description of the litter in the Thames, now that "the nymphs are departed," appears in a slightly altered form in Lewis's *That Hideous Strength* when Lewis describes the river at Edgestow after the establishment of N.I.C.E.

> The grip of the N.I.C.E. on Edgestow was tightening. The river itself which had once been brownish green and amber and smooth-skinned silver, tugging at the reeds and playing with the red roots, now flowed opaque, thick with mud, sailed on by endless fleets of empty tins, sheets of paper, cigarette ends and fragments of wood, sometimes varied by rainbow patches of oil.[26]

Two passages in particular suggest Eliot's "Dead mountain mouth of carious teeth that cannot spit" (l. 339). In *Out of the Silent Planet*, Ransom and Augray encounter the carious teeth of the mountain: "like the jagged teeth of a giant—a giant with very bad teeth—the topmost peaks of the mountain wall down which they must pass loomed up over the edge of their gully."[27] In *Perelandra*, Ransom and the Lady "were faced with a little bit of real rock work—a neck of stone about eight feet high which joined, like a gum of rock, the roots of the two monstrous teeth of the mountain" (*P*, 79).

Although Lewis's novels bear some superficial resemblances to *The Waste Land* in his use of the Fisher King, descriptions of modern blight, and implications of the barrenness of post-war civilization, Lewis carefully refrained from the "negativism" which he found in Eliot. Instead of focusing on the more dismal traits of modern life, as Eliot did in the first four sections of *The Waste Land*, Lewis briefly stated the problem and then emphasized the solution. If the two men differed greatly in their perception of the state of the world and the spiritual condition of man, the difference was more in emphasis than in substance. They agreed that man had blinded himself to the eternal truths, and that it was within the grasp of individual men to solve their problems. They approached the same problems, proposed essentially the same solution, and exaggerated the significance of the slight difference in their viewpoints. Had Lewis noticed traces of Eliot's lines in his trilogy, he would undoubtedly have obliterated them in revision.

Although Williams's novels are unique to his genius, following his own preferences and applying his peculiar theology to the modern situation, one cannot deny the presence of Eliot in Williams's novels.

Because of similar outlooks and fascinations with myth and the occult, Eliot and Williams took hints from each other. Since Williams had formed his perspective and had determined the ways by which to communicate it before he advanced into his career as a novelist, he already knew what he sought before borrowing motifs, imagery, themes, and phrases from a poem published eight years before his first novel appeared. In a letter to Theodora Bosanquet dated 5 October 1940, Williams did indicate that Eliot participated directly in the genesis of *All Hallows' Eve*.[28] Considering writing another novel, and having difficulty finding an appropriate form and subject to follow *Descent into Hell*, he presented his ideas to Eliot. According to Williams, Eliot approved the ideas and Williams then planned to develop the novel. Two years later, however, also writing to Bosanquet, Lewis insisted that Eliot have no part of Williams's work, on the grounds that Eliot was incapable of appreciating it.[29] Perhaps Lewis was justified, for writing to Conrad Aiken on 1 May 1946, Eliot indicated that his favorite Williams novels were *War in Heaven, The Place of the Lion*, and *All Hallows' Eve*.[30] The first used the Grail, the second the speaking thunder, and the third the "Unreal City," so that perhaps Eliot's appreciation was based on reflected glory as much as on Williams's talent.

Lewis wrote to Eliot on 22 February 1943, mentioning that "Charles Williams is always promising (or threatening!) to confront us with each other,"[31] and Williams arranged a meeting. It did not go at all well:

> Though Lewis can hardly be said to have been a vain man regarding his physical appearance, and once told Walter Hooper how much easier he would find life when his hair fell out, he was anything but amused by Eliot's opening remark: "Mr Lewis, you are a much *older* man than you appear in photographs." Whatever possessed Eliot to say such a thing no one knows. Lewis stood facing him with the poker-face he sometimes assumed. Having botched it the first time, Eliot tried again: "I must tell you, Mr Lewis, that I consider your *Preface to 'Paradise Lost'* your best book." This being the very book in which he had attacked him, Lewis could not believe Eliot meant him any good will. After that the conversation dwindled to small-talk and, according to Fr Mathew, a very bad time was had by all except Charles Williams who is said to have enjoyed himself hugely.[32]

Apparently the "small-talk" included a request from Eliot, for Lewis entered a brief note in one of his notebooks: " 'Mr. Eliot,' he scribbled, 'has asked me not to write about his literary criticism. Very well. I obey.' Beyond that, he seems to have put Eliot out of his mind till they met years later under more congenial circumstances."[33] After Williams's death, shortly following the meeting of Lewis and Eliot, Lewis wrote to Eliot concerning the publication of a *Festschrift* for Williams, which would focus on *mythopoeia* and was to include essays by J. R. R. Tolkien and Dorothy Sayers. If Lewis hoped that Eliot would publish the book under the Faber & Faber imprint, he was disappointed, but the book was published by Oxford University Press in 1947 and by Eerdmans in 1966. Lewis's estimate of Eliot's poetry had not improved. In 1954,

> in a poem published in *Punch*, Lewis, writing under the pseudonym "N. W.", remarks about himself that he is so coarse that ". . . things the poets see are obstinately invisible to me. / For twenty years I've stared my level best / To see if evening—any evening—would suggest / A patient etherized upon a table / In vain. I simply wasn't able."[34]

In his letter to Alastair Fowler (7 January 1961), however, Lewis revealed that he considered Eliot worthy to receive the Nobel Prize for Literature:

> In confidence if you were asked to nominate a candidate for the Nobel Prize (literature) who wd be your choice? Mauriac has had it. Frost? Eliot? Tolkien? E. M. Forster? Do you know the ideological slant (if any) of the Swedish Academy? Keep this all under your hat.[35]

There was no need for secrecy on Eliot's account—he had already won the Nobel Prize thirteen years before, in 1948.

8

GRAHAM GREENE

Heaps of Broken Images

Graham Greene's development as a novelist paralleled his growing understanding of *The Waste Land*, and his recognition of a theological orientation in *The Waste Land* occurred before Cleanth Brooks's 1939 article appeared. In 1938, with the publication of *Brighton Rock*, Greene successfully combined *The Waste Land*'s imagery with themes derived partly from his reading of the poem and partly from his growing appreciation of Eliot's criticism. Before *Brighton Rock*, Greene used Eliot's poem rather clumsily in such works as *Rumour at Nightfall* (the title of which comes from *The Waste Land*'s l. 146), *Stamboul Train* [*Orient Express*], *England Made Me*, and *A Gun for Sale* [*This Gun for Hire*], but after *Brighton Rock*, in which the imagery and the theological interpretation of *The Waste Land* merge, Greene proceeds to adapt *The Waste Land*'s lines consistently in his novels and in what he refers to as "entertainments." In the later novels, Greene's characters confront the dilemma of *The Waste Land*, struggling to find meaning in an empty world. In the later "entertainments," Greene borrows imagery from *The Waste Land* to advance plot and to embellish atmosphere.

Greene's use of Eliot was so apparent to Eliot scholars that E. K. Brown, making a point about the memorable quality of Eliot's imagery, relegated the fact to a footnote as early as 1938: "Anyone whose mind is well-stored with Mr Eliot's images, if he reads widely in recent fiction, will be startled by the frequency with which these recur. The novels of Mr Graham Greene, to name but one writer, abound in them."[1] Nathan A. Scott, Jr., notes that

> In his earlier novels—*Stamboul Train* (1932), *It's a Battlefield* (1934), *England Made Me* (1935), and *A Gun for Sale* (1936)—Greene created (as did T. S.

Eliot in his early poems) a kind of abstract of our modern Inferno, and it is the adjective "seedy", recurring again and again, which is the focally descriptive term.[2]

Philip Stratford establishes a relationship between Eliot's criticism and Greene's developing "in his own critical articles a theological orientation."[3] Lynette Kohn finds parallels between "the tradition of the godless women of T. S. Eliot" in *The Waste Land* and Ida Arnold in *Brighton Rock*.[4] A. A. DeVitis notes Eliot's heavy influence in the novels of the 1930s, and concludes "Graham Greene believes that the way out of the waste land is belief in God," adding that Greene drew heavily from *The Waste Land*'s "atmosphere and symbols" in *Stamboul Train* and *A Gun for Sale*.[5] And Robert O. Evans notes that Greene adds "a distinct dimension to his meaning, by attempting, like T. S. Eliot, to fuse disparate areas of experience into an organic, meaningful unity, and, thereby, to emphasize the kind of religious truth with which the book [*Brighton Rock*] is concerned."[6]

Gwenn R. Boardman, in her discussion of *Journey Without Maps* (1936), comes closest to explaining the transition which occurred between the early and post-*Brighton Rock* writing of Graham Greene:

> Greene had yet to discover, through the subtleties and disappointments of Africa, that life was not simply divided into the polarities represented by Conrad's world and T. S. Eliot's. Only at the end of his creative journey, after he was back in the familiar English scene, could Greene begin to evaluate and apply all that he had learned in Liberia.[7]

Examining the Conrad/Eliot polarities, Boardman finds that

> Usually Greene underscores ironic comment with lines from Eliot, as in his description of Major Grant "Having to construct something upon which to rejoice," i.e., "Ordering a woman, as one might order a joint of meat, according to size and cut and price." . . . Greene uses Conrad's words to emphasize the romantic aspects of Africa.[8]

When Greene wrote of the contaminating effect of the white man's civilization in Africa, he entitled his article "The Waste Land," and in his *Journey Without Maps*,

> Greene added T. S. Eliot's lines on "fishing in the dull canal . . . round behind the gashouse" to express his sense of all that we have done but ought not to have done, and all that we have left undone.
> Yet Greene's conclusion was essentially optimistic.[9]

Greene's association of Eliot's poem with the contamination of modern civilization becomes evident as well in such later novels as *The Heart of the Matter* (1948) and *A Burnt-Out Case* (1960).

Greene's early reading of Eliot's criticism and poetry, which began when Greene was still at Oxford, provided an explanation and memorable imagery for "the real world . . . full of lust, betrayal, violence, and exploitation" which dominates his work.[10] Yet because he did not understand *The Waste Land*'s relation to his own ideas until he had read Eliot's critical essays, particularly the essay on Baudelaire, Greene's early attempts to profit from *The Waste Land* were less successful than in his later writing. Only when he placed *Waste Land* imagery into its proper context could he create his own Waste Land. Once he had accomplished this, Greene was able to select specific aspects of Eliot's poem to fit his purpose as a writer.

Greene's applications of *The Waste Land* in *Rumour at Nightfall* (1932) are awkward, but in *Stamboul Train* [*Orient Express*] (1932) Greene is more successful. Much of Myatt's character imitates Eliot's "Mr. Eugenides, the Smyrna merchant / Unshaven, with a pocket full of currants / C. i. f. London" (ll. 209–11). Myatt, a currant merchant with "the small eyes, the large nose, the black oiled hair" is Jewish, but his features may suggest one from Smyrna. Carrying a partitioned box of currants in his pocket, he samples those of his competitors: "He chose another currant and without a glance placed it. One of our own. Myatt, Myatt and Page. For a moment with the currant upon his tongue he might have been one of the lords of the world, carrying destiny with him. This is mine and this is good, he thought."[11]

In *A Gun for Sale* [*This Gun for Hire*], published in 1936, Greene creates the physical Waste Land of Nottwich without introducing the spiritual or philosophical concerns which such a Waste Land implies. As an adventure story it is dynamic and exciting, but its characterizations are unconvincing except in the case of the murderer Raven, the forerunner of Pinkie in *Brighton Rock*. Mather is wooden, unimaginative, and mechanical, a policeman whose emotions are conspicuous by their absence, while his fiancée Anne Crowder acts so irrationally that she seems made of cardboard. When Raven informs her that he has a gun and wants her ticket, she merely says "I like he-men. My name's Anne. What's yours?"[12] After going through a series of adventures which includes being stuffed up a chimney, Anne deduces that Raven is evil; she nevertheless helps him to evade the police, wondering only afterwards how she will explain this to Mather. (Since a policeman has died during Raven's escape, a direct result of Anne's intervention as Raven's decoy, she might well wonder.) In this book,

Greene uses Eliot's imagery to describe a physical Waste Land, although the characters themselves are not directly involved in the meaning of their experiences.

The Hanged Man, a major motif of Eliot's poem, occurs frequently in *This Gun for Hire*, but the frequency of the repetitions detracts from the desired effect. Raven continually recalls that his father was hanged. He hates the sight of the Madonna and Child, and he gives his reason when he recalls the religious training he received in an orphanage:

> They twisted everything, even that story in there. It was historical, it had happened, but they twisted it to their own purposes. They made him a god because they could feel fine about it all; they didn't have to consider themselves responsible for the raw deal they'd given him. He'd consented, hadn't he? That was the argument, because he could have called down "a legion of angels" if he'd wanted to escape hanging there. On your life he could, he thought, with bitter lack of faith; just as easily as his own father, taking the drop at Wandsworth, could have saved himself when the trap opened. He stood there, with his face against the glass, waiting for somebody to deny *that* reasoning, staring at the swaddled child with a horrified tenderness—"the little bastard"—because he was educated and knew what the child was in for: the damned Jews and the double-crossing Judas, with no one even to draw a knife on his side when the soldiers came for him in the garden. (*Gun*, 76)

Raven pities the child who will be hanged, and he associates the hanged god with his own hanged father. Anne has occasion to bring in another reference to hanged men when Raven refers to dreams:

> "It seems as how your dreams mean things. I don't mean like tea leaves or cards."
>
> "I knew someone once," Anne said. "She was so good with the cards it gave you the creeps. She used to have those cards with queer pictures on them. The Hanged Man—" (*Gun*, 106–07)

The allusion to Madame Sosostris's cards, after repeated references to Raven's hanged father and Christ as the hanged god, combines Eliot's uses of the motif but overworks it.

Other deaths occur frequently in this "entertainment." Mather's brother has committed suicide. The diplomat whom Raven has murdered, like Raven, spent his youth in an orphanage because his father was a thief and his mother a suicide. Anne reveals much about the diplomat to Raven, including another death by water:

"His father was a thief and his mother committed—"
"Suicide?" Raven whispered. "Did you read how she—"
"She drowned herself." (*Gun*, 105)

Although the Death by Water and the Hanged Man motifs are over-worked throughout the book, at least the relationship of the motifs to Raven's struggle is explicit: "A small aged voice whispered agonizingly in his memory through a closed door. Memories had never troubled him. He didn't mind death: it was foolish to be scared of death in this bare, wintry world" (*Gun*, 41). Unlike Eliot's *The Waste Land*, which offers some potential hope for an individual willing to set his lands in order, the only escape from Greene's Waste Land for Raven is death.

The spirit of the city in *The Waste Land* appears at the end of *This Gun for Hire*. Eliot's description of litter in the Thames introduces a memorable image:

A rat crept softly through the vegetation
Dragging its slimy belly on the bank
While I was fishing in the dull canal
On a winter evening round behind the gashouse (ll. 187–90)

When Anne considers how foolish she has been to believe that her efforts could prevent a war, looking at the world around her in Nott-wich, she sees the *Waste Land* world in Eliot's terms:

In this waste through which she travelled, between the stacks of coal, the tumbledown sheds, abandoned trucks in sidings where a little grass had poked up and died between the cinders, . . . the dusk came up from the dark wounded ground and the glow of furnaces became visible beyond the long black ridge of slag heaps. This was war too—this chaos through which the train moved slowly, grinding over point after point, like a dying creature dragging itself painfully away through no man's land from the scene of battle. (*Gun*, 157)

Finally, "it occurred to her, staring out at the bleak, frozen countryside, that perhaps, even if she had been able to save the country from a war, it wouldn't have been worth the saving" (*Gun*, 158). Another recurrent motif is that of the Metropole, named in *The Waste Land*. The Metropole serves as a landmark in Nottwich for Mather, but it is also the scene for Mr. Cholmondeley's encounters with various members of the chorus line. In *The Waste Land*, Mr. Eugenides invites the narrator "To luncheon at the Cannon Street Hotel / Followed by a weekend at the

Metropole" (ll. 213–14). Cholmondeley invites actresses to the Metropole for luncheon in an "intimate" setting. His idea of intimacy, however, is "one table set among two hundred tables," and his purpose is not seduction but gluttony. His use of the Metropole parodies Mr. Eugenides's. When Anne leaves the Metropole she hears "the shrill voices of children singing a tuneless carol" (*Gun*, 50), recalling Eliot's use of Verlaine's line *"Et O ces voix d'enfants, chantant dans la coupole!"* which appears in *The Waste Land* immediately after the Mr. Eugenides passage. (Greene includes the Metropole in almost all his works, even placing a Metropole in Saigon in *The Quiet American*.)

Greene alludes to Eliot's poem throughout, but he manages only to create a physical atmosphere similar to that of *The Waste Land*. The applications of Eliot's Hanged Man and Death by Water motifs to the characterization of Greene's figures fail because they are too obviously allusions, they occur too often, and they have no direct bearing on the characters of Anne Crowder or Mather. With Raven the motif becomes too pointed, although the memory of his hanged father, suicidal mother, and orphanage upbringing explains much of his bitterness. When applied to such a mechanism as Mather, however, the motif fails.

In other early novels and "entertainments," notably *England Made Me*, Greene integrated his characters and Eliot's poem more successfully, but the problems of *Rumour at Nightfall* and *This Gun for Hire* were present in other early works. According to Philip Stratford, a major change in Greene's technique derives from reading Eliot's criticism:

> Greene was particularly impressed by *After Strange Gods* which he reviewed for *Life and Letters* in April, 1934, and from which he quoted passages in several subsequent articles. The gist of these was the same and coincided with his conclusions about the Jacobeans: that the strength of metaphysical poets lay in the fact that they had retained a spiritual dimension in their work, and that the loss of this dimension in life and literature in modern times was a crippling one. . . . when he did turn to the open treatment of Catholic themes in his fiction, it was as though to illustrate some of Eliot's critical pronouncements. And when, in 1938, he began to give his own critical articles a theological orientation, he again had Eliot's example in mind.[13]

In 1938 Greene published *Brighton Rock*, his first novel openly religious in theme, successfully combining Eliot's imagery with *The Waste Land's* perspective for the first time.

Greene's use of Eliot's poem is important to the atmosphere and setting of this novel, but it is no longer set apart from the movement of the plot or the meaning of the work as a whole. In terms of character-ization, Greene learned to distinguish between the inhabitants of the Waste Land and fully developed characters. The less-developed charac-ters resemble Eliot's figures, while the more fully realized characters struggle with the spiritual dilemma of modern man. According to Strat-ford,

> Indeed Eliot's statement,
>
>> "Most people are only a very little alive; and to awaken them to the spiritual is a very great responsibility; it is only when they are so awakened that they are capable of real Good, but at the same time they become first capable of Evil,"
>
> which Greene had quoted in an early review, might have been the direct inspiration for the theme of *Brighton Rock*.[14]

The principle of division, however, between Rose and Pinkie on the one hand and Ida Arnold on the other, is more likely the reaction of Greene to Eliot's essay on Baudelaire, which includes the distinction more finely drawn:

> Baudelaire has perceived that what distinguishes the relations of man and woman from the copulation of beasts is the knowledge of Good and Evil (of *moral* Good and Evil which are not natural Good and Bad or puritan Right and Wrong). Having an imperfect, vague romantic con-ception of Good, he was at least able to understand that the sexual act as evil is more dignified, less boring, than as the natural, "life giving," cheery automatism of the modern world.[15]

(Cleanth Brooks found this same passage crucial to his theological in-terpretation of *The Waste Land*.) Eliot's statement suggests not only the opposition of Ida's puritanical attitudes regarding Right and Wrong to Pinkie and Rose's conception of Good and Evil, but it also relates Ida's "cheery" attitudes about life and sex to Pinkie's deep-seated disgust with both. Pinkie's spiritual condition is that which Eliot ascribes to Baudelaire:

> The worst that can be said of most of our malefactors, from statesmen to thieves, is that they are not men enough to be damned. Baudelaire was man enough for damnation. . . . In all his humiliating traffic with other beings, he walked secure in this high vocation, that he was capable of a damnation denied to the politicians and the newspaper editors of Paris.[16]

In her relentless pursuit of vengeance on behalf of the murdered "Fred" Hale, Ida Arnold indicates that Right and Wrong are more significant to her than Good and Evil. As soon as she has decided to investigate Hale's death, she summarizes her attitude in these terms:

> "I'm going to make those people sorry they was ever born. . . . Right and wrong," she said, "I believe in right and wrong," and delving a little deeper, with a sigh of happy satiety, she said: "It's going to be exciting, it's going to be fun, it's going to be a bit of life, Old Crowe," giving the highest praise she could give to anything. . . .[17]

Later, reflecting on her dissatisfaction with Phil Corkery as a lover, Ida reviews her own behavior:

> It did no one any harm, it was just human nature, no one could call her really bad—a bit free and easy, perhaps, a bit Bohemian; it wasn't as if she got anything out of it, as if like some people she sucked a man dry and cast him aside like a cast-off—threw him aside like a cast-off glove. She knew what was Right and what was Wrong. God didn't mind a bit of human nature—what He minded—and her brain switched away from Phil in pants to her Mission, to doing good, to seeing that the evil suffered. . . . (BR, 218)

Challenged by Phil, who feels that the murder of Hale is the business of the police, Ida, who values life above all else and who cannot see beyond the moral vacuity of right and wrong, remains completely satisfied that Pinkie's death will serve the cause of simple justice.

Both Pinkie and Rose, however, know that much more is at stake. When Rose attempts to explain Ida's attitude to Pinkie, she reveals that she understands Ida's limitations.

> "What does she know about us? . . .
>
> "Right and wrong. That's what she talks about. I've heard her at the table. Right and wrong. As if she knew." She whispered with contempt: "Oh, she won't burn. She couldn't burn if she tried. . . .
>
> "I'd rather burn with you than be like Her." Her immature voice stumbled on the word: "She's ignorant." (BR, 162)

Attempting to force Rose to betray Pinkie, Ida unintentionally reveals her own limitations (with the help of Greene's narrative comment):

> "I know one thing you don't. I know the difference between Right and Wrong. They didn't teach you that at school."
>
> Rose didn't answer; the woman was quite right; the two words meant

nothing to her. Their taste was extinguished by stronger foods—Good
and Evil. The woman could tell her nothing she didn't know about
these—she knew by tests as clear as mathematics that Pinkie was evil—
what did it matter in that case whether he was right or wrong? (*BR,* 292)

Ida's optimism blinds her to the shortcomings of the Waste Land life
she values. "There was something dangerous and remorseless in her
optimism, whether she was laughing at Henneky's or weeping at a
funeral or a marriage" (*BR,* 47). Pinkie and Rose, unlike Ida or the
inhabitants of Eliot's Waste Land, are aware that life has little to offer,
and that the price of enjoying this life is spiritual, not moral. Pinkie's
spiritual awareness, however, does not make him optimistic about a
future world. He cannot accept a happy afterlife because ". . . he
couldn't believe in it. Heaven was a word; Hell was something he
could trust. A brain was capable only of what it could conceive, and it
couldn't conceive what it had never experienced . . ." (*BR,* 331). After
he has already decided to murder Spicer, Pinkie reflects on the afterlife:

> Why, it was even possible that old Spicer was not set for the flames,
> he'd been a loyal old geezer, he hadn't done as much harm as the next
> man, he might slip through the gates into—but the Boy couldn't picture
> any eternity except in terms of pain. (*BR,* 137)

Pinkie conscientiously invites his own damnation. Although he constantly remembers that repentance even at the moment before death
could save him, he painstakingly inverts each of the seven sacraments
in the seven parts of the novel.[18] His initial purpose in marrying Rose is
to prevent her testifying against him in court, but he sets out deliberately to corrupt her.

Rose, unlike Pinkie, is capable of hope, but she knows the price of
her "happiness." After she and Pinkie are married, outside the church,
Rose begins to consider the consequences:

> What have I done to deserve to be so happy? She'd committed a sin;
> that was the answer; she was having her cake in this world, not in the
> next, and she didn't care. She was stamped with him, as his voice was
> stamped on the vulcanite [recording]. (*BR,* 286)

When Pinkie eventually proposes a suicide pact, intending thus to rid
himself of Rose so that he can return to living solely for himself, Rose
reluctantly agrees. Although she knows that suicide will result in her
damnation, she pities Pinkie and decides that "He was going to damn
himself, but she was going to show them that they couldn't damn him

without damning her too" (*BR*, 332). While Ida is completely ignorant of such concerns, Rose, who realizes fully the consequences of her actions, is as consciously willing in her damnation as Pinkie is in his: "she wouldn't let him go into that darkness alone" (*BR*, 332).

To establish the contrast between Ida's spiritual vacuity on the one hand, and Pinkie and Rose's knowledge on the other, Greene draws extensively from *The Waste Land*. Greene believes "that the way out of the waste land is belief in God."[19] In Eliot's poem, however, hope is only offered near the end—the earlier description of the arid plain finds a contrast in "What the Thunder Said" to emphasize the emptiness of the world. Greene, however, presents this emptiness through Ida and contrasts her ignorance with Pinkie and Rose's knowledge. The result is a spiritual Waste Land which exists both in Ida's ignorance and indifference at one extreme, and Rose and Pinkie's active rejection of their knowledge at the other.

Ida's attitudes towards life echo those of the women in *The Waste Land*:

> Death shocked her, life was so important. She wasn't religious. She didn't believe in heaven or hell, only in ghosts, ouija boards, tables that rapped and little inept voices speaking plaintively of flowers. Let Papists treat death with flippancy; life wasn't so important perhaps to them as what came after; but to her death was the end of everything. (*BR*, 46)

Ida's values are almost entirely sensory. "Life was sunlight on brass bedposts, ruby port, the leap of the heart when the outsider you have backed passes the post and the colours go bobbing up. Life was poor Fred's mouth pressed down on hers in the taxi, vibrating with the engine along the parade" (*BR*, 47). For Ida, the sexual act is the "game" which offers pleasure in an otherwise dull life. Her pursuit of vengeance for Hale offers her excitement, but otherwise she is content with a few glasses of stout and the attentions of a passing lover. Despite Ida's attempts to convince Rose to betray Pinkie, Rose, in her "ignorance," knows more than Ida, who believes that the end of human life is pleasure rather than happiness. Eliot's women ask "What shall I do now? What shall I do?" Ida's pursuit of Pinkie and of the sexual relationship is the best answer she can provide for herself. Immediately after Hale's funeral,

> a determination grew. . . . Somebody had made Fred unhappy, and somebody was going to be made unhappy in turn. An eye for an eye. If you believed in God, you might leave vengeance to Him, but you couldn't trust the One, the universal spirit. Vengeance was Ida's, just as

much as reward was Ida's, the soft gluey mouth affixed in taxis, the warm handclasp in cinemas, the only reward there was. And vengeance and reward—they were both fun. (*BR*, 47–48)

Ida's apparent goodness of heart and belief in justice might mislead many of her friends, but beneath everything she does is a selfish desire to alleviate her boredom.

Pinkie, although he should be more aware of spiritual reality, actively repudiates the hope offered by Christianity. While his conception of good and evil owes much to Eliot's essay on Baudelaire, his specific refusal to accept the Christian answer to the horrors of modern life and his absolute horror of sexuality serve as a commentary on the human condition. Pinkie's attitudes towards sex exaggerate those of a reader confronting the sexual episodes of the early sections of Eliot's poem. Pinkie's rejection of Christianity keeps him in the Waste Land of Brighton.

Eliot's Tiresias episode ends with quotations from both St. Augustine's *Confessions* and Buddha's *Fire Sermon*, combining Eastern and Western images of the fire of lust and the purifying fire. Pinkie repeatedly makes the same connection. Thinking of the "game," "the Boy's mind turned with curiosity and loathing to the small cheap ready-for-anyone face, the bottles catching the moonlight on the bin, and the word 'burn,' 'burn' repeated" (*BR*, 166), an echo of Eliot's "Burning burning burning burning" (l. 308). In another reflection after his unsuccessful attempt at the "game" with Sylvie, "Fear and curiosity ate at the proud future, he was aware of nausea and retched. Marry, he thought, hell, no; I'd rather hang" (*BR*, 196). While departing from St. Paul's "It is better to marry than to burn," this introduces that association as well as calling up the image of the Hanged Man, particularly the Nazarene, who was "hanged" and who did not marry. Pinkie's refusal to escape the Waste Land through belief results from his horror of life itself, but ironically Pinkie's ability to perceive the horror of others' pleasure and pain is the result of his training in the church.

Pinkie's background as a choirboy, his repetition of Latin phrases from the Mass, his knowledge that repentance can save a sinner "between the stirrup and the ground," and his deliberate pursuit of evil ("*Credo in unum Satanum*") make his situation pathetic, although his end is hardly tragic. As the priest implies to Rose at the end of the novel, "*Corruptio optimi est pessima*" describes Pinkie's situation. *Brighton Rock* has taken its theme and the motives of its characters from Eliot's critical writings and *The Waste Land*. For the first time in Greene's work, Eliot's imagery contributes directly to plot, character, and setting without calling undue attention to itself. In one instance where Greene uses a phrase from Eliot's "Sweeney Among the Nightingales," the passage functions on both literal and allusive levels. Ida hears Colleoni's secretary reading from a list:

> "Bananas, oranges, grapes, peaches . . ."
> "Hothouse?"
> "Hothouse."
> "Who's that?" Ida Arnold said. (*BR*, 210)

One answer to Ida's question is Mr. Colleoni, who has walked into the room, although the reader who recalls "The waiter brings in oranges / Bananas figs and hothouse grapes" will answer "Eliot." In a similarly unobtrusive manner, Greene employs Eliot's imagery to delineate character, advance his plot, and create a Waste Land atmosphere.

DeVitis notes that "The grotesque images of evil . . . owe a good deal to Eliot's *The Waste Land*: the broken windows, the ouija boards, the gramophone, the Cosmopolitan Hotel, death by water—all have their counterparts in Eliot's poem."[20] Except for the "broken windows," each of these images is vital to Greene's plot and character development, as well as to the Waste Land atmosphere of Brighton. The ouija board, as Ida uses it, tells the reader much about her as she is in the process of embarking on her "Mission," but Waste Land superstition occurs elsewhere in the novel. After the death of Spicer, another member of Pinkie's gang, Cubitt, reflects on Spicer's passing and reveals that, like others of the Waste Land, he believes in ghosts:

> Cubitt thought of Spicer, who'd liked a good tune. Poor old Spicer. The mist blew in, heavy compact drifts of it like ectoplasm. Cubitt had been to a séance once in Brighton; he had wanted to get in touch with his mother dead twenty years ago. It had come over him quite suddenly—the old girl might have a word for him. She had: she was on the seventh plane where all was very beautiful; her voice had sounded a little boozed, but that wasn't really unnatural. The boys had laughed at him about it, particularly old Spicer. Well, Spicer wouldn't laugh now. He could be summoned himself any time to ring a bell and shake a tambourine. It was a lucky thing he liked music. (*BR*, 226)

Ida's refusal to take a moral stand, to experience genuine love for others, or to put her faith in something other than superstition allies her with those around her. They resemble the completely neutral Mrs. Equitone, who consults Madame Sosostris regularly. Pinkie, despite his more theological orientation, shares Ida's concern over spilled salt.

When Hale's horse, Black Boy, wins the Derby, Pinkie has serious misgivings:

> Pinkie was silent. He told himself: Fred's horse. If I was one of those crazy geezers who touch wood, throw salt, won't go under ladders, I might be scared to— . . .
>   . . . —To go on with what he'd planned with care. (BR, 149)

The omen disturbs Pinkie, and his constant memory of phrases from the Mass, uttered throughout the novel, serves as a talisman rather than as a reminder of spiritual truth.

The gramophone, another device from *The Waste Land*, is crucial to Greene's final effect, although he goes far beyond the mechanical indifference of the typist and her young man carbuncular. At Rose's insistence that he make a vulcanite recording for her, Pinkie complies but his message is of hatred:

> "God damn you, you little bitch, why can't you go back home for ever and let me be?"; he heard the needle scratch and the record whir, then a click and silence.
>   Carrying the black disk he came out to her. "Here," he said, "take it. I put something on it—loving." (BR, 257)

Although Rose has no gramophone, she treasures the recording. After Pinkie's death Rose goes to a priest, retorts angrily to his refusal to understand Pinkie's "goodness," and wrings one admission from the priest: "If he loved you, surely, . . . that shows . . . there was some good . . ." (BR, 357). At this point Rose acts exactly as the typist in Eliot's *The Waste Land*:

> When lovely woman stoops to folly and
> Paces about her room again, alone,
> She smoothes her hair with automatic hand,
> And puts a record on the gramophone. (ll. 253–56)

Rose, who has willingly risked her soul for Pinkie by living in a marriage outside the church and by agreeing to a suicide pact, has "stooped to folly." Now that she is going to play Pinkie's message on the gramophone, "She walked rapidly in the thin June sunlight towards the worst horror of all" (BR, 358). The gramophone device shows Pinkie at his worst, Rose at her most vulnerable, and the horror of the two youngsters.

In addition to the Cosmopolitan Hotel, which owes much to Eliot's

Metropole and Cannon Street Hotel of the Mr. Eugenides section of
The Waste Land, Greene includes a Metropole in *Brighton Rock*. His
Metropole contributes to the decayed atmosphere of Brighton. Descrip-
tions of the Metropole in the Brighton setting combine sea and Met-
ropole as Eliot combined Mr. Eugenides with Phlebas the Phoenician:
"The pale green sea curdled on the shingle and the green tower of the
Metropole looked like a dug-up coin verdigrised with age-old mould"
(*BR*, 203).

The Death by Water motif, prominent in *The Waste Land*, also appears often in *Brighton Rock*. Eliot's

> Phlebas the Phoenician, a fortnight dead,
> Forgot the cry of gulls, and the deep sea swell
> And the profit and loss.
>   A current under sea
> Picked his bones in whispers. (ll. 312–16)

The function of Greene's use of the motif is to associate Pinkie with
death by water, utlimately revealing that the peace of Phlebas's repose
is the only peace Pinkie can expect. Early in the novel Pinkie sees
notices plastered on a wall: "Found drowned. A dead face met his eye
staring from the wall, unnaturally pasty. Unbrushed hair. A scar by
the mouth" (*BR*, 92). Later another notice varies slightly on the same
theme: "Woman Found Drowned at Black Rock" (*BR*, 239). When Pinkie
sees it among the other notices, including an advertisement for *Married Love* by Marie Stopes, he is greatly disturbed. Talking with Dallow,
Pinkie confides,

> "When I was a kid, I swore I'd be a priest."
> "A priest? You a priest? That's good," Dallow said. He laughed with-
> out conviction, shifted his foot uneasily, so that it trod in a dog's ordure.
> "What's wrong with being a priest?" the Boy said. "They know what's
> what. They keep away—" his whole mouth and jaw loosened; he might
> have been going to weep; he beat out wildly with his hands towards the
> window: Woman Found Drowned; two-valve, *Married Love*, the horror—
> "from this." (*BR*, 240)

In a series of nightmares, Pinkie encounters death by water:

> A piece of blanket fell across his mouth; he breathed with difficulty. He
> was upon the pier and he could see the piles breaking—a black cloud
> came racing up across the Channel and the sea rose; the whole pier
> lurched and settled lower. He tried to scream; no death was so bad as
> drowning. (*BR*, 270)

Yet when he regards the irrevocability of even a registry office marriage, he concludes "Only death could ever set him free" (BR, 272). Eliot's "Death by Water" section appears in the combination of Pinkie's fear of death, disgust with sexuality, and knowledge that his only peace will result from death. Eliot's Phlebas

> As he rose and fell
> . . . passed the stages of his age and youth
> Entering the whirlpool. (ll. 316–18)

Pinkie approaches a similar oblivion when he meets his own death by water: "he was at the edge, he was over; they couldn't even hear a splash. It was as if he'd been withdrawn suddenly by a hand out of any existence—past or present, whipped away into zero—nothing" (BR, 352).

In Greene's later "novels" (as distinguished from "entertainments"), the conflict between characters represents a conflict between belief and unbelief. The Power and the Glory (1940) presents a Waste Land in which the Catholic faith has been declared illegal by secular forces in Mexico. Belief's champion is the novel's protagonist, a whiskey priest who has sired an illegitimate child, constantly questions his own worthiness, and refuses to renounce his vocation. Unbelief has its representative in the secular lieutenant, who desires to help the people by disposing of their traditional oppressors—the Church, the foreigner, and the politician. The novel's plot consists of the efforts of the whiskey priest to evade capture and execution by finding his way out of the state, but the priest's efforts are thwarted by the relentless pursuit of the lieutenant and the requirements of the priest's office—once a summons to perform last rites prevents his leaving by boat, and ultimately, only miles from the border and safety, the priest responds to another summons to perform last rites although he knows that this call is a trap which will result in his capture.

John Atkins, writing about this novel, is clearly not entirely happy with it:

> DEATH! DEATH! DEATH! What a way to start a novel! And what a way to continue it! But that's what he wanted—it was certainly no accident, for Greene doesn't make slips, except intentional ones—and death's ubiquity is the slogan he drives home, like a particularly beastly nail. As literary drumming, The Power and the Glory ranks very high indeed.[21]

Atkins argues that Greene's use of death imagery is excessive, but in order to establish the contrast between those who believe that death is the end of everything and the priest (and those who risk death to help him) who believes that death is only a transition to a better world, the issue of death is crucial. In his handling of images of death and decay in the novel, Greene states Eliot's themes and occasionally echoes lines of *The Waste Land*.

Since the secular powers have eliminated all outer vestiges of worship, destroying the churches and making it extremely difficult to obtain wine for the Mass, the state of the Church in the novel recalls lines from "What the Thunder Said":

> There is the empty chapel, only the wind's home.
> It has no windows, and the door swings,
> Dry bones can harm no one. (ll. 389–91)

When the priest tries to buy wine and finds himself forced to drink it with the Chief of Police and the Governor's cousin (the latter of whom had sold him the illegal wine in the first place), Greene's narrative intrusion suggests the contrast between Eliotian thunder and the spiritual Waste Land below it:

> The lightning shot down over the harbour and the thunder beat on the roof: this was the atmosphere of a whole state—the storm outside and the talk just going on—words like "mystery" and "soul" and "the source of life" came in over and over again, as they sat on the bed talking, with nothing to do and nothing to believe and nowhere better to go.[22]

In another narrative comment, Greene suggests Madame Sosostris's "I see crowds of people, walking round in a ring" (l. 55):

> The young men and women walked round and round the plaza in the hot electric night: the men one way, the girls another, never speaking to each other. In the northern sky the lightning flapped. It was like a religious ceremony which had lost all meaning, but at which they still wore their best clothes. (*Power*, 96)

These suggestions of *The Waste Land*, however, are comparatively minor. In *The Power and the Glory*, as in other "novels," Greene is more concerned with themes and motifs of *The Waste Land* than with specific lines or images.

The Heart of the Matter (1948) draws more directly from *The Waste Land* than does *The Power and the Glory*. Scobie, a Catholic policeman garrisoned in West Africa, caught between pity for his wife and love for another woman, ultimately commits suicide. Helen Rolt, survivor of a shipwreck, is the other woman. Referring to her father, she comments that "he believes in God and heaven, all that sort of thing. . . . I gave up all that when I left school."[23] Had she been left to her own devices, had there been no Scobie, Helen confesses, "Perhaps I'd have slutted with Bagster, or killed myself, or both. I think both" (*Heart*, 204). Wilson, who has been sent to investigate Scobie but who has also fallen somewhat ridiculously in love with Scobie's wife Louise, expresses attitudes which might have come directly from *The Waste Land*: "He thought sadly, as lust won the day, what a lot of trouble it was; the sadness of the after-taste fell upon his spirits beforehand" (*Heart*, 188).

The most overt use of Eliot in this novel, besides the "godless women" tradition to which Helen Rolt belongs, is Scobie's perception of death in a Hanged Man motif. When he goes to Bamba after Pemberton has committed suicide, he must cross a river identified as a Styx. Pemberton, a comparative youngster, has hanged himself. Greene includes Pemberton in a motif of hanged men which dominates Scobie's thinking. The association links Pemberton's death with Scobie's suicide. Scobie, like Eliot, connects hanging with the crucifixion:

> But they [the priests] taught also that God had sometimes broken his own laws, and was it more impossible for him to put out a hand of forgiveness into the suicidal darkness and chaos than to have woken himself in the tomb, behind the stone? Christ had not been murdered: you couldn't murder God: Christ had killed himself: he had hanged himself on the Cross as surely as Pemberton from the picture rail. (*Heart*, 206–07)

Greene does not pursue these associations too far, however, when alluding to *The Waste Land* in the novel. When Greene uses Eliot in *The Heart of the Matter*, he does so to underscore Scobie's specific attitude or mood and to develop the relatively minor characters such as Wilson and Bagster.

Allusions to *The Waste Land* appear much more frequently in the "entertainments." *The Third Man* (1950) develops Eliot's imagery and includes several motifs from the poem. Rollo Martins, who journeys to Vienna to meet his old friend Harry Lime, learns that Lime has died. However, discrepancies in witnesses' accounts indicate that a "third man" was present at the "fatal" automobile accident, and Martins sets out to solve this mystery. Along the way he loses much of his idealism, especially when he learns that Lime, much admired by Martins, traffics in black-market penicillin and therefore is responsible for many deaths. Finding Lime still alive, Martins betrays and ultimately kills Lime. Mar-

tins's disillusionment resembles that implied in *The Waste Land*. When
Martins learns Lime's true nature,

> a world for Martins had certainly come to an end, a world of easy
> friendship, hero-worship, confidence that had begun twenty years be-
> fore—in a school corridor. Every memory—afternoons in the long grass,
> the illegitimate shoots on Brickworth Common, the dreams, the walks,
> every shared experience was simultaneously tainted, like the soil of an
> atomized town.[24]

The title of this work alludes to Eliot's line—"Who is the third who
walks always beside you?"—referring to Christ's appearance to his
disciples on the road to Emmaus. The identity of the third man is a
mystery until it becomes evident that Lime has not died. The setting
of the entertainment, Vienna, specifically labeled in Eliot's poem as
"Unreal," is an Unreal City in Greene's description, too. A "Great
Wheel," reminiscent of Madame Sosostris's wheel among her cards
and the wheel referred to in "Death by Water," towers over the unreal landscape of the Russian zone. When Martins meets Lime on the
wheel, Lime reveals his indifference to his victims. "'Victims?' he
asked. 'Don't be melodramatic, Rollo. Look down there,' he went on,
pointing through the window at the people moving like black flies at
the base of the Wheel" (*Third*, 233). The wheel of fortune dwarfs the
city of man and its crowds. Greene adapts another connection Eliot
makes involving the Unreal City, comparing the modern city with
hell, by placing the final action in the "underground" city of Vienna's
sewers.

The descriptions of Lime's two burials evoke Eliot's "The Burial of
the Dead." In the mock funeral, although Lime is "vaulted in" by snow
and frozen earth, "resurrection" occurs. The second burial, however,
proceeds more easily and has been made more ugly by the snow's
melting:

> A thaw set in that night, and all over Vienna the snow melted, and the
> ugly ruins came to light again: steel rods hanging like stalactites, and
> rusty girders thrusting like bones through the grey slush. Burials were
> much simpler than they had been a week before when electric drills had
> been needed to break the frozen ground. (*Third*, 243)

There is also a suggestion of influence from *The Waste Land* in Martins's
relationship with Anna. At one point Martins's actions recall the "assault" of the young man carbuncular on the passive typist of "The Fire
Sermon."

Our Man in Havana (1958), the story of an English vacuum cleaner

salesman pressed into the British Secret Service, who justifies his expense account by creating fictitious assistants and sending drawings of
vacuum cleaner parts as secret plans, includes more comedy than any
of Greene's other "entertainments." Yet the comedy becomes serious
as Wormold's assistants, whose names he drew from the local tele-
phone directory, begin to die, and Wormold becomes enmeshed in a
world of international intrigue. While the plot and characterization of
this work owe little to Eliot, the atmosphere owes a great deal to *The
Waste Land*. As he has done in the other "entertainments," Greene
draws a sharp line between the worlds of reality and imagination,
belief and unbelief. Hasselbacher tells Wormold, "You should dream
more, Mr. Wormold. Reality in our century is not something to be
faced."[25] The harsh reality of atomic warfare dominates modern life for
Wormold and for Hasselbacher, who is an actual secret agent. Hasselbacher asks Wormold "Do you ever have a desire, Mr. Wormold, to go
back to peace? Oh no, I forget, you're young, you've never known it.
This was the last peace for any of us" (*Our*, 367). Hasselbacher's youth
was spent before World War I—he is constantly aware of modernity's
post-war blight.

Those who consider the atomic horror are either indifferent to it or
have abandoned hope in everything. Carter, who kills Hasselbacher
and whom Wormold finally kills, in answer to Wormold's question
"What do you hope?" replies "Nothing" (*Our*, 419). Beatrice blames
part of this on such bureaucrats as those in the Secret Service who
cross-examine Wormold in London about his activities: "They haven't
left us much to believe, have they?—even disbelief. I can't believe in
anything bigger than a home, or anything vaguer than a human being"
(*Our*, 433). Wormold, who himself believes in nothing, reports to Hasselbacher that "Father Mendez spent half an hour describing the effect
of the hydrogen bomb. Those who believe in heaven on earth, he said,
are creating a hell; he made it sound that way too—it was very lucid"
(*Our*, 251). Despite this awareness, however, the horror continues. The
chief bureaucrat in the London office, excited by Wormold's drawings
of a gigantic vacuum cleaner, says in a Waugh-like exchange,

> "I believe we may be on to something so big that the H-bomb will
> become a conventional weapon."
> "Is that desirable, sir?"
> "Of course it's desirable. Nobody worries about conventional weap-
> ons." (*Our*, 313)

Hasselbacher advises Wormold to tell his government nothing: "They
don't deserve truth" (*Our*, 294). Yet Wormold notices that something is

lacking. "Dr. Hasselbacher never talked in terms of morality; it was outside the province of a doctor" (*Our*, 294).

While Wormold does not accept the teaching of any specific religion, he regrets the spiritual decline of the modern world. He thinks of the problems of the world in terms of human cruelty and associates this with images of "ruins," as Eliot has associated spiritual vacuity with the blight on the Waste Land. "The cruel come and go like cities and thrones and powers, leaving their ruins behind them. They had no permanence" (*Our*, 270). The only solution for Wormold, once taken abruptly out of the Cuban world, is to marry Beatrice. Beatrice has said that she believes in home and human beings, and perhaps Wormold can also create order on that small a scale. Beatrice suggests another possibility, however, echoing *The Waste Land*'s solution to the modern dilemma—regeneration similar to that at the end of "The Fire Sermon." Once Wormold's fraud has emerged, he asks Beatrice,

> "I wonder where you'll be sent next."
> "The Persian Gulf perhaps. Basra."
> "Why the Persian Gulf?"
> "It's their idea of purgatory. Regeneration through sweat and tears."
> (*Our*, 426)

This proves unnecessary, however.

The atmosphere of Wormold's world owes much to *The Waste Land*, although the allusions to specific lines are less frequent than in other "entertainments." The "one-eyed merchant," for example, which Madame Sosostris sees in her Tarot pack and which combines Phlebas and Mr. Eugenides, appears often under different guises in *Our Man in Havana*. One, a purveyor of pornography, combines elements of the one-eyed merchant and Phlebas: "The Negro was blind in one eye . . . and his ribs showed through his torn shirt like a ship's under demolition . . ." (*Our*, 249). The Chief of the Secret Service, himself a merchant of death, also has one eye. Even Wormold is part of this motif, described as "an old-fashioned merchant King" (*Our*, 237). The treatment of love and sexuality in this book has counterparts in *The Waste Land*. Attempting to warn his "agents" after realizing that at least one man had died because of his bogus reports, Wormold warns Teresa, a stripper, and Sanchez, a professor. Beatrice (herself a typist) and Wormold sit through a pornographic film before finding Teresa backstage. The major problem Tiresias witnesses in the typist's encounter with her young man carbuncular is absence of sentiment, leaving only the act of lust, and watching the movie both Beatrice and Wormold draw

Tiresias's conclusion. They realize that "The act of lust and the act of love are the same; it cannot be falsified like a sentiment" (*Our*, 350). When Wormold finds Professor Sanchez with his young mistress, the girl "stooped and turned off the gramophone" (*Our*, 356), an echo of the end of the Tiresias episode in "The Fire Sermon." Other *Waste Land* echoes occur when Beatrice and Wormold consider their former spouses, hers "fading away" and his running off with an American. When Hasselbacher plays a recording of *Tristan*, Wormold immediately thinks of his wife (*Our*, 342), connecting her with Isolde. The complaints he remembers hearing from his former wife recall the questions of Eliot's neurasthenic woman: Wormold's wife asked "Why don't you do something, act some way, any way at all? You just stand there . . ." (*Our*, 268).

In his "entertainments," Greene borrowed the Unreal City motif regularly to describe the physical bleakness of the modern world, employed Eliot's imagery to describe the disillusionment of such characters as D, Rowe, Martins, and Wormold, and occasionally used episodes from *The Waste Land* to advance his plot, as when he included fortune-telling and séances as significant actions in *The Ministry of Fear*. Greene does not attempt, however, to resolve the dilemma of his disillusioned characters by providing the answer of faith. When disillusionment is overcome, usually the character has tried to create a more limited order: D finds temporary contentment with Rose Cullen, Rowe with Anna Hilfe, Martins with Anna Schmidt, and Wormold with Beatrice. In the novels, including *The Power and the Glory*, *The Heart of the Matter*, *The End of the Affair*, and *The Honorary Consul*, several allusions to *The Waste Land* assist atmosphere and plot, but other allusions apply to the struggles of the major characters as they look towards Christianity to resolve the modern plight. Of the characters who realize that they are in a Waste Land, some reject the Christian solution, and others try, with varying degrees of success, to achieve belief. The characters look to theology for an answer and deeply feel the consequences when they fail to believe. From Greene's point of view, the significant difference between an "entertainment" and a novel is the emphasis placed on development of character. In his use of Eliot, the significant difference is whether he uses *The Waste Land* descriptively, without trying to resolve the Waste Land dilemma beyond the realm of immediate circumstance, or thematically, providing a spiritual solution to the problems of his characters.

PART III

The Waste Land's Influence
After World War II

The Waste Land's influence on British novelists declined considerably after World War II. As novelists of the 1950s began to write, *The Waste Land* was more than thirty years old and the problems of modernity, particularly after the Great Depression and the nuclear bombing of Hiroshima, took on an even more frightening aspect. Many novelists who were familiar with *The Waste Land* did not find the poem particularly useful to their art. Muriel Spark, for example, found Eliot's poetic drama more interesting than his earlier work. She described *The Cocktail Party* as "a marriage feast wherefor the funeral baked meats of Eliot's *Waste Land* are coldly furnished forth. For although the *Waste Land* meats were certainly baked for consumption at the funeral, at least they were not."[1] Spark's novels include counterparts of the "neurasthenic woman" of "A Game of Chess" which seem to owe nothing to Eliot, and in *The Prime of Miss Jean Brodie* she has one of her characters, an author, deny Eliot's influence during an interview:

> "what would you say was your greatest influence during the 'thirties? I mean, during your teens. Did you read Auden and Eliot?"
> "No," said Sandy. . . . "But there was a Miss Jean Brodie in her prime."[2]

(The denial, of course, demands that the novelist, if not the character, be conscious of Eliot's presence.)

As Eliot's poem became associated with the "beginning" of "modern" poetry, it also began to harden into literary artifact. Varied readings of *The Waste Land,* provided by Edmund Wilson, I. A. Richards, F. R. Leavis, F. O. Matthiessen, and Cleanth Brooks, offered salient interpretations of the poem without limiting the uses to which the poem had been put, for no single interpretation has succeeded in excluding another. Perhaps the greater understanding of the poem's potential meanings has robbed it of much of its power. In any case, more recent authors, like Paul Theroux, allude to *The Waste Land* only in passing, or use the poem to make a point totally unrelated to *The Waste Land's* content. John Fowles, for example, refers pointedly to *The Waste Land* at the beginning and end of *Daniel Martin.* Early in the novel, Eliot's poem becomes part of the bantering of Daniel and Jenny:

> "Then you need your eyesight tested."
> "Not really. If you want to know what the shored fragments are worth, ask the ruin."
> " 'Why then I'll fit you. Hieronymo's mad again.' " She sits away and grins at him in the night, raises a reproving finger. "You'd forgotten that was the next line. Right? You shouldn't get literary with actresses. We may be cows, but we can always cap you."
> "Stage point. Not a real one."[3]

Near the end of the novel, "The wretched dog began barking again somewhere outside, and he thought once more of T. S. Eliot: *oh keep the Dog far hence* . . . but couldn't stop to remember how it went on. . . ."[4]

Such use of *The Waste Land* suggests allusion for its own sake, and occasionally provokes the disapproval of reviewers. Samuel Ludu, reviewing Lawrence Durrell's *Livia, or Buried Alive,* criticizes Durrell's echoes of Eliot:

> Even more seriously, Durrell sees his world too often through the eyes of others. "A swarm of violins started up somewhere and through half-closed eyes he saw fiddlers performing their hieratic arabesque—girls combing out their long hair."
>
> > A woman drew her long black hair out tight
> > And fiddled whisper music on those strings—Eliot's *The Waste Land.*
>
> Earlier, as Blanford sits conversing with his "semblable and frere," his character Sutcliffe (echoes of Baudelaire and of Eliot's references to him in *The Waste Land*), he hears the question which characterizes the inertia of Eliot's own figures in "A Game of Chess." "My God, Blanford, what is to become of us? We shall go on sitting about regretting our lack of talent; we shall go on trying to convince people."[5]

Some of the parallels Ludu finds are not very convincing precisely because they are only parallels, but Ludu's point is clear: a novelist ought not to borrow from a literary source so generally known as *The Waste Land* unless he wishes to be regarded as trite or unimaginative. However, the two novelists of this section, Iris Murdoch and Anthony Burgess, respectively demonstrate two continuing uses of *The Waste Land*: applying *The Waste Land* to modern dilemmas and alluding to *The Waste Land* to emphasize specific themes.

9

IRIS MURDOCH

Murmurs of Maternal Lamentation

Although fully aware of the conditions that had inspired it, Iris Murdoch flatly rejects the moralism of Eliot's viewpoint. Her Waste Land implies a sympathy for moderns which Eliot's poem appears to lack. Murdoch avoids Eliot's moral tone when depicting sexual relationships, and she provides a different explanation for the difficulties which human beings have when trying to understand, accept, and love one another. While she, like Eliot, blames the problem on man, she focuses on individual failure rather than on widespread social or moral problems. Murdoch has always been an admirer of Eliot's work but only recently has she felt that she understands it. As a result, she feels that Eliot has not influenced her work directly.[1] While she has not developed *The Waste Land*'s implicit morality in her novels, she has borrowed images and situations from the poem to place them in a context which often contradicts Eliot's use of them.

In her essay "T. S. Eliot as a Moralist," Murdoch focuses on the issues of disagreement between herself and Eliot. She asks "How can one be a moralist in this age? What does one appeal to? To appreciate the nature of Mr Eliot's moral appeal it is necessary to see the basis of his opposition to 'liberalism.'"[2] After defining Eliot as an "eclectic moralist," Murdoch specifies her objections to his philosophy as he expressed it in "The Pensées of Pascal":

> One feels this disillusioned tone in Mr Eliot's political writings, especially in his attitude to "the mob." He declares, alarmingly, that he would prefer an illiterate audience to an audience of ill-educated or half-educated persons such as are now available. And it is significant

that he extends no sympathy to the English Non-conformist tradition, with its wide-reaching utilitarian and socialist connections. . . .

With hair-raising thoroughness Mr Eliot rejects the "stuff" of our liberal world.[3]

Yet "In his poetry Mr Eliot is no Jansenist,"[4] and Murdoch does not find Eliot's convictions detrimental to the power of his imagery.

Despite Murdoch's rejection of Eliot's stance, references to his work appear in her novels. In *The Italian Girl* (1964), David comments, "It is better to do the wrong thing for the right reasons than the right thing for the wrong reasons,"[5] quoting *Murder in the Cathedral*. Hilary Burde, in *A Word Child* (1975), thinks often of Eliot near the end of the novel. "Just before I reached Gloucester Road I noticed the church, St Stephen's, at which, Clifford once told me, T. S. Eliot served for many years as a churchwarden."[6] Reflecting that "Tragedy belongs in art. Life has no tragedies" (*WC*, 382), Hilary spies

> a memorial tablet which asked me to pray for the repose of the soul of Thomas Stearns Eliot. How is it with you, old friend, the intolerable wrestle with words and meanings being over? Alas, I could not pray for your soul any more than I could for Clifford's. You had both vanished from the catalogue of being. But I could feel a lively gratitude for words, even for words whose sense I could scarcely understand. (*WC*, 383–84)

In the process of thinking of Eliot, Hilary echoes *East Coker*, recalling Murdoch's statement that "Unlike other poets in the Imagist tradition, Mr Eliot has never lost his respect for words."[7] Such direct references to Eliot, however, appear rarely and are not necessary either to plot or to theme.

General references to the modern Waste Land are more frequent. In *A Severed Head* (1961), "civilization" becomes the acceptance of the unconscionable in the absence of ethics or values. Alexander, who was Antonia's lover long before Palmer was, defines Palmer as "an imitation human being: beautifully finished, exquisitely coloured, but imitation."[8] *The Time of the Angels* (1966) recalls *The Waste Land* in its description of physical setting as well as of human relationships. Early in the novel Pattie, a black domestic servant and cast-off mistress of Carel Fisher, explores the area around the new Rectory. Unable to see any other buildings in the fog, "she found herself in a waste land. There were no houses, only a completely flat surface of frozen mud, through which the roadway passed, with small humps here and there under stiff frozen tarpaulins."[9] This Waste Land passage combines the desolation, ruined chapel, shelter under the "red rock," and "waste land" of

Eliot's poem. A reference to Christopher Wren's tower, which will be
torn down in the novel, recalls Eliot's note to "Magnus Martyr" (l. 264):
"The interior of St. Magnus Martyr is to my mind one of the finest
among Wren's interiors. See *The Proposed Demolition of Nineteen City
Churches. . . .*" Similar imagery appears when Muriel, another character, explores the same area, which is again labeled a "waste land" (*TA*,
62). In the novel, the general condition of empty modern man, the
physically blighted world, and the absence of order establish a Waste
Land setting.

The opening of Eliot's poem introduces April "mixing / Memory and
desire, stirring / Dull roots with spring rain" (ll. 2–4), a nostalgic memory of earlier summers, and a Hyacinth Girl. Murdoch suggests these
images in *The Flight from the Enchanter* (1956): "For the first time that
year Rainborough could feel the sun on his neck, stirring memories of
other summers; and through his reflections he began at last to see the
flowers. Hyacinths, . . ."[10] Speaking of his mistress Georgie, Martin
recalls aspects of April which made it "the cruellest month" in *The
Waste Land*: "a miraculous April without its pangs of transformation
and birth" (*SH*, 21). Eliot used the image of dust in "I will show you
fear in a handful of dust" (l. 30) as a symbol of mortality. Murdoch
often uses dust to stress the physical limitations of the human being,
and in *The Black Prince* (1973), Pearson relates fear and dust: "As I stood
there in that thick oppressive urban dusk breathing the breath of fear,
smelling the dunes of dust, . . ."[11] In *The Time of the Angels*, after Muriel
has passed through a Waste Land, "It was strange to Muriel to think
that they were surrounded by invisible domes and towers and spires.
She had ceased to think that she was in a city at all" (*TA*, 64), suggesting Eliot's Unreal City. In *The Black Prince*, London and its inhabitants
are as dispirited as they are in Eliot's poem:

> The sun was shining and there was a dusty defeated smell of mid-
> summer London: oily, grimy, spicy, melancholy and old. A number of
> tousled and rather elderly-looking pigeons stood around us, staring
> at us with their hard insentient eyes. Despairing people sat on other
> benches. The sky above Oxford Street was a sizzling unforgiving blue.
> (*BP*, 143)

In *A Word Child*, London is specifically labeled "unreal": "London is
unreal north of the park and south of the river. Unreality reaches its
peak on the horrible hills of Hampstead. For me the park was the great
divide between myself and a happier land . . ." (*WC*, 5). An episode
similar to "That corpse you planted last year in your garden" (l. 71)

occurs in *The Flight from the Enchanter*. Stefan and Jan, refugees from Poland, live with their aged mother and constantly revile her. When she dies, the sons plant her in their garden and Stefan declares *"gaudeamus igitur"* (*FFE*, 247). Stefan's words echo the spirit of Stetson and the narrator, who take every precaution to keep the body in the ground. Murdoch's borrowings from "The Burial of the Dead," used in several of her novels, include the "pangs" of April, the Unreal City, and the burials.

Murdoch does not appear to draw from "A Game of Chess," with its neurasthenic woman and pub scene; Eliot's lack of sympathy for women would not appeal to her. However, Eliot's "The Fire Sermon" is a source of both imagery and episode in Murdoch's novels. Eliot's description of the "violet hour, the evening hour that strives / Homeward" (ll. 220–21) has its counterpart in *The Black Prince*:

> It was evening now, twilight time, the evening of that same lengthy fantastic eventful day.
> The evening was overcast, the dour thick light turning a little purple, the air warm and motionless. (*BP*, 243)

The quest for the Grail becomes somewhat perverted in *The Time of the Angels*. Leo, who has stolen his father's religious icon to pawn it, strikes an agreement with Muriel to return the icon in exchange for an introduction to Muriel's cousin Elizabeth: "A quest! A quest! It's on. I'll take my chance. I'll even take my chance on your estimate of her beauty" (*TA*, 113). Confronted by Arnold and Rachel concerning his relationship with Julian, Pearson in *The Black Prince* says he feels as responsible for Julian "as if—I'd been given . . . the bloody Grail" (*BP*, 241).

The Waste Land's typist appears frequently in Murdoch's work. The typist's passivity, her indifference to her lover and to the sexual act, and her lack of awareness of the pleasures and values of sexuality are characteristic of several women in Murdoch's novels. However, in the novels, the women are clearly victims. In *The Flight from the Enchanter*, Annette, Rosa, and Miss Casement share some traits of Eliot's typist and Thames Maidens. Annette

> had been deflowered at seventeen by a friend of her brother on the suggestion of the latter. Nicholas would have arranged it when she was sixteen, only he needed her just then for a black mass. "You must be rational about these things, Sis," he told her. "Don't build up an atmosphere of mystery and expectation, it'll only make you neurotic." Since

that time Annette had had a number of adventures attended by neither delight nor grief. (*FFE*, 64)

In one of her "adventures," Annette shows that she is more sensitive to her situation than is *The Waste Land*'s typist to hers. Rainborough, undressing Annette, is nettled by her detachment and indifference. Unlike the young man carbuncular, whose "vanity requires no response, / And makes a welcome of indifference" (ll. 241–42), Rainborough demands that Annette admit a share of responsibility for his assault. Offended, she resists his attempts violently rather than acknowledge complicity by remaining passive. Rosa, initially horrorstricken by the suggestion that she become the lover of both Jan and Stefan (because the brothers share everything), struggles to suppress her reaction: "It was nearly gone, it was gone; and now as she sat rigid, like a stone goddess, and as she felt herself to be there, empty of thoughts and feelings, she experienced a kind of triumph" (*FFE*, 78). Rosa's state of mind resembles that of the typist, who is

> Hardly aware of her departed lover;
> Her brain allows one half-formed thought to pass:
> "Well now that's done: and I'm glad it's over." (ll. 250–52)

Rosa's mind is "empty of thoughts," although this is the result of will.

However, Miss Casement resembles the typist in a different manner. Rainborough visits her flat, deliberately arriving early to catch her and her one-room flat in a state of unpreparedness. *The Waste Land*'s typist returns home from work,

> clears her breakfast, lights
> Her stove, and lays out food in tins.
> Out of the window perilously spread
> Her drying combinations touched by the sun's last rays,
> On the divan are piled (at night her bed)
> Stockings, slippers, camisoles, and stays. (ll. 222–27)

Miss Casement's room includes unwashed sauce-pans, a divan bed, and disorder:

> The floor and most of the furniture was covered with underclothing and silk dresses, the latter no doubt the record of Miss Casement's earlier indecisions. The dressing-table was stacked with creams, powders, rouges, lipsticks, tonics, fresheners, varnishes, removers, cleaners and other kinds of cosmetics. (*FFE*, 196)

There is an important distinction between Eliot's and Murdoch's descriptions of women, however; Eliot does not invite sympathy for the women, whereas Murdoch emphasizes the pathetic and sympathetic traits of Annette, Rosa, Miss Casement, Dora Greenfield, Julian, and others. Eliot's women are indifferent by nature, but Murdoch's women have been forced to adopt indifference in order to survive.

"What the Thunder Said" has suggested to Cleanth Brooks a spiritual solution to modern problems. The opening description of Gethsemane and the speaking thunder's "Give, Sympathize, Control" suggest a moral solution to *The Waste Land's* dilemma. Although Murdoch does not wholly accept this solution, she does indicate that the major problem with human relationships results from failure to give, sympathize, and control. Such power-oriented figures as Julius in *A Fairly Honourable Defeat*, Mischa in *The Flight from the Enchanter*, Paul Greenfield in *The Bell*, and Carel Fisher in *The Time of the Angels* are "villains" to the extent that they will not give or sympathize, while Julian in *The Black Prince*, Hilary in *A Word Child*, and Morgan in *A Fairly Honourable Defeat* notably lack control. Although Murdoch seems to agree that the ability to give, sympathize, and control is essential if modern man is to overcome the Waste Land in which he lives, the two writers view these traits from different perspectives.

In *Under the Net* (1954), the narrator offers as a worthy purpose "To save my soul," but Dave responds, "Precisely it is not to think of your soul, but to think of other people."[12] This is the major difference between Eliot's vision and Murdoch's, the poet emphasizing personal belief and the novelist expressing the importance of human relationships. However, insensitive and unsympathetic characters in Murdoch's novels frequently repudiate faith. In *A Severed Head* the narrator, Martin, comments, "It may be relevant here to add that I hold no religious beliefs whatever. Roughly, I cannot imagine any omnipotent sentient being sufficiently cruel to create the world we inhabit" (*SH*, 14). The perversion of morality becomes evident when Julius says to Rupert, in *A Fairly Honourable Defeat*,

"In fact experience entirely contradicts this assumption. Good is dull. What novelist ever succeeded in making a good man interesting? It is characteristic of this planet that the path of virtue is so unutterably depressing that it can be guaranteed to break the spirit and quench the vision of anybody who consistently attempts to tread it. Evil, on the contrary, is exciting and fascinating and alive. It is also very much more mysterious than good. Good can be seen through. Evil is opaque."[13]

As a result of this attitude, Julius becomes responsible for the death of Rupert and for the misery of at least four other people as well. The absence of hope in the modern world, which Eliot emphasized as a denial of religion, also is important in Murdoch's world. When Isabel tries to convince the narrator of *The Italian Girl* to stay, she indicates that she has awaited a secular savior:

> "We all need you. Who else could I have talked to like this? I was so much looking forward to your coming. You are the only person who can heal us."
> "I am no healer," I said. I could not add: I cannot heal you. Perhaps no one can. (*IG*, 36)

Isabel's desire for a healer, and the narrator's awareness that in her present condition no one can help her, may imply that lack of faith prevents Isabel from coping with her problems.

Throughout her work, Murdoch echoes images taken from the fifth section of *The Waste Land*. Thunder cracks at appropriate moments, as when Morgan feels remorse for having aborted her child. The Unreal City of Eliot's fifth section concludes:

> What is the city over the mountains
> Cracks and reforms and bursts in the violet air
> Falling towers
> Jerusalem Athens Alexandria
> Vienna London
> Unreal (ll. 372–77)

One passage in *The Black Prince* suggests the mystery of the city, "violet" air, and an equation of Jerusalem and London:

> The evening had darkened to an intense blue, but it was not yet night. The forms of London, some already chequered with yellow light, glided onward through a dim shimmering corpuscular haze. The Albert Hall, the Science Museums, Centre Point, the Tower of London, St. Paul's Cathedral, the Festive Hall, the Houses of Parliament, the Albert Memorial. The precious and beloved skyline of my own Jerusalem processed incessantly behind that dear mysterious head. Only the royal parks were already places of darkness, growing inkily purple with nighttime and its silence. (*BP*, 202)

Such similarities in imagery aside, however, most of what Murdoch draws from "What the Thunder Said" concerns the philosophy of give, sympathize, and control, which she then expresses in her own terms.

Eliot has not been a major influence on the philosophy of Iris Murdoch's novels despite the presence of episodes, motifs, and images from *The Waste Land*. Murdoch deplores Eliot's rejection of liberalism and does not accept any overtly Christian solution to the problems of the modern world. She rejects Eliot's implicit misogyny, creating instead sympathetic counterparts for Eliot's memorable women, and she has profited from a judicious use of Eliot's imagery and characters. While *The Waste Land* no longer seems to provide novelists with apt statements of contemporary problems, it still contributes powerful descriptions of human beings under emotional stress.

10
ANTHONY BURGESS
One Must Be So Careful These Days

Anthony Burgess's original interest in *The Waste Land* stems from the impulse that has inspired thousands of adolescents to race to the library for furtive readings of *Lady Chatterley's Lover, Tropic of Cancer,* and *Catcher in the Rye.* When Burgess was fifteen, after reading a column by James Douglas, editor of the *Sunday Express,* warning youth against reading *The Waste Land,* Burgess borrowed the book from the public library. "By the time I got to Manchester University, I understood *The Waste Land* pretty well. Without boasting, I can say that I knew the poem better than any of my English lecturers: they did not have it by heart, and I did."[1] Responding to the question of Eliot's influence on the prose of his generation, Burgess wrote that *The Waste Land* has had an immense influence on his generation, that echoes of the poem occur frequently because the poem is almost universally known, and that many who quote Eliot's lines apply them inappropriately.[2] Burgess, however, limits his use of Eliot's poem to the purpose of his novels. Burgess notes that

> It was, I discovered myself when I first began to write seriously, hard to get the Eliotian voices out of my ears and my prose. It was so delightful to conjoin mock-pomposity with deliberate vulgarity, to throw in recondite literary allusions for ironic effects, to make statements conveying an authority somehow both professorial and parsonic, and yet, at the same time, tinged with self-mockery.[3]

Independent of Eliot's poem's content, "the quality of his phrase-making is so insidious that it cannot easily be rejected."[4] In *Clockwork*

Orange (1962), which depicts a futuristic Waste Land peopled by spiritually empty men, and in *Enderby's End* (1975), which places the poet in the midst of a modern Waste Land, Burgess does not quote Eliot's poem despite the appropriate atmosphere of each novel. In *Enderby's End*, Burgess does use part of the last line of Eliot's "The Hollow Men": "Noise of impending victory. Not with a bang but."[5] The one allusion, however, is sufficient—Burgess does not indulge in overkill. Similarly *MF* (1971) includes a reference pertinent to *The Waste Land's* philosophy, "a question relevant to the sick times and leprous state we live in,"[6] but there are no verbal echoes of Eliot's poem in the novel. Although Burgess occasionally sprinkles his novels with pointed references to modern writers, these references add a playful touch to the novels and rarely include direct quotation. When direct quotations do appear, they reflect a major motif of the novel. Burgess is not only a creator of imaginative fiction but also a scholar and critic, and as such he is familiar with *The Waste Land* interpretations developed by Edmund Wilson, I. A. Richards, F. R. Leavis, F. O. Matthiessen, and Cleanth Brooks. When Burgess alludes to *The Waste Land*, he is very careful to subordinate echoes to a specific function in his novels.

In some novels, Burgess often refers directly to T. S. Eliot and to *The Waste Land* to emphasize the intellectual and literary awareness of selected characters. In *A Vision of Battlements* (written in 1949), the atmosphere and structure of the novel parody Vergil's *Aeneid,* with easily recognizable correspondences. Ennis (Aeneas), for example, suffers a "shipwreck" by falling from a boat, accidentally throws Turner (Turnus) from the Rock of Gibraltar, and descends into "Hell," a town outside the British zone. Ennis, responsible for the "cultural" activities of the soldiers, constantly thinks in terms of Eliot's *The Waste Land*. In the middle of an attempted seduction, Ennis "was nerveless, beyond such control. Then spoke the thunder. The awful daring of a moment's surrender and all the rest of it. Now, this afternoon, an age of prudence faced him, a desert."[7] This quotes the final section of *The Waste Land*:

Then spoke the thunder
. . . .
My friend, blood shaking my heart
The awful daring of a moment's surrender
Which an age of prudence can never retract (ll. 400, 403–5)

When Ennis surveys a bookshelf he notes only a "few new volumes of interest—*Animal Farm, Four Quartets, The Unquiet Grave, Brideshead Re-*

visited—" (*VB*, 140), and to Ennis, the drunken Turner resembles "a broken Colossus," possibly an echo of Eliot's "a broken Coriolanus" (l. 417). Near the end of the novel, Mrs. Carraway tells Ennis's fortune. Ennis recalls Madame Sosostris: "The Tarot, to Ennis, had so far merely been a literary reference. 'The wisest woman in Europe,' he now quoted, 'with a wicked pack of cards'" (*VB*, 213). Draughts enter the room as the wind entered the chapel perilous (l. 388), the thunder rolls, and Ennis recognizes cards mentioned in Eliot's poem, including the Hanged Man. While parts of the plot, particularly Ennis's seductions, resemble episodes of Eliot's poem, the allusions reflect Ennis's recognition of the parallels rather than the reader's recognition.

Similarly Howarth, in *The Worm and the Ring* (1961), finds Eliot's *The Waste Land* relevant to the events of his own life. When his wife declares that she will not even discuss having more children, she says, "'I don't want another baby. I nearly died of Peter.' Howarth grinned at that: Veronica had never read Mr Eliot."[8] Howarth thinks of Eliot's line "(She's had five already, and nearly died of young George.)" (l. 160). In contrast, Turton recalls having acted in *Murder in the Cathedral*, but his memories are more of his problems acting than of the lines of the play. Howarth later reflects on Amfortas (from *Parsifal*, to which *The Waste Land* alludes), and reveals in his observations an awareness of the sterility and barrenness which Eliot stressed in his poem.

Enderby, of *Inside Mr Enderby* (1963), is a poet, and as such is more than familiar with Eliot's poem. When he finds he must travel to London, "Along with other memories that made him wince (including one excruciating one of a ten-shilling note in the Café Royal) came gobbets from *Oliver Twist*, *The Waste Land*, and *Nineteen Eighty-Four*."[9] Most of Enderby's thoughts, however, are of Eliot as a public poet. "Gloomily, Enderby reflected that most modern poets were not merely sufficiently clean but positively natty. T. S. Eliot, with his Lloyd's Bank nonsense, had started all that, a real treason of clerks" (*IME*, 39). After dressing for his journey, Enderby views himself in a mirror: "Urban, respectable, scholarly—a poet-banker, a poet-publisher" (*IME*, 47), recognizing two aspects of Eliot's career. As Rawcliffe leaves, "Enderby sadly watched him join a group of important poets who had not been above cynically taking a free meal—P. S. ffolliott, Peter Pitts, Albert Death-Stabbes, Rupert Tombs, or some such names" (*IME*, 64). Reading one of his earlier verses, Enderby encounters a possible echo of Eliot's "violet hour" motif—"When the violet air blooms about him" (*IME*, 115)—and Vesta asks Enderby, in protest, "But there's no need to regale us with poetic drama in the style of early Mr Eliot, is there?" (*IME*, 137). Even the criticism directed against Enderby suggests Eliot.

Enderby hears that there is "Too much meaning in your poetry, Enderby. Always has been" (*IME*, 149). As in other overt uses of Eliot and *The Waste Land*, these distinguish Enderby's character rather than provide atmosphere for the novel.

More often, however, Burgess uses Eliot's poem to establish a dominant motif. *The Malayan Trilogy*, consisting of *Time for a Tiger* (1956), *The Enemy in the Blanket* (1958), and *Beds in the East* (1959), uses *The Waste Land* to emphasize a major theme. In the first novel Nabby Adams, an alcoholic policeman stationed in Malaya, befriends Victor and Fenella Crabbe. Crabbe, a schoolmaster, had nearly drowned when his car plunged into water. He escaped but his first wife did not, and his recurrent nightmares of drowning are important to all three novels. When Fenella discovers that Crabbe has been unfaithful to her, she tests his love by pretending to drown. After Crabbe has proven incapable of swimming out to "rescue" her, she leaves him. In the third novel, after an encounter with a man who knew his first wife, Crabbe himself drowns. Throughout the trilogy numerous references to *The Waste Land* occur, firmly establishing the death by water motif that is introduced early in *Time for a Tiger*:

> Victor Crabbe woke up sweating. He had been dreaming about his first wife whom, eight years previously, he had killed. At the inquest he had been exonerated from all blame and the coroner had condoled with him all too eloquently and publicly. The car had skidded on the January road, had become a mad thing, resisting all control, had crashed through the weak bridge-fence and fallen—his stomach fell now, as his sleeping body had fallen time and time again in the nightmare reliving of the night-mare—fallen, it seemed endlessly, till it shattered the ice and the icy water beneath, and sank with loud heavy bubbles. His lungs bursting, he had felt the still body in the passenger-seat, had torn desperately at the driver's door, and risen, suffocating, through what seemed fathom after fathom of icy bubbling lead. It was a long time ago. He had been exonerated from all blame but he knew he was guilty.[10]

The dream recurs once again in the novel, still so disturbing to Crabbe that he fears his dream as much as he fears the watery death itself. Crabbe follows Eliot's Madame Sosostris's advice to "Fear death by water" to the letter.

Yet the directness of the connection between Crabbe's fear and Eliot's poem does not become apparent until halfway through this novel. Burgess refers to several modern writers when Crabbe surveys his library, but Eliot does not appear until Fenella, a poetess on the fringe of literature, opens a book to read "the whole of Mr Eliot's *The Waste*

Land" to Alladad Khan and Nabby Adams. Adams pointedly comments
on "The Man With Three Staves," the Three of Wands in the traditional Tarot, focusing the reader's attention on the Madame Sosostris
episode which introduces the Drowned Phoenician Sailor and the
warning "Fear death by water":

> "He's got that wrong about the pack of cards, Mrs Crabbe. There isn't
> no card called The Man With Three Staves. That card what he means is
> just an ordinary three, like as it may be the three of clubs."
>   And when they came to the dark thunder-speaking finale of the poem,
> Alladad Khan had nodded gravely.
>   "Datta. Dayadhvam. Damyata.
>   Shantih. Shantih. Shantih."
>   "He says he understands that bit, Mrs Crabbe. He says that's what the
> thunder says." (*Time*, 133)

(In Burgess's *Earthly Powers* (1980), the protagonist Kenneth Toomey,
a well-known novelist, contemptuously cites Eliot's "misuse" of the
Tarot, attributing the presence of "The Man With Three Staves" to
Eliot's ignorance.)

   After *The Waste Land* has appeared, Burgess shows that the characters are in a Waste Land without realizing it. Reflecting on the quality
of his own life ("Always owing, often drunk, sometimes incapable. . . .
What had he achieved?"), Nabby concludes, "There was nothing to
show, nothing. Only moral debts and debts of money, only imagined
miles of empties and cigarette-ends" (*Time*, 177). *The Waste Land* asserts
the superiority of death to life throughout its first four sections. Winter
is preferable to "cruellest" April, the buried corpse must not rise, and
Phlebas reaches peace in death. Nabby's situation is similar: "Nabby
Adams heard the *bilal* calling over the dark, saying that there was no
God but Allah. Another day was starting for the faithful. But for the
faithless, it was better that the night should prolong itself, even into
the sunlight of Sunday morning" (*Time*, 177). At the end of *Time for a
Tiger*, as Fenella sobs with misery at the quality of her life in Malaya,
the comfort Crabbe can offer her is bleak: "Fenella sobbed. Crabbe took
her in his arms and comforted her. Then midnight sounded from the
half-drowned town clock. Above the broken meats, the drained bottles, the insect noises, the gunfire, the snores and the retchings he
wished her a merry Christmas" (*Time*, 203). By the end of the novel,
The Waste Land contributions have emphasized the spiritual emptiness
of the major characters and Crabbe's fear of drowning.

   In *The Enemy in the Blanket*, the second novel in the trilogy, the (fear)
death by water motif that echoed *The Waste Land* in the previous novel

not only continues but becomes an essential plot element: Crabbe's fear of drowning leads directly to Fenella's leaving him. Crabbe has a recurrence of the drowning nightmare that had haunted him in *Time for a Tiger*, and the dream leaves him convinced that Fenella has somehow let him down and that the marital relationship can become another form of drowning: "he shuddered at the thought of water closing over his head again, of his being enclosed by the element of another woman" (*Enemy*, 300). Crabbe nevertheless tells Fenella that he will do anything for her, but when she asks him to swim with her, he refuses. Deciding to test his love for her, Fenella goes in alone and pretends to drown. When Crabbe hears her cry for help, he tries to enter the water to save her, but his fear is too great and he returns, panic-stricken, "frantically trying not to hear the thin distant voice."

> "All right, darling." Fenella was beside him, comforting him with her wet body. "Perhaps that wasn't fair, really. But I just had to know." (*Enemy*, 372–73)

Crabbe's protest that indeed this was not fair is to no avail. He has failed the test, and Fenella leaves him.

The death by water theme is not the only evocation of *The Waste Land* in *Enemy in the Blanket*. There is, for example, at least one unmistakable allusion to "What the Thunder Said" in a description of Hardman, an Englishman who in a frenzy "danced up and down, sweating violently, incoherent, croaking obscenities, ending with a refrain like the end of an Upanishad. 'Bitch! Bitch! Bitch!'" (*Enemy*, 346). But this is an isolated instance; a far more recurrent, and important, echo of *The Waste Land* can be seen in the spiritual emptiness of the novel's characters and the world they inhabit. There is religion, but no belief, and in such a world only hypocrites can profess faith. Hardman, for example, is a convert to Islam who eats pork in private, fully aware of how this reflects on his spiritual condition. And in his disregard of the doctrines of his adopted religion Hardman is no worse than those around him who were born to the faith:

> They themselves were too fond of the bottle to be good Muslims; they even kissed women and ate doubtful meat. They did not really know what they wanted. The middle-class of Kenching who carried Muslim names and were not too dark, not too light, were unified by the most tenuous of bonds. One of these bonds was 'Che Guru Abdul Kadir, the hairy-legged goat who carried their sins on his back, who defined a vague smoky image of the true Malay (who did not exist), the true Islam (not truly desirable) in terms of what these things were not. (*Enemy*, 252)

(The parenthetical qualifiers of the last two lines echo Forster's description of Islam in India). A typically flippant attitude appears in a comic passage reminiscent of Waugh:

> "Where is your bangle?" asked Mohinder Singh. "You are not wearing the bangle on your wrist. A Sikh should not be without his bangle."
> "I found a way of using it to open beer bottles, brother. By ill luck it broke. But I shall get another one." (*Enemy*, 285)

The Hanged Man, in the sense that he provides focus for spiritual hope and awareness, is as absent in Burgess's Malaya as he is in Madame Sosostris's fortune-telling.

In *Beds in the East*, Burgess continues the motifs of the first two novels of the trilogy, focusing particularly on the absence of values and the lack of human warmth that are prevalent in *The Waste Land*. Among the characters who most clearly evidence these traits are Robert Loo, the young musical student whose inability to understand affection disturbs Crabbe, and Syed Hassan, a juvenile delinquent who despises his father for having attacked an enemy with his fists to avenge an insult. Syed's complaint is that the method was not contemporary, but it also appears that direct physical contact, albeit with fists and feet, is too personal for him:

> His dad shouldn't have done it. It was old-fashioned, that business of punching and kicking, it was Wild West. And his dad was an old man, too. It was a bit undignified. Fish-hooks, knives, razors, bicycle-chains— that was different, that was modern. He felt ashamed of his dad and wanted to change the subject. (*Beds*, 443)

The force of his father's anger is beyond Syed's comprehension. Later when Syed is caught in a clumsy burglary attempt, he shows himself devoid of loyalty, too: "Syed had betrayed his three friends very readily, arguing that, as the four shared responsibility for the crime, so they must equally share the quantum of the punishment. The English had taught him arithmetic but no ethics" (*Beds*, 500). Crabbe, who has tried to extend English values to Malaya, is less important to the Malayans than Tommy Jones, purveyor of alcohol. Jones tells Crabbe,

> "You'd hardly believe the things they put up with back in England. I've not been back for thirty years. And I'm buggered if I'm going back. But," he said in triumph, "you've got to, haven't you? They're kicking you lot out. But not old Tommy. Beer's much too important." (*Beds*, 524)

The response of the Chinese to the garish juke box which Robert Loo's father has installed recalls *The Waste Land*'s inhabitants' confusion of the "Shakespeherian Rag" with culture: "Ten-cent pieces shone everywhere in eager waiting fingers. What was rice, what was coffee compared to the solace of art?" (*Beds*, 464). Superstition is as prevalent among the expatriate British as among the regular clients of Madame Sosostris. Moneypenny, who blames the scorpion's maiming of Crabbe's foot on Crabbe's having laughed at a butterfly, warns Crabbe, "if we get any thunder today, for God's own sweet sake don't choose that time to run a comb through your hair" (*Beds*, 544).

The reactions to Crabbe's death similarly reveal the lack of humanity in the novel's characters. Everyone thinks of Crabbe only in terms of opportunity gained or lost.

> Anyway, there was little trouble about writing Crabbe off. Crabbe was dead. His death, though little mourned, was resented by a few. Rosemary felt that he might have, sooner or later, introduced her to somebody eligible, or, perhaps in an ultimate weariness matching hers, have been tossed legitimately to her breast. Robert Loo felt, in a way, let down, for Crabbe had promised much and fulfilled little. And Syet Omar remembered something about the possibility of a situation in the Education Department, now not likely to be realized. The white man lies, or dies, or goes away, or forgets. Moreover, money cannot be borrowed from a dead man. Crabbe's cook-boy had some weeks of unemployment, which was rather a nuisance. Lim Cheng Po said an Anglican prayer or two, not too perfunctorily. The Malay whom Crabbe had been training to take over his job now took over his job with trumpets and cocktails, finding it convenient to blame missing letters and mislaid files on a defunct infidel. (*Beds*, 605–06)

The death by water motif, however, is more central to the plot of this novel than are the *Waste Land*-like aspects of atmosphere and characterization. Crabbe accidentally discovers a poem by Fenella which includes "a proleptic Eliotian image of an aged eagle with tiring wings demanding to be released from the dressing mirror" (*Beds*, 521). The reference recalls the rape of Philomel by Tereus, depicted in the carved mirror frame of the dressing table in "A Game of Chess." (Crabbe cannot understand why Fenella, aged twenty-eight or twenty-nine, would write a poem called "Lines for Middle Age," as others have wondered why Eliot chose to write "Gerontion" at age thirty-two.) Shortly thereafter, Crabbe, filled with foreboding at the prospect of a trip to the Durian Estate, realizes that "the feeling of apprehension had, for some reason, come over him on reading Fenella's poem" (*Beds*,

525). The combination of Crabbe's fear and Fenella's Eliotian imagery, borrowed from *The Waste Land*, functions to reintroduce the death by water motif. Crabbe considers his own death unlikely, however, dismissing the possibility as "absurd" (*Beds*, 550). The foot injury he suffers from the scorpion bite leads him to compare himself with Oedipus Rex, but he quickly reminds himself that he has not committed Oedipus's sins: "I am now Club-Foot the Tyrant. . . . But I didn't kill my father and I didn't marry my mother" (*Beds*, 578). Crabbe then discovers that his first wife had planned to leave him for a man named Costard, as he learns from Costard himself in an angry encounter. Costard accuses him of wanting to be rid of his wife and letting her drown. Crabbe defends himself by claiming "It was an accident," and complains "Christ, I've suffered enough" (*Beds*, 590). His suffering is now nearly over, however; after he leaves Costard he unexpectedly finds the forgetful slumber of Phlebas the Phoenician. Watching from the shore, Vythilingam, a veterinarian,

> saw Crabbe try to board the launch. He put his foot clumsily on the gunwhale. The foot seemed to crumple underneath him. Still carrying his stick and his bag, he faltered in the air for an instant and fell. Vythilingam saw water, green and white, shoot up long fingers of protest as the weight crashed the surface. He heard faint human noises, and then animal noises, and, hearing the animal noises, he rose to his feet in compassion. He stood undecided. And then, as noise subsided and the river settled and the launch moved in again, he sat down on the grass once more. Human lives were not his professional concern. Humanity? Yes, humanity, but humanity was altogether a different matter. He sat for a time thinking about humanity, seeing the great abstractions move and wave in the fronds of the jungle over the river. (*Beds*, 593–94)

As Raj has predicted, Crabbe will remain upriver (as Phlebas remained at the bottom of the sea): "Bodies, it was well-known, were near-irrecoverable in that river of deep-set weeds. Nobody felt inclined to give orders to drag: let the river keep them" (*Beds*, 602).

Throughout *The Malayan Trilogy* Burgess alludes to *The Waste Land* to establish a death by water motif. Acknowledging Eliot's influence in *Time for a Tiger*, Burgess offered two explanations. First, he wanted to establish a death by water motif through the entire trilogy and, second, he was translating *The Waste Land* into Malay at the time he worked on *Time for a Tiger*.[11] His introduction of Eliot into his trilogy is gradual. In *Time for a Tiger*, the presence of *The Waste Land* is minimal, restricted to the death by water motif, Fenella's reading of the poem, and the demonstration that Fenella, Crabbe, and Adams are in the Waste Land.

The Enemy in the Blanket introduces Eliotian episodes while continuing themes established in the first novel, and *Beds in the East* extends the modern departure from values before presenting Crabbe's death by water. Excessive borrowing from *The Waste Land* would have obscured the relevance of the death by water motif. However, the pointedness of allusion to the poem in *Time for a Tiger* makes further development of *The Waste Land*'s theme, atmosphere, and characters both appropriate and plausible.

Devil of a State (1961) satirizes the developing nation of Dunia's pretense to civilization and the British pretense to civilize in the manner of Evelyn Waugh's *Black Mischief*. In the novel Burgess refers to other works which have criticized British imperialism. Carruthers Chung invites Lydgate to a "blidge party" which has no more to do with cards than Turton's "bridge" party in *A Passage to India*. Burgess refers directly to *John Bull's Other Island* and has Covendry tell Brethren, " 'You and your hearing voices. . . . Bad as bloody Joan of Arc.' It was considered appropriate for a State Officer to lard his talk with literary allusions."[12] Lydgate comments that "you can't live very long in a place like Africa without coming to the conclusion that sin really exists" (*Devil*, 43), echoing Greene's Scobie in *The Heart of the Matter* (appropriately, since the novel is dedicated to Greene). "African morning. A terrible beauty is born" (*Devil*, 193) quotes Yeats's "Easter, 1916." Of those who have written about British rule, however, Waugh has inspired the largest number of absurdities in Burgess's novel. The unit of currency in Dunia is "ONE BUCK." When the natives shrink a head, they include the victim's horn-rimmed glasses and "put Brylcreem on his hair" (*Devil*, 106). Covendry mentions that he prefers J. B. Priestley and Hugh Walpole (antagonists, respectively, of Graham Greene and Somerset Maugham), but when Lydia asks Convendry about Evelyn Waugh, he replies, "I never really cared for women writers much" (*Devil*, 201). Burgess also mentions D. H. Lawrence's *Kangaroo*, Joyce's Stephen Dedalus, and *The Jew of Malta* (from which Eliot drew the epigraph for "Portrait of a Lady"). While the writers Burgess has referred to either criticized the British directly or painted a dismal picture of contemporary life, none contributed to *Devil of a State* as much as Eliot. The dominant motif of the novel, developed from *The Waste Land*, is the rain that will not come to the blighted land. Several images from "What the Thunder Said" reinforce this motif.

At the beginning of the novel, the search for a key is of paramount importance. Lydgate cannot find a key for his new quarters and shouts "The key! The key! Somebody *must* have the key!" (*Devil*, 3). After spending the day tracing the stewardship of the missing key, Lydgate learns "The key not fit. No need for key. The door open all the time" (*Devil*, 13), recalling the *Dayadhvam* section of "What the Thunder Said":

> I have heard the key
> Turn in the door once and turn once only
> We think of the key, each in his prison
> Thinking of the key, each confirms a prison (ll. 412–15)

Late in the novel, Paolo Tasca locks himself in the minaret and the officials look for a key to allow them to force Paolo out. "Bishopspawn thought: 'The key. Somebody must have the key.' But that small sun of hope went in; this was Dunia: there would be no key" (*Devil*, 246). When the storm breaks at the end of the novel,

> the Caliph asked for the key to the massy doors of the Mosque.
>   "The key!"
>   "Who has the key?"
>   "The key, the key!"
>   "Does nobody know where the key is?"
>   "Somebody *must* have the key!"
>   "The key, the key, the key!" (*Devil*, 281)

The relation of the key to Eliot's Fisher King, the rain, and what the thunder said is explicit in the novel. Even before Lydgate has finished his quest for the key to his quarters, the Fisher King appears in a descriptive passage: Lydgate "stretched himself as it were in pain, like a dusky Fisher King" (*Devil*, 11). Hope for rain is constant, but when water comes Lydgate meets disappointment: even during a rainstorm Lydgate's shower will not work, and he must bathe himself by standing under a leak in his roof. Expressions of hope for rain echo Eliot's "Then a damp gust / Bringing rain" (ll. 394–95).

> But stay. Is it hope that cooleth? Is it sweet water coming to refresh your soul? For a wind shaketh the louvers and the trees are writhing in that wind. The parched grass looks up to be fed. Is it rain? Is it indeed rain, long looked-for? Shall the dried-up streams sing again and ride in high pride of water? It looks like it. How cool the air as dawn approaches. With a glory as of thunder and a loud, proud laughing, with a hiss and a roar, here is the rain. (*Devil*, 69)

The relief is temporary, however. Burgess echoes Eliot's "water-dripping song" shortly after Lydgate's hope seems fulfilled:

He dreams that he is in hell and that Lazarus (though he is indeed no Dives) comes at regular intervals and drops water in his open mouth. He wakes to find the roof leaking. The cigarettes on his side-table are soaked. He has no others. Water is dripping on him with the regularity of a Roman water-clock that thinks the Empire will last for ever. God curse them all. (*Devil*, 70)

However, "In the State Council Chamber it was as if there were no rain" (*Devil*, 73).

Before the rain comes, however, the thunder speaks. In Eliot's poem the thunder says "Give, Sympathize, Control" in a foreign tongue. In the novel, Paolo, a marble cutter, speaks in thundering Italian from the minaret: "He switched the microphone on, and his sobs began to pump themselves, sobs of a giant, from loudspeakers all round the town. God was crying. Then he sang, for a bar or two, 'Stardust' in Italian, changing 'stardust' to 'marble-dust'" (*Devil*, 226). The voice of the thunder becomes hostile as Paolo curses his father. Carruthers Chung links the acts of men with the lack of rain: "I wonder if it will lain. . . . We play for lain but lain does not come. Our sin must be velly gleat" (*Devil*, 251–52). When the rain finally does arrive in the last paragraph of the novel, it comes not as a gift of relief but as an expression of profound disgust with man: "The rain cracked, hurled and kettle-drummed, vomited like a whole sick heaven over the Mosque and the whole black kingdom, heedless of human time or of any time but its own" (*Devil*, 282).

The key, the Fisher King, the speaking thunder, the water-dripping song, and the withheld rain recall the fifth section of *The Waste Land*. These echoes occur frequently and establish the motif clearly for the reader. Other echoes of the fifth section appear in the novel to reinforce the dominant motif, although they are less frequent. The contrast between the first four sections of *The Waste Land*, which present the lack of spiritual values in modern life, and the fifth section, which for Brooks implies that man is in a Waste Land because he has denied the hope of resurrection, also appears in the novel. The death-wish Paolo overhears from Lydgate echoes the lack of hope expressed in the first lines of *The Waste Land*: "'God,' went the words from next door. 'God, let me sleep. Let me sleep and let me not wake up again. Make it easy. Make it as easy as that'" (*Devil*, 66). Two pages later a stylized address to Lydgate provides an explanation for his despair: "Thou has a sense of guilt, meseemeth, which thy neighbour lacketh. Thy neighbour is saved. He hath thrown his guilt on to the shoulders of One who will bear the guilt of all mankind, and that gladly" (*Devil*, 68). Tomlin, the

UN Adviser, reinforces this contrast in his awkward attempt to explain Christianity to the Caliph:

> "If Christians want to be immoral that is entirely their own affair. I mean, it's something they have to sort out with their own consciences. Nobody can stop a Christian committing adultery or getting drunk. Unless, of course, he interferes with law and order when he does these things." (*Devil*, 78)

The modern spirit, barren in its rejection of Christianity's promised hope, is the subject of the opening lines of "What the Thunder Said":

> He who was living is now dead
> We who were living are now dying
> With a little patience (ll. 328–30)

The corruption of religion and the modern spiritual squalor appear in a poem, written by "Some disaffected person . . . in heroic couplets," which echoes Pope's style and Eliot's lines:

> "Dunia, the little world of the misled,
> A deadly living for the living dead.
> All mortal sins are venal here; the least
> Of public works officials is a priest
> Ordained by the traditions of his tribe
> For one sole rite—the blessing of the bribe." (*Devil*, 251)

And the last line of Eliot's poem, "Shantih shantih shantih," has its parodic equivalent in Burgess's Upanishad ending of a chapter: "Shut up, shut up, shut up" (*Devil*, 189).

Yet only one *Waste Land* episode from the first four sections of the poem appears in the novel, that of Tiresias's witnessing the typist and the young man carbuncular. Eileen Forbes, who sells herself not for money but because she enjoys meeting different people, becomes drunk and disappears into a shed with Paolo. Forbes, her Australian husband, enlists the aid of Lydgate to look for her. Burgess emphasizes the association of this episode with the liaison of the typist and the young man carbuncular by introducing Tiresias. Addressing Paolo, the narrator of the novel asks,

> But, stay, who are these? One man is from the Antipodes but, contrary to the superstition of the vulgar, he is like other men. His companion is the eternal wanderer; he acknowledgeth neither kin nor birthplace. He

approacheth eld, he hath experience. . . . With somewhat of envy he heareth, but with somewhat more of loathing. (*Devil*, 136–37)

The attitudes of this "eternal wanderer," envy and loathing, resemble those of Tiresias, who "Perceived the scene and foretold the rest" (l. 229). Lydgate, the Tiresias figure in this passage, later reflects on the liaison of Paolo and Forbes's wife in an attitude similar to Tiresias's: "Disgusting, ridiculous, when other people did it" (*Devil*, 156). Burgess lays the groundwork for making this association by alluding to *The Waste Land* immediately before this episode: "Eileen was not by the dust-bins, not by the slag-heap, not by the abandoned tractor on the waste land, not in the thicket of scrub among the tin-cans" (*Devil*, 134). When the reader subsequently encounters the description of the eternal wanderer, he is more likely to think of Tiresias because the reference to Waste Land has prepared him for it.

In *Devil of a State*, Burgess introduces the major elements of "What the Thunder Said" so that the climax of the novel, with the heavens vomiting on the earth, parodies *The Waste Land*. Except for the Tiresias episode, his borrowings from Eliot serve to satirize the characters in the novel. Eliot's poem provides a parallel that points to the relationship between the blight on the human spirit and the blight on Dunia, and Burgess therefore focuses on the one section of Eliot's poem which makes that relationship explicit (according to Cleanth Brooks's interpretation). Use of Eliot's imagery from the first four sections of *The Waste Land* is not developed fully, allowing the thunder motif to remain dominant.

The Wanting Seed (1962), a "Malthusian comedy," refers directly to many contemporary works, including Bernard Shaw's *St. Joan* and Graham Greene's *The Power and the Glory*. Several authors' names appear, including Auden, Isherwood, Maugham, Baudelaire, Shakespeare, and Eliot. While *The Wanting Seed* is part of the tradition of dystopian novels, it owes part of its central theme to *The Waste Land*, for Burgess again directly relates a blight on the land to a blight on the human spirit. The novel presents a world of overpopulation which encourages birth control, sterility, homosexuality, and wars which systematically slaughter every soldier. Man has changed somewhat—teeth are "atavistic," God has given way to Livedog, and a whiskey priest in the tradition of Greene's tells Tristram Foxe "I was a priest. Do you know what that is?"[13] Tristram, a history teacher, and his wife Beatrice-Joanna, an *Urmutter*, are unhappy in this sterile world: Tristram resents the preference homosexuals receive over "heteros" like himself, and Beatrice-Joanna cannot stifle her urge to reproduce despite the strict penalties for giving "unlicensed" birth. Derek Foxe, Tristram's brother and Beatrice-Joanna's lover, highly placed in the Population Police because he affects homosexuality, impregnates Beatrice-Joanna when she neglects to take contraceptives after her first child has died of meningitis. Beatrice-Joanna flees to safety and gives birth to twins, whom she names Derek and Tristram, after their biological and legal fathers. The elder Tristram, arrested by mistake and allowed to remain in prison by his brother, escapes and seeks Beatrice. In the course of his wanderings, Tristram observes a complete reversal from worship of sterility to striving for fertility.

The novel opens with a Burial of the Dead. Beatrice-Joanna's son's body receives "treatment" at the Phosphorus Reclamation Department, and an attendant informs her that her son will return to her, not because of resurrection but because his phosphorus pentoxide will return to the soil. Early in the novel a homosexual recites a popular ballad that includes, in four lines, the major themes of Eliot's "The Burial of the Dead" (as well as an allusion to Greene's *The Third Man*):

"My dead tree. Give me back my dead dead tree.
Rain, rain, go away. Let the earth be still
Dry. Kick the gods back into the cakey earth,
Making a hole for that purpose, with a drill." (*WS*, 33)

The verse, expressing the desire of the prominent members of society, recalls Eliot's characters' resentment of life-giving April and their desire that the corpse buried in the garden remain undisturbed. Soon after, the members of Burgess's futuristic world realize that the land labors under a curse. The *Daily Newsdisc* announces an "inexplicable failure to breed" (*WS*, 47), Tristram's sister Emma writes from China that the rice crop has failed, and Tristram's brother George reports a similar occurrence in Ohio. The failure of crops becomes drastic, "a blight never known before" (*WS*, 87). Ultimately the Prime Minister realizes the seriousness of the situation, but he is at a loss. Wahab, the Prime Minister's assistant, approaches a solution when he recalls the practice of sacrificing to a deity, but the Prime Minister dismisses the "facetious" notion on the grounds that there is no one to accept the sacrifice.

Pockets of resistance endure in the provinces, however. Although Beatrice-Joanna's sister Mavis remains noncommittal, Mavis's husband Shonny believes in God. When Beatrice-Joanna flees to them after discovering that she is pregnant, Shonny tells her that she can give birth in one of the outbuildings: "A greater mother than you gave birth in a——" (*WS*, 84). Mavis stops "that sentimentality" short, but when

Shonny continues with his analysis of the world's blight, he states the true source of the famine: "There's a curse settling on us, God forgive us all, with our blaspheming against life and love" (WS, 84). Ambrose, an unfrocked priest, informs Tristram that fear has led to a return to the catacombs, and then equates fertility with God: "All dirty words are fundamentally religious. They are all concerned with fertility and the processes of fertility and the organs of fertility. God, we are taught, is love" (WS, 95). Finally the Governor reads an apostrophe, directed not at God but at whatever intelligent force is ravaging the planet. Although it falls somewhat short of being a true prayer, it does mention sin and imply repentance:

> "It is conceivable that the forces of death which at present are ravaging the esculent life of this planet have intelligence, in which case we beseech them to leave off. If we have done wrong—allowing in our blindness natural impulse to overcome reason—we are, of course, heartily sorry. But we submit that we have already suffered sufficiently for this wrong and we firmly resolve never to sin again. Amen." (WS, 95–96)

The Christianity that ultimately saves the world from sterility is not what Shonny or Ambrose expects. The image of Christ that triumphs is not one of redemption, but of cannibalism: To Shonny's surprise, his own son has it that "this chap was born, you see. Then he was killed by being hung up on a tree, and then he was eaten" (WS, 98). After men combine fertility rites, cannibalism, and human sacrifice, the effects on the land are almost immediate: "a vast communal nocturnal gorge of man-flesh had been followed by a heterosexual orgy in the ruddy light of the fat-spitting fires and, . . . the morning after, the root known as salsify was seen sprouting from the pressed earth" (WS, 104). The effect on Shonny's hens recalls Shaw's St. Joan:

> "We found some eggs in the henhouse and gave her those."
> "Eggs? Eggs? Is everybody going mad, including myself?" (WS, 114)

The narrator's summary of the land's problem is essentially Shonny's version: "That blight had been man's refusal to breed" (WS, 139). Eliot's premise that a wasted human spirit has caused the waste of modern civilization operates throughout the novel. Although the Christianity of Burgess's characters differs from the resurrection motif of Eliot's poem, the way out of Burgess's Waste Land is essentially Christian.

To create and support the Waste Land atmosphere and theme, Burgess frequently echoes lines from *The Waste Land*. For example, Burgess describes "Tristram, joining the I-had-not-thought-death-had-undone-so-many workward rush" (*WS*, 49). Echoing Donne as well as Eliot's "voices singing out of empty cisterns and exhausted wells" (l. 385), Burgess describes feedback from loudspeakers "set like doomsday trumpets at the imagined corners of each round tiered gallery, [which] blasted a noise of eructation that fell into the empty belly of the well" (*WS*, 95). Burgess also includes an echo of Eliot's thunder: "Tiny Tristram alone said, like Upanishadian thunder, 'Da da da'" (*WS*, 171). Elsewhere Burgess refers to the Metropole, the Fisher King, and even Frazer's *The Golden Bough*, cited by Eliot in his notes. The novel abounds in Eliot's imagery to support the *Waste Land* theme.

Eliot himself appears twice in the novel, first to identify his importance to *The Wanting Seed*. A statue by the water, Protean in its nature, has represented many people, including Pelagius. The statue had also been, at one time, "Eliot (a long-dead singer of infertility)" (*WS*, 15). Later, a long list of couples participating in a heterosexual orgy includes "Tommy Eliot and Kitty Elphick" (no doubt "Old Possum and Fickle Kitty," if "Fickle Kitty" is Burgess's equivalent of "Practical Cat"). Eliot is thus connected both with the sterility of the blighted land and the lifting of the curse. In *The Wanting Seed*, Burgess has expressed Cleanth Brooks's interpretation of *The Waste Land*, referred directly to Eliot in relation to that reading, and supported that theme with several allusions to other aspects of the poem relevant to sterility.

In *A Vision of Battlements*, *The Worm and the Ring*, and *Inside Mr Enderby*, T. S. Eliot and his poetry form an essential part of selected characters' knowledge. In *The Malayan Trilogy*, *Devil of a State*, and *The Wanting Seed*, Burgess borrows from *The Waste Land* to provide major themes, atmosphere, and episodes for his novels. Burgess has understood Eliot's poem and its traditional readings more fully than any other contemporary novelist. This has enabled him to borrow from *The Waste Land* with an unprecedented degree of sophistication. Burgess's attention to relevance when combining *Waste Land* imagery with a novel's theme, the care with which he has limited allusion to the poem in a given novel, and the variety of effects he has achieved show that, even after half a century, a novelist can draw effectively from *The Waste Land*.

PART IV
Conclusion

The influence of T. S. Eliot's *The Waste Land* has not been to shape the modern British novel. However, considering the extent to which the poem has influenced the thought, art, and language of succeeding generations, the impact of *The Waste Land* on modern British fiction is a unique literary phenomenon. That one poem should appear in so many works in another genre, that an American author should so profoundly affect British writing, and that one work should impress so many novelists are startling literary facts. Why has *The Waste Land* enjoyed its lasting vitality?

Part of *The Waste Land*'s power results from its timing. Eliot described the psychological and physical condition of modern man immediately after World War I had laid bare the harshest realities of industrialized civilization. For succeeding generations the descriptions of nostalgic longing for the pre-war way of life, the litter in the Thames, the loss of individuality of crowds streaming anonymously to work, the absence of faith, and the indifferent quality of human relationships have been verified beyond the most malign expectations. The passing years have served to intensify the poem's relevance, for *The Waste Land* suggests prototypes for almost every modern problem. In a sense Eliot defined the modern age when that age was only beginning to become aware of its identity, and his description was accurate enough and complete enough to embrace developing attitudes and situations. Albert and Lil's relationship was as realistic in the era of Vietnam as in the era of World War I.

Another source of *The Waste Land*'s vitality is that while it is easy to remember specific lines, it is difficult to understand the poem. One can

attribute this partly to Ezra Pound, whose ruthless cutting of the manuscript allowed memorable phrases to survive but who often ignored the
context in which those phrases occurred. When a reader encounters a
phrase such as "the awful daring of a moment's surrender" or "bats
with baby faces in the violet light," he can apprehend the denotation of
the words and can recognize the powerful effect the phrase has on
him, but he still must grapple with the meaning of the phrase in the
context of the poem. Such elusiveness invites the reader to return
repeatedly until he is immersed in the poem's expressions.

A third source of *The Waste Land*'s vitality is the poem's thematic
ambiguity, which allows readers to draw diverse conclusions regarding
the poem's meaning. A nihilist approaching the poem finds confirmation for his nihilism, a sociologist confirmation for his approach to the
problems of modern civilization, and a Christian affirmation of his
faith. For instance, the lines "He who was living is now dead / We who
were living are now dying / With a little patience" lend themselves to
different interpretations. To some these lines mean that the Nazarene
has died, leaving no hope for others, and the lines thus repudiate the
Christian myth. To others they mean that the Fisher King mourns the
loss of a beloved friend. To others they mean that man should take
hope in resurrection. One can support virtually any interpretation the
reader brings to the poem by reading controversial lines in a manner
consistent with the reader's expectations: many value the poem for its
apparent support of their preconceived notions.

Another source of *The Waste Land*'s vitality is the enduring quality of
the poem's symbols and descriptions. While Eliot's use of myth can
account for part of this, the manner in which he has presented various
episodes very carefully excludes external detail. The reminiscence of
Marie, except for one reference to "archduke," is timeless. The episodes of the neurasthenic woman and the narrator, the typist and the
young man carbuncular, the Thames Maidens, and Mr. Eugenides similarly occur with no references to place the poem's action too specifically. The focus of these episodes is purely psychological, emphasizing
the human relationships independent of time or place. The intensity of
such encounters, almost universal, makes the figures of the poem truly
abiding.

Why would these traits impel novelists, as well as poets, to borrow
from *The Waste Land*? Whereas poets are primarily interested in words
as a medium to evoke emotional response, valuing the powerful effects
of economical expression and savoring words as words, novelists are
more interested in an interpretation of life, in human nature, and in
the interaction of their characters. As a result *The Waste Land*, which

can be read as a narrative of people who confront and fail to cope with the meaninglessness inherent in modern life, is congenial to the novelist. Although the *manner* of Eliot's poem can inspire a poet to adopt Eliotian phrases or images, the *matter* of *The Waste Land* is more appropriate to the novelist, who tends to regard description, atmosphere, plot, and language subordinate to the development of character and the examination of the meaning of existence. Given the scene of the neurasthenic woman and the narrator in "A Game of Chess," or the encounter of the typist and the young man carbuncular in "The Fire Sermon," a novelist can explore the nature of their relationships, speculate on the origins of their psychological states, and develop a plot which demonstrates the probable consequences of their natures. For a novelist, *The Waste Land* provides a series of intense moments which can be placed into the perspective of an entire life, and a novel provides sufficient space for such expansion. Whereas a poet can find poetic techniques and effective images in *The Waste Land*, the novelist can find the characters and situations upon which many novels can focus. Also, the "rhetoric of fiction" is especially receptive to the many meanings implicit in *The Waste Land*, so that novelists can use Eliot's figures and situations to offer their own interpretations of the poem and of life. Poetry less often can carry that burden. That *The Waste Land* can confine an epic to only 434 lines is itself phenomenal.

Whether novelists will continue to draw from *The Waste Land* remains to be seen. While several novelists wrote under *The Waste Land*'s influence in the 1920s and 1930s, there are signs that the poem's influence is waning. As Iris Murdoch demonstrates, much of *The Waste Land*'s tone, including its implicit misogyny, has become unfashionable and uncongenial since the poem was written, although the women who inspired that tone—the neurasthenic woman, the typist, Lil—remain hauntingly real. As Anthony Burgess has shown, however, sophisticated allusion to *The Waste Land* can create fresh effects despite the familiarity of the poem's lines. As long as novelists such as Theroux, Durrell, and Fowles allude to the poem, *The Waste Land* will continue to demonstrate some measure of utility, but after sixty years the poem is less likely to affect novelists as profoundly as it did in the 1930s. *The Waste Land* retains great power, but familiarity has made it too easy for readers to dismiss its effects as "literary."

NOTES

The following abbreviations are used in references to published and unpublished letters:

A.B.   Alan Bird   J.A.   John Atkins
A.L.   Amy Lowell   J.C.P.   John Cowper Powys
C.S.L.   C. S. Lewis   R.A.   Richard Aldington
F.M.F.   Ford Madox Ford   T.S.E.   T. S. Eliot
Arents   The John Cowper Powys Collection, George Arents Research Library for
              Special Collections at Syracuse University
Beinecke   The Beinecke Library, Yale University Libraries
Berg   The Henry W. and Albert A. Berg Collection, New York Public Library,
              Astor, Lenox and Tilden Foundations
Houghton   The Houghton Library, Harvard University
HRC   Humanities Research Center, University of Texas at Austin
Huntington   The Huntington Library
UCLA   Department of Special Collections, Research Library, University of Cali-
              fornia at Los Angeles
Wade   The Marion E. Wade Collection, Wheaton College

All quotations from unpublished correspondence are used with the permission of the
copyright holder and the repository library.

PREFACE

1. James E. Miller, Jr., *T. S. Eliot's Personal Waste Land: Exorcism of the Demons* (University Park, Pa.: Pennsylvania State Univ. Press, 1977), p. 8.

2. T. S. Eliot, "What Dante Means to Me," *To Criticize the Critic* (New York: Farrar, Straus & Giroux, 1965), p. 128.

INTRODUCTION

1. Paul Theroux, *The Great Railway Bazaar* (New York: Houghton Mifflin, 1975), p. 24.

2. Roger Sale, *Modern Heroism: Essays on D. H. Lawrence, William Empson, and J. R. R. Tolkien* (Berkeley: Univ. of California Press, 1973), p. 109.

3. Myra Buttle, pseud., *The Sweeniad* (New York: Sagamore Press, 1957), p. 14.

4. Ibid., p. 15.

5. Ibid., p. 19.

6. Harold Bloom in "American Writers: Who's Up, Who's Down?" *Esquire* 88 (August 1977), 77.

7. Karl Shapiro, "The Death of Literary Judgment" in *Storm Over The Waste Land*, ed. Robert E. Knoll (Chicago: Scott, Foresman, 1964), p. 137.

8. E. K. Brown, "Mr Eliot and Some Enemies," *The University of Toronto Quarterly* 8 (1938), 82n.

9. B. Murdoch, "The Overpopulated Wasteland: Myth in Anthony Burgess's *The Wanting Seed*," *Revue des Langues Vivantes* (Bruxelles), 39 (1973), 203–17.

10. Audrey T. Rodgers, "Eliot in the 70's: A Mosaic of Criticism," *T. S. Eliot Review* 2 (Spring 1975), 10.

11. M. C. Bradbrook, *T. S. Eliot: The Making of "The Waste Land"* (London: F. Mildner & Sons, 1972), p. 22.

12. C. P. Snow to Fred Crawford, 21 April 1976.

13. Rumer Godden to Fred Crawford, 20 January 1977.

14. Quentin Bell, *Virginia Woolf: A Biography* (New York: Harcourt Brace Jovanovich, 1972), II, 63.

15. Leon Edel, *Bloomsbury: A House of Lions* (New York: J. B. Lippincott, 1979), p. 247.

16. T.S.E. to Virginia Woolf, 22 May 1924; Berg.

17. Mary Graham Lund, "The Androgynous Moment: Woolf and Eliot," *Renascence* 12 (1960), 75.

18. Samuel Hynes, *The Auden Generation: Literature and Politics in England in the 1930s* (New York: Viking Press, 1977), p. 25.

19. Ibid., p. 163.

Part I

1. Roger Poole, *The Unknown Virginia Woolf* (London: Cambridge Univ. Press, 1978), p. 178.

2. Ibid., p. 180.

Chapter 1

1. R.A. to A.L., 18/20 (?) November 1917; Houghton.

2. "Modern American Poetry," *TLS* (6 May 1920), 277–78.

3. R.A. to A.L., 14 May 1920; Houghton.

4. R.A. to A.L., 17 June 1920; Houghton.

5. R.A. to A.L., 7 April 1921; Houghton.

6. R.A. to A.L., 26 August 1921; Houghton.

7. R.A. to A.L., 27 September 1921; Houghton.

8. R.A. to A.L., 5 May 1922; Houghton.

9. R.A. to A.L., 7 July 1922; Houghton.

10. R.A. to A.L., 18 July 1922; Houghton.

11. A.L. to R.A., 4 April 1923; Houghton.

12. R.A. to J.A., 22 January 1958; HRC.

13. Valerie Eliot, ed., *T. S. Eliot: The Waste Land: A Facsimile and Transcript of the Original Drafts Including the Annotations of Ezra Pound* (New York: Harcourt Brace Jovanovich, 1971), p. xvii.

14. Richard Aldington, *Life for Life's Sake: A Book of Reminiscences* (New York: Viking Press, 1941), pp. 268–69. Subsequent references to *Life* are to this edition.

15. R.A. to J.A., 5 June 1957; HRC.

16. V. Eliot, *The Waste Land Facsimile*, pp. xiv–xv.

17. R.A. to J.A., 22 June 1957; HRC.

18. T.S.E. to Henry Treece, 19 February 1952; HRC.

19. R.A. to Rachel Annand Taylor, 6 January 1950; Berg.

20. R.A. to A.B., 7 October 1954; in *A Passionate Prodigality: Letters to Alan Bird from Richard Aldington: 1949–1962*, ed. Miriam J. Benkovitz (New York: New York Public Library, 1975), p. 139.

21. R.A. to A.B., 25 August 1951; *Prodigality*, p. 39.

22. R.A. to A.B., 15 March 1953; *Prodigality*, p. 87.

23. T.S.E. to R.A., 17 July 1922; HRC.

24. T.S.E. to R.A., 18 November 1922; HRC.

25. R.A. to Harold Monro, 8 May 1924; UCLA.

26. T.S.E. to John Quinn, 12 March 1923; *The Waste Land Facsimile*, pp. xxvi–xxvii.

27. John Peter, "A New Interpretation of *The Waste Land*," *Essays in Criticism* 2 (July 1952), 245. Quoted in Miller, *Eliot's Personal Waste Land*, p. 12.

28. Miller, *Eliot's Personal Waste Land*, passim.

29. T.S.E. to R.A., 15 November 1922; *The Waste Land Facsimile*, p. xxv.

30. Conrad Aiken, "An Anatomy of Melancholy," in *T.S. Eliot: 1888–1965, Sewanee Review* (Special Issue) 74 (Jan.–Mar. 1966), 190.

31. R.A. to F. S. Flint, 8 (?) April 1923; HRC.

32. R.A. to Harold Monro, 14 July 1925; UCLA.

33. *A Passionate Prodigality*, p. 19n.

34. Richard Aldington, *Death of a Hero* (Garden City, NY: Garden City Publishing Co., 1929), p. 111. Subsequent references to *DH* are to this edition.

35. Richard Aldington, *The Colonel's Daughter* (Garden City, NY; Doubleday, Doran, 1931), p. 17. Subsequent references to *CD* are to this edition.

36. R.A. to A.B., 6 January 1954; *Prodigality*, p. 105.

37. T.S.E. to Richard Church, 2 August 1963; HRC.

38. Valerie Eliot to Fred Crawford, 18 January 1977.

39. Richard Aldington, *Stepping Heavenward: A Record* (Florence: G. Orioli, 1931), p. 35. Subsequent references to *SH* are to this edition.

40. T. S. Eliot, *The Sacred Wood* (London: Methuen, 1960), p. 58.

41. R.A. to A.B., 18 July 1955; *Prodigality*, p. 191.

42. Miller, *Eliot's Personal Waste Land*, p. 25.

43. R.A. to A.B., 19 October 1952; *Prodigality*, p. 62.

44. Richard Aldington, *All Men Are Enemies* (Garden City, NY: Doubleday, Doran, 1933), p. 6. Subsequent references to *AM* are to this edition.

45. Richard Aldington, *Rejected Guest* (New York: Viking Press, 1939), pp. 118–19. Subsequent references to *RG* are to this edition.

CHAPTER 2

1. George H. Thomson, *The Fiction of E. M. Forster* (Detroit: Wayne State Univ. Press, 1967), p. 204.

2. E. M. Forster, *Abinger Harvest* (New York: Harcourt, Brace & World, 1964), p. 76.

3. E. M. Forster, "Some of Our Difficulties," The New York *Herald Tribune*, 12 May 1929, Section 11, p. 6.

4. Ibid.

5. Ibid.

6. Oliver Stallybrass, "Forster's 'Wobblings': The Manuscripts of *A Passage to India*," in *Aspects of E. M. Forster: Essays and Recollections Written for His Ninetieth Birthday*, ed. Oliver Stallybrass (New York: Harcourt, Brace & World, 1969), p. 149.

7. Ibid., p. 153.

8. E. M. Forster, *A Passage to India* (New York: Harcourt, Brace & World, 1952), pp. 149–50. Subsequent references to *PI* are to this edition.

9. T.S.E. to F.M.F., 14 August 1923; in R. W. Lid, *Ford Madox Ford: The Essence of His Art* (Berkeley: Univ. of California Press, 1964), p. 20.

10. T.S.E. to F.M.F., 4 October 1923; *Ford: Essence*, p. 20.

11. Ibid.

12. Paul L. Wiley, *Novelist of Three Worlds: Ford Madox Ford* (Syracuse: Syracuse Univ. Press, 1962), pp. 255–56.

13. Robert J. Andreach, *The Slain and Resurrected God: Conrad, Ford, and the Christian Myth* (London: Univ. of London Press, 1970), p. 205.

14. Ford Madox Ford, *Some Do Not . . . & No More Parades* (New York: New American Library, 1964), p. 221. Subsequent references to *SDN* and *NMP* are to this edition.

15. Reprinted in C. B. Cox and Arnold Hinchcliffe, *T. S. Eliot, The Waste Land: A Casebook* (New York: Macmillan, 1968), p. 55.

16. Ford Madox Ford, *A Man Could Stand Up— & Last Post* (New York: New American Library, 1964), p. 171. Subsequent references to *Man* and *LP* are to this edition.

17. James C. Cowan, *D. H. Lawrence's American Journey* (Cleveland: Press of Case Western Reserve Univ., 1970), p. 81; Samuel A. Eisenstein, *Boarding the Ship of Death: D. H. Lawrence's Quester Heroes* (The Hague: Mouton, 1974), p. 92; William York Tindall, *D. H. Lawrence and Susan His Cow* (New York: Columbia Univ. Press, 1939), p. 192.

18. C. E. Baron, "Lawrence's Influence on Eliot," *The Cambridge Quarterly* 5 (1971), 236.

19. Mark Schorer, "Introduction" to D. H. Lawrence, *Lady Chatterley's Lover* (New York: Grove Press, 1957), p. 30. Subsequent references to *LCL* are to this edition.

20. Edmund Wilson, *Axel's Castle: A Study in the Imaginative Literature of 1870–1930* (New York: Scribner's, 1969), p. 106.

Chapter 3

1. Hynes, *The Auden Generation*, p. 60.

2. Aldous Huxley, *Crome Yellow* (New York: Harper & Brothers, 1922), p. 270.

3. Aldous Huxley, *Point Counter Point* (New York: Harper & Row, 1965), pp. 306, 321. Subsequent references to *PCP* are to this edition.

4. Aldous Huxley to Grover Smith, 3 March 1952, in *Letters of Aldous Huxley*, ed. Grover Smith (New York: Harper & Row, 1959), p. 640.

5. Hynes, *The Auden Generation*, pp. 63–64.

6. Aldous Huxley, *Antic Hay* (New York: Modern Library, 1932), p. 65. Subsequent references to *AH* are to this edition.

7. Wilson, *Axel's Castle*, p. 106.

8. Aldous Huxley, *Brave New World* (New York: Bantam Books, 1955), p. x. Subsequent references to *BNW* are to this edition.

9. Aldous Huxley, *Eyeless in Gaza* (New York: Bantam Books, 1954), p. 17. Subsequent references to *EG* are to this edition.

10. Sybille Bedford, *Aldous Huxley: A Biography* (New York: Harper & Row, 1974), p. 463.

11. Ibid., p. 524.

12. Ibid., p. 722.

13. Ibid., p. 684.

PART II

1. Cleanth Brooks, "The Beliefs Embodied in the Work," in *Storm Over The Waste Land*, ed. Robert E. Knoll (Chicago: Scott, Foresman, 1964), p. 79.

2. Ibid., p. 80.

3. Ibid., p. 82.

4. Ibid., p. 83.

5. Ibid., p. 86.

6. Ibid., p. 87.

7. T.S.E. to Cleanth Brooks, 15 March 1937; Beinecke.

CHAPTER 4

1. Evelyn Waugh, *A Little Learning: An Autobiography: The Early Years* (Boston: Little, Brown, 1964), p. 76.

2. Ibid., pp. 77–78.

3. Christopher Sykes, *Evelyn Waugh: A Biography* (Boston: Little, Brown, 1975), p. 316.

4. James F. Carens, *The Satiric Art of Evelyn Waugh* (Seattle: Univ. of Washington Press, 1966), pp. 13–14.

5. Ibid., pp. 91–92.

6. Ibid., p. 16.

7. Evelyn Waugh, *Decline and Fall & A Handful of Dust* (New York: Dell, 1959), p. 294. Subsequent references to *D&F* and to *HD* are to this edition.

8. Hynes, *The Auden Generation*, pp. 57–58.

9. Evelyn Waugh, *Vile Bodies* (Boston: Little, Brown, 1930), p. x. Subsequent references to *VB* are to this edition.

10. Evelyn Waugh, *Black Mischief* (Boston: Little, Brown, 1946), p. 170. Subsequent references to *BM* are to this edition.

11. Sykes, *Evelyn Waugh*, pp. 138–39.

12. Stephen Jay Greenblatt, *Three Modern Satirists: Waugh, Orwell, and Huxley* (New Haven: Yale Univ. Press, 1965), p. 32.

13. Ibid., p. 4.

14. The Earl of Birkenhead, "Fiery Particles," in *Evelyn Waugh and His World*, ed. David Pryce-Jones (Boston: Little, Brown, 1973), p. 45.

15. Evelyn Waugh, *Brideshead Revisited: The Sacred and Profane Memories of Captain Charles Ryder* (Boston: Little, Brown, 1945), p. 33. Subsequent references to *BR* are to this edition.

16. Evelyn Waugh, *Men at Arms and Officers and Gentlemen* (New York: Dell, 1961), p. 14. Subsequent references to *MA* are to this edition.

17. Evelyn Waugh, *The End of the Battle* [American edition of *Unconditional Surrender*] (Boston: Little, Brown, 1961), p. 57. Subsequent references to *EB* are to this edition.

CHAPTER 5

1. George Orwell, "Review: *Burnt Norton, East Coker, The Dry Salvages* by T. S. Eliot," in *The Collected Essays, Journalism and Letters of George Orwell,* ed. Sonia Orwell and Ian Angus (New York: Harcourt, Brace & World, 1968), II, 242.

2. Peter Stansky and William Abrahams, *The Unknown Orwell* (New York: Alfred A. Knopf, 1972), p. 121.

3. Ibid., p. 208.

4. Ibid., p. 300.

5. Orwell, *The Collected Essays,* II, 239.

6. George Orwell, *A Collection of Essays* (Garden City, NY: Doubleday, 1954), p. 318.

7. George Orwell, *Keep the Aspidistra Flying* (New York: Harcourt, Brace & World, 1956), pp. 12–13. Subsequent references to *KAF* are to this edition.

8. George Orwell, *Coming Up for Air* (New York: Harcourt, Brace & World, 1950), p. 23. Subsequent references to *CUA* are to this edition.

9. George Orwell, *1984* (New York: New American Library, 1961), p. 7. Subsequent references to *1984* are to this edition.

10. Peter Hutchinson, "Tales of the Lower Depths in 'Men and [sic] Darkness,'" New York *Times Book Review* (24 January 1932), p. 18.

11. James Hanley, *The Furys* (New York: Macmillan, 1935), p. 442. Subsequent references to *Furys* are to this edition.

12. James Hanley, *Levine* (London: MacDonald, 1956), p. 46. Subsequent references to *L* are to this edition.

13. James Hanley, *The Closed Harbour* (London: Chatto & Windus, 1952; 1971), p. 25. Subsequent references to *CH* are to this edition.

14. James Hanley, *An End and a Beginning* (London: MacDonald, 1958), p. 220. Subsequent references to *E&B* are to this edition.

15. James Hanley, *The German Prisoner* (Muswell Hill: Privately printed by the author, 1950), p. 9.

16. James Hanley, *The Last Voyage* (London: Furnival, 1931), p. 58.

17. Jocelyn Brooke, "Wauchop Agonistes," *Time and Tide* 34 (17 Jan. 1953), 86.

18. Anthony Powell to Fred Crawford, 17 January 1976.

19. Anthony Powell, *Afternoon Men* (Boston: Little, Brown, 1963), p. 62.

20. Anthony Powell, *Venusberg* (London: Heinemann, 1955), p. 181.

21. Neil Brennan, *Anthony Powell* (New York: Twayne, 1974), p. 101.

22. Anthony Powell, *Casanova's Chinese Restaurant* (Boston: Little, Brown, 1960), p. 33. Subsequent references to *CCR* are to this edition.

23. Robert Towers, "Hearing Secret Harmonies," New York *Times Book Review* (11 April 1976), p. 1.

24. Anthony Powell, *A Question of Upbringing,* in *A Dance to the Music of Time* (Boston: Little, Brown, 1955), p. 14.

25. Anthony Powell, *The Acceptance World,* in *A Dance to the Music of Time,* p. 153.

26. Anthony Powell, *A Question of Upbringing,* p. 171.

27. Ibid., p. 208.

28. Ibid., p. 217.

29. Anthony Powell to Fred Crawford, 17 January 1976.

CHAPTER 6

1. John Cowper Powys, *Autobiography* (Hamilton, NY: Colgate Univ. Press, 1934; 1968), p. 527.

2. John Cowper Powys, "England Revisited," *Scribner's Magazine* 98 (Sept. 1935), 143.

3. J.C.P. to Eric Barker, 10 November 1934; Arents.

4. J.C.P. to Eric Barker, 10 July 1951; Arents.

5. John Cowper Powys, *Weymouth Sands* (New York: Simon & Schuster, 1934), p. 564. Subsequent references to *WS* are to this edition.

6. Giorgio Melchiori, *The Tightrope Walkers: Studies of Mannerism in Modern English Literature* (London: Routledge & Kegan Paul, 1956), p. 190.

7. John Russell, *Henry Green: Nine Novels and an Unpacked Bag* (New York: Rutgers Univ. Press, 1960), p. 206.

8. Melchiori, *The Tightrope Walkers*, p. 194n.

9. Russell, *Henry Green*, p. 138.

10. Melchiori, *The Tightrope Walkers*, pp. 189–90. The italics are Melchiori's.

11. Ibid., pp. 188–89. The italics are Melchiori's.

12. Ibid., p. 194n.

13. Hynes, *The Auden Generation*, p. 28.

14. Christopher Isherwood, *Lions and Shadows: An Education in the Twenties* (Norfolk, CT: New Directions, 1947), p. 191.

15. Christopher Isherwood, *All the Conspirators* (London: Jonathan Cape, 1957), unnumbered.

16. Alan Wilde, *Christopher Isherwood* (New York: Twayne, 1971), p. 44.

17. Christopher Isherwood, *The Memorial: Portrait of a Family* (Norfolk, CT: New Directions, 1946), p. 175. Subsequent references to *Memorial* are to this edition.

18. Wilde, *Christopher Isherwood*, p. 50.

19. Ibid., p. 51.

20. Christopher Isherwood, *The World in the Evening* (New York: Random House, 1954), p. 9. Subsequent references to *World* are to this edition.

21. Christopher Isherwood, *Down There on a Visit* (New York: Simon & Schuster, 1962), pp. 78–79. Subsequent references to *Down* are to this edition.

22. Wilde, *Christopher Isherwood*, pp. 116–17.

23. Ibid., p. 124.

CHAPTER 7

1. Charles Williams, *All Hallows' Eve*, with an introduction by T. S. Eliot (New York: Pellegrini & Cudahy, 1948), pp. ix, x.

2. Elizabeth Wright, "Theology in the Novels of Charles Williams," *Stanford University Honors Essays in Humanities* 5/6 (1962), pp. 36–38.

3. Mary McDermott Shideler, *The Theology of Romantic Love: A Study in the Writings of Charles Williams* (Grand Rapids: Eerdmans, 1962), p. 121.

4. Charles Moorman, *Arthurian Triptych: Mythic Materials in Charles Williams, C. S. Lewis, and T. S. Eliot* (Berkeley: Univ. of California Press, 1960), p. 31.

5. Charles Williams, *War in Heaven* (London: Faber & Faber, 1962), p. 101. Subsequent references to *WIH* are to this edition.

6. David W. Evans, "T. S. Eliot, Charles Williams, and the Sense of the Occult," *Accent* 14 (1954), 152.

7. Ibid., p. 154.

8. Charles Williams, *The Greater Trumps* (New York: Pellegrini & Cudahy, 1950), p. 19. Subsequent references to *GT* are to this edition.

9. Charles Williams, "The Image of the City in English Verse," *Dublin Review* 207 (July 1940), 50.

10. Gunnar Urang, *Shadows of Heaven: Religion and Fantasy in the Writing of C. S. Lewis, Charles Williams, and J. R. R. Tolkien* (London: S C M Press, 1971), p. 62.

11. Charles Williams, *All Hallows' Eve*, p. xiii. Subsequent references to *AHE* are to this edition.

12. Wright, "Theology in the Novels of Charles Williams," p. 26.

13. Charles Williams, *Shadows of Ecstasy* (London: Faber & Faber, 1965), p. 160. Subsequent references to *SE* are to this edition.

14. Charles Williams, *The Place of the Lion* (New York: Pellegrini & Cudahy, 1951), p. 65. Subsequent references to *PL* are to this edition.

15. T. S. Eliot, "The Dry Salvages," *Complete Poems and Plays, 1909–1950* (New York: Harcourt, Brace & World, 1952), p. 133.

16. Charles Williams, *Many Dimensions* (New York: Pellegrini & Cudahy, 1949), p. 70.

17. C.S.L. to Bede Griffiths, 1931 or 1932; Wade.

18. Roger L. Green and Walter Hooper, *C. S. Lewis: A Biography* (New York: Harcourt Brace Jovanovich, 1974), p. 130.

19. Corbin Scott Carnell, *Bright Shadow of Reality: C. S. Lewis and the Feeling Intellect* (Grand Rapids: Eerdmans, 1974), pp. 129–30.

20. Ibid., p. 130.

21. C.S.L. to Sr. Magdelena, 7 June 1934; Wade.

22. C.S.L. to Charles Williams, 20 July 1940; Wade.

23. C.S.L. to Theodora Bosanquet, 27 August 1942; Houghton.

24. C.S.L. to E. R. Eddison, 16 November 1942; Wade.

25. C. S. Lewis, *Perelandra* (New York: Macmillan, 1965), p. 205. Subsequent references to *P* are to this edition.

26. C. S. Lewis, *That Hideous Strength* (New York: Macmillan, 1965), p. 121.

27. C. S. Lewis, *Out of the Silent Planet* (New York: Macmillan, 1965), p. 104. Subsequent references to *OSP* are to this edition.

28. Charles Williams to Theodora Bosanquet, 5 October 1940; Houghton.

29. C.S.L. to Theodora Bosanquet, 27 August 1942; Houghton.

30. T.S.E. to Conrad Aiken, 1 May 1946; Huntington.

31. C.S.L. to T.S.E., 22 February 1943; Wade.

32. Green and Hooper, *C. S. Lewis*, pp. 223–24.

33. Ibid., p. 224.

34. Carnell, *Bright Shadow*, p. 129.

35. C.S.L. to Alastair Fowler, 7 January 1961; Berg.

CHAPTER 8

1. E. K. Brown, "Mr. Eliot and Some Enemies," p. 82n.

2. Nathan A. Scott, Jr., "Graham Greene: Christian Tragedian," in *Graham Greene: Some Critical Considerations*, ed. Robert O. Evans (Lexington, KY: Univ. of Kentucky Press, 1967), pp. 28–29.

3. Philip Stratford, *Faith and Fiction: Creative Process in Greene and Mauriac* (Notre Dame: Univ. of Notre Dame Press, 1964), p. 132.

4. Lynette Kohn, "Graham Greene: The Major Novels," *Stanford Honors Essays in Humanities* 4 (1961), p. 4.

5. A. A. DeVitis, *Graham Greene* (New York: Twayne, 1964), pp. 41, 54.

6. Robert O. Evans, "The Satanist Fallacy of *Brighton Rock*," in *Graham Greene: Some Critical Considerations*, pp. 153–54.

7. Gwenn R. Boardman, *Graham Greene: The Aesthetics of Exploration* (Gainesville, FL: Univ. of Florida Press, 1971), p. 7.

8. Ibid., p. 7n.

9. Ibid., p. 31.

10. Harvey Curtis Webster, "The World of Graham Greene," in *Graham Greene: Some Critical Considerations*, p. 9.

11. Graham Greene, *Orient Express* (New York: Pocket Books, 1975), p. 19.

12. Graham Greene, *This Gun for Hire*, in *Triple Pursuit: A Graham Greene Omnibus* (New York: Viking Press, 1971), p. 35. Subsequent references to *Gun* are to this edition.

13. Stratford, *Faith and Fiction*, p. 132.

14. Ibid., p. 166.

15. T. S. Eliot, *Selected Essays* (New York: Harcourt, Brace & World, 1952), p. 380.

16. Ibid.

17. Graham Greene, *Brighton Rock* (New York: Viking Press, 1956), p. 58. Subsequent references to *BR* are to this edition.

18. H. R. Haber, "The Two Worlds of Graham Greene," *Modern Fiction Studies* 3 (Autumn 1957), 256–68.

19. DeVitis, *Graham Greene*, p. 41.

20. Ibid., p. 80.

21. John Atkins, "Altogether Amen: A Reconsideration of *The Power and the Glory*" in *Graham Greene: Some Critical Considerations*, p. 181.

22. Graham Greene, *The Power and the Glory* (New York: Bantam Pathfinder Editions, 1972), p. 107. Subsequent references to *Power* are to this edition.

23. Graham Greene, *The Heart of the Matter* (New York: Viking Press, 1960), p. 169. Subsequent references to *Heart* are to this edition.

24. Graham Greene, *The Third Man* in *Triple Pursuit*, p. 219. Subsequent references to *Third* are to this edition.

25. Graham Greene, *Our Man in Havana* in *Triple Pursuit*, p. 252. Subsequent references to *Our* are to this edition.

PART III

1. Muriel Spark to Derek Stanford, 14 March 1950; HRC.

2. Muriel Spark, *The Prime of Miss Jean Brodie* (New York: Dell, 1961), p. 43.

3. John Fowles, *Daniel Martin* (Boston: Little, Brown, 1977), p. 14.

4. Ibid., p. 598.

5. Samuel Ludu, "*Livia* by Lawrence Durrell," *San Francisco Review of Books* (July 1979), p. 22.

CHAPTER 9

1. Iris Murdoch to Fred Crawford, postmarked 12 January 1975.

2. Iris Murdoch, "T. S. Eliot as a Moralist," in *T. S. Eliot: A Symposium for His Seventieth Birthday*, ed. Neville Braybrooke (New York: Farrar, Straus & Cudahy, 1958), p. 152.

3. Ibid., pp. 157–58.
4. Ibid., p. 160.
5. Iris Murdoch, *The Italian Girl* (New York: Viking Press, 1964), pp. 187–88. Subsequent references to *IG* are to this edition.
6. Iris Murdoch, *A Word Child* (New York: Viking Press, 1975), p. 387. Subsequent references to *WC* are to this edition.
7. Iris Murdoch, "T. S. Eliot as a Moralist," p. 156.
8. Iris Murdoch, *A Severed Head* (New York: Viking Press, 1961), p. 46. Subsequent references to *SH* are to this edition.
9. Iris Murdoch, *The Time of the Angels* (New York: Viking Press, 1966), p. 20. Subsequent references to *TA* are to this edition.
10. Iris Murdoch, *The Flight from the Enchanter* (New York: Viking Press, 1956), p. 131. Subsequent references to *FFE* are to this edition.
11. Iris Murdoch, *The Black Prince* (New York: Viking Press, 1973), p. 244. Subsequent references to *BP* are to this edition.
12. Iris Murdoch, *Under the Net* (New York: Viking Press, 1954), p. 25.
13. Iris Murdoch, *A Fairly Honourable Defeat* (New York: Viking Press, 1970), pp. 215–16.

CHAPTER 10

1. Anthony Burgess, "The Waste Land Revisited," *Horizon* 14 (Winter 1972), 105.
2. Anthony Burgess to Fred Crawford, postmarked 22 May 1976.
3. Anthony Burgess, "The Waste Land Revisited," p. 109.
4. Ibid.
5. Anthony Burgess, *The Clockwork Testament or Enderby's End* (New York: Bantam Books, 1976), p. 130.
6. Anthony Burgess, *MF* (New York: Alfred A. Knopf, 1971), p. 73.
7. Anthony Burgess, *A Vision of Battlements* (New York: W. W. Norton, 1965), p. 58. Subsequent references to *VB* are to this edition.
8. Anthony Burgess, *The Worm and the Ring* (London: Heinemann, 1970), p. 22.
9. Anthony Burgess, *Inside Mr Enderby* (London: Heinemann, 1963), p. 37. Subsequent references to *IME* are to this edition.
10. Anthony Burgess, *The Malayan Trilogy* (Harmondsworth, Middlesex: Penguin Books, 1972), p. 40. Subsequent references to *Time*, *Enemy*, and *Beds* are to this edition.
11. Anthony Burgess to Fred Crawford, postmarked 22 May 1976.
12. Anthony Burgess, *Devil of a State* (New York: W. W. Norton, 1975), p. 99. Subsequent references to *Devil* are to this edition.
13. Anthony Burgess, *The Wanting Seed* (New York: Ballantine Books, 1962), p. 33. Subsequent references to *WS* are to this edition.

INDEX

172

Index

Wilde, Oscar, ix

Wiley, Paul L., 26, 160

Williams, Charles, 48, 90–97, 98, 99, 100–1, 102, 163–64; *All Hallows' Eve*, 90, 93–94, 97, 99, 101, 163, 164; *Descent Into Hell*, 97, 101; *The Greater Trumps*, 90, 92–93, 94, 97, 164; "The Image of the City in English Verse," 93, 164; *Many Dimensions*, 96, 164; *The Place of the Lion*, 95, 96, 101, 164; *Shadows of Ecstasy*, 93, 95, 97, 164; *War in Heaven*, 90, 91–92, 94, 95, 96, 97, 101, 163

Williams, William Carlos, 7

Wilson, Edmund, xi, xvii, 31, 39, 46, 47, 48, 64, 78, 126, 137, 160

Wilson, John Anthony Burgess. *See* Burgess, Anthony

Woolf, Leonard, xvi

Wolf, Virginia, xvi, xvii, 1–2, 77, 85, 158; *Beginning Again*, 1; *Mrs. Dalloway*, 1; *Orlando*, 77; *To the Lighthouse*, xvi, xvii; *The Waves*, xvi, xvii, 1

Wordsworth, William, ix, 51; "Intimations of Immortality, " 51

Wren, Sir Christopher, 130

Wright, Elizabeth, 90, 93, 163, 164

Yeats, W.B., 4, 24, 65, 145; "Easter, 1916," 145

Yorke, Henry Vincent. *See* Green, Henry